DESCARTES

The Arguments of
the Philosophers

EDITOR: TED HONDERICH
Reader in Philosophy, University College London

The group of books of which this is one will include an
essentially analytic and critical account of each of the
considerable number of the great and influential
philosophers. Each book will provide an ordered exposition
and an examination of the contentions and doctrines of the
philosopher in question. The group of books taken together
will comprise a contemporary assessment and history of the
entire course of philosophical thought.

Already published in the series

Plato	J. C. B. Gosling
Meinong	Reinhardt Grossman
Santayana	Timothy L. S. Sprigge
Wittgenstein	R. J. Fogelin
Hume	B. Stroud
Berkeley	George Pitcher

DESCARTES

Margaret Dauler Wilson

Routledge & Kegan Paul
London, Boston, Melbourne and Henley

First published in 1978
by Routledge & Kegan Paul Ltd
39 Store Street,
London WC1E 7DD,
9 Park Street,
Boston, Mass. 02108, USA,
296 Beaconsfield Parade, Middle Park
Melbourne, 3206, Australia and
Broadway House,
Newtown Road,
Henley-on-Thames,
Oxon RG9 1EN
Photoset in 11 on 12 Garamond
Reprinted (with corrections) 1982
and first published as a paperback
Printed in the United States of America

British Library Cataloguing in Publication Data

Wilson, Margaret Dauler

Descartes.—(The arguments of the philosophers).
1. Descartes, Rene
I. Series
194   B1875
ISBN 0 7100 9208 3

Contents

CONTENTS

Preface

There are already more books on Descartes's philosophy than anyone other than a near-maniacal specialist could assimilate in a single lifetime. A very large number of these are good books. Quite a few are—by any reasonable standard of historical philosophical writing—both erudite and brilliant. Apart from the specific intentions of the series in which it appears, the present volume can hardly claim to fill some painful 'gap' in the existing philosophical literature.

My reason for writing a book on Descartes is that I believe I have a somewhat different over-all reading of his philosophy, and particularly of the *Meditations*, from other commentators—especially those writing in English. Also, I believe the interpretations I have developed of certain aspects of his system, or particular arguments, are either novel or overly neglected. It will probably be clear to the reader that I have been especially strongly influenced by two English-language commentaries—the books on Descartes by Frankfurt and Kenny. For all I have learned from them, I have ended up disagreeing with Frankfurt and Kenny on very many issues of criticism and interpretation.

My interpretation is presented in the form of a sort of semi-commentary on Descartes's *Meditations Concerning First Philosophy*. I follow the general line of argument of the *Meditations*, introducing material from other works where appropriate. The analysis is in some cases very detailed. However, I do not attempt to comment on every feature—or even every major feature—of the *Meditations* argument.

In view of the contemporary orientation of the series, readers may be disappointed that this book is not more systematically oriented toward evaluating Descartes's system in relation to the powerful anti-Cartesian currents in recent philosophical writing. But these currents are both so powerful and so various that it's difficult to imagine dealing with them in any organized way, while also producing anything like a coherent interpretation of Descartes's thought. I have been more concerned with the latter task. It is certain, I think, that Descartes had virtually no sense of the problems of 'privacy' and meaning, of identity and reference that have occupied many philosophers in recent decades, and have come to seem increasingly fundamental to epistemological and metaphysical issues. He had little understanding of, or respect for, the concept of formalization. His quaint physiological theories led him to some strange and naïve accounts of what goes on when we perceive, imagine or understand. He had very little notion of 'conceptual change' or the possibility of historical evolution of the categories of scientific understanding. (He consistently explained his own 'conceptual revolution' in terms of the 'removal of prejudice'!) In these and many other respects Descartes's philosophical system could fairly be called old-fashioned. There would even be little *point* in solemnly wondering what Descartes might have to say about the private language argument, or the Freudian unconscious, or the problem of 'individuating' 'pure Cartesian egos.'

Despite these limitations, I believe, Descartes ranks among the very greatest philosophical intelligences in history, and the careful study of his thought remains overwhelmingly interesting. (That's the *reason*, of course, for all those books mentioned above.) In the first place, he had an extraordinarily powerful, disciplined and well-organized mind. His arguments are usually thought out in great detail, and he responds tirelessly (if often irritably) to criticisms, objections and simple questions. He is, in effect, his own best commentator. As a result one can often obtain a complex and well-rounded conception of the 'logic' of his philosophical claims. More important, Descartes somehow grasped in a very deep way the relations between modern scientific concepts and certain fundamental philosophical problems, especially those having to do with knowledge and the self. The spare yet relaxed Latin of the *Meditations* presents us with a tightly-constructed problematic that has proved pervasive, durable, and very hard to shake or completely dissolve, however much we may try. It is the sole aim of the present volume to offer some slight advance in our understanding of this strong position, which still troubles (at least) our philosophical unconscious.

Acknowledgments

Students, colleagues, colloquia participants and others have contributed more to the formation and improvement of ideas and arguments in this book than I could possibly acknowledge individually. They have also contributed immensely to the pleasure I've had in the work—for which I'm equally grateful. I would like to express special thanks, though, to those who have offered detailed criticisms of parts of the book in earlier versions, and to those who have made available unpublished bibliographies, papers, or longer works (from which I've often profited). I am particularly indebted, in these respects, to the following: Willis Doney, Harry Frankfurt, Michael Hooker, Robert Sleigh, Ruth Mattern, Janet Broughton, Peter DeVos, Norman Malcolm, Edwin Curley, Jean-Marie Beyssade, Alan Donagan, Mark Sagoff, Eric Rosen, Richard Watson, Nancy Newman† and David Lachterman. Whatever its remaining deficiencies, the book would have been poorer, less informed and more erroneous without the contributions of these individuals.

Christopher Mogil, Lawrence Remmel and Jay Behmke have provided most valuable and reliable assistance in preparing the manuscript. Laura Bell produced a beautifully typed penultimate draft with great efficiency, and Helen Wright did a superbly accurate job with the final version, catching numerous mistakes that might otherwise have gone unnoticed. I also wish to thank Lee Ritins, Beverley Juhl and other past and present members of the Princeton Philosophy Department secretarial staff for miscellaneous clerical assistance in connection with the project. A grant from the Humanities Research Council of Princeton University helped cover typing and other expenses. A significant part of the remaining clerical expenses was borne by the Philosophy Department.

I am grateful to Princeton University for giving me a crucial year of leave with partial support, and to the Institute for Advanced Study, under the Directorship of Carl Kaysen, for the haven of a peaceful office and other facilities and support during that year. I'm especially grateful to my former teacher, Morton White, for his immensely thoughtful and generous assistance in this connection. Together with his earlier instruction and guidance, it constitutes a debt that could never be repaid.

Before making final revisions on the manuscript, I was privileged to have a chance to talk with a number of outstanding Descartes scholars in France. I own thanks to the Ministère des Affaires Etrangères of the French Government, to Professor Jules Vuillemin, and once again to Princeton, which gave me a short leave, for this marvelous opportunity. I am also grateful to Professors L. Guillermit, J-M. and M. Beyssade, Y. Belaval, H. Gouhier, G. Rodis-Lewis, J. Vuillemin, and their families and colleagues, for their hospitality and courteous availability.

Most of section 3 of Chapter VI consists of material previously published in *Noûs* under the title, 'Descartes: The Epistemological Argument for Mind–Body Distinctness' (vol. X (1976), pp. 3–17); it is reprinted by kind permission of the Editor. A version of section 2 of Chapter VI, 'Cartesian Dualism,' is to appear in *Descartes: Critical and Interpretive Essays*, edited by Michael Hooker.

Both Professor Honderich and the editors at Routledge also deserve thanks, for bearing with me without remonstrance through a formidable series of delays.

My friend Jim Ross has discussed and criticized my ideas on Descartes with unfailing insight and patience, over a period of several years. He has also read and criticized parts of the manuscript. He has not only saved me from countless logical and stylistic mistakes, but has provided encouragement, interest—and occasional skepticism— just when these were most needed. Discussions with him have especially affected my treatments of the *cogito*, the Dreaming Argument and the creation of the eternal truths doctrine—though I have no reason to suppose he would be sympathetic to the final versions.

Finally, my husband Emmett has sustained far more inconvenience and trouble in connection with this book than anyone else, in matters both large and small. The only reward for him is having the Descartes books finally out of the living room (but this may be sufficient). I am very deeply grateful for his patience, understanding and kindness.

I dedicate this book to my parents and maternal grandparents.

A Note on the Texts

I follow almost exclusively the Latin, rather than the French texts of the *Meditations, Objections and Replies* and *Principles*. There are two main reasons for this policy. The more interesting is that—particularly with respect to the *Meditations*—the Latin text seems to me philosophically much more lucid and coherent. Where the French text departs from the Latin the result, in my judgment, is far more often difficulties and confusion than illumination or improvement. The more obvious reason—which one might have thought would be sufficient—is that the Latin texts were written by Descartes himself, whereas the French is the work of translators. I am aware, of course, that Descartes 'approved' the French translations (but what exactly does that mean?), and that he is supposed himself to have introduced some changes in the French versions, to improve the argument or make his meaning clearer. There are even a few places where I personally would guess that this has occurred. The problem though, is that we generally have no way of knowing for sure whether a given change is Descartes's or his translator's. And here the consideration mentioned first is relevant.

Like most English-speaking students of Descartes, I have greatly profited from the very convenient two-volume edition of his works translated and edited by E. S. Haldane and G. R. T. Ross. Their contribution to Descartes studies in English-speaking countries has been immense. But I think it is time for the limitations of these translations to be more widely recognized. First, Haldane and Ross almost always follow the French translation of the *Meditations, Objections and Replies* and *Principles*, rather than the Latin original. Second, they do occasionally contribute errors of their own. Third, the language of their translation is by now rather archaic, whereas (for some reason I do not fully understand) Descartes's Latin usually seems as direct and immediate as good contemporary journalism. (I realize my own translations do not preserve this quality; for purposes of philosophical analysis and commentary I've been perhaps excessively concerned to achieve 'literalness.') As a result, when one turns from the Haldane and Ross translations to the Cartesian originals one seems to come across almost a different mind. Descartes's Latin, for all its elegance, is not especially difficult. I hope serious students of Descartes, and especially publishing scholars, will begin to study it more—and become perhaps a little less trusting of the authority of 'H & R.'

I add a brief note on Descartes's life and works that should aid in following the text. (For more detailed accounts—and for the references—see the commentaries by Kemp Smith, Boyce Gibson, Beck and M. Beyssade listed in the Bibliography.).

Errors and misprints in the first printing have been pointed out to me by several people, some of whom have generously provided lists of needed corrections. I wish to thank Vere Chappell, E. M. Curley, Willis Doney, Thomas M. Lennon, Hoke Robinson, J. W. Smith, Richard Watson, and above all Roger Montague for valuable assistance in this regard.

A Note on Descartes's Life and Works

Descartes was born in 1596 in Touraine. His father was a provincial government official and a landholder. His mother died when he was one year old. He was educated primarily at the leading Jesuit academy La Flèche, where he received a grounding in traditional Aristotelian-Scholastic philosophy and developed a profound admiration for the 'clarity and distinctness' of mathematical knowledge. He later studied law at the University of Poitiers. After leaving the University in 1616 he traveled extensively in Europe as a volunteer in first a Dutch, and then a Bavarian army. In 1618 he became friendly with a Dutch scientist, Isaac Beeckman, under whose influence he began to do a good deal of creative work in mathematics and physics. In 1619 he arrived at the great ambition that was to guide his life's work: that of producing a complete or universal science of nature according to modern mathematical and mechanical principles. A dramatic series of dreams on the evening of 10 November 1619 seemed to Descartes to indicate divine approval of his project.

Subsequently Descartes spent a number of years in Paris, where he became acquainted with the intellectual leaders of the time. Among his friends were certain theologians of Augustinian bent—rivals of the Jesuits—whose views concerning God and the will he seems to have found especially congenial. In 1628 he moved to Holland where he lived with only brief interruptions until 1649, when Queen Christina of Sweden persuaded him to come to Stockholm to grace her court. He died there in February 1650.

Descartes's major philosophical and scientific works were written in Holland. As the present study will stress, Descartes conceived his scientific system as the successor and replacement of the great Aristotelian-Scholastic synthesis that had dominated European thought for centuries. His philosophy (or 'metaphysics') was conceived as the 'foundation' of this science.

Throughout his career Descartes and his work were surrounded by controversy. He used many strategies to try to win approval and acceptance for his views—especially among the theological authorities of the day. He withheld publication of his heliocentric world system (*Le Monde*) in response to the condemnation of Galileo. His first published work, consisting of the *Discourse on Method* and three scientific essays, was written in French rather than Latin—apparently in the hope of gaining popular support and recognition. He repeatedly asked his well-connected friend Mersenne to obtain soundings on the likely reception of specific views, or to collect systematic criticisms from leading thinkers so that Descartes could reply to them. He dedicated the *Meditations* to the theological faculty of the Sorbonne, addressing to them several pages of hopeful and flattering remarks. When he finally published a version of his complete system—metaphysics plus 'universal physics'—it was in the form of a Jesuit school text (*Principles of Philosophy*). From the theologico-political point of view, this campaign was largely unsuccessful. It did not spare him official hostility, rejection and censure during his lifetime—and has left him open to charges of hypocrisy, cowardice and 'guile' by scholars writing in a more enlightened age. His works were placed on the Index in 1663. From another point of view, however—that of the history of thought—it is hard to imagine a more formidable triumph. Quite simply, Descartes's 'principles' *did* overcome and replace the Aristotelian ones—despite Leibniz's rather desperate efforts to retain some of the more 'spiritual' features of the latter. Although Descartes's specific contributions to mathematics and physics were soon dated by the work of Leibniz, Huygens and (above all) Newton, among others, the Western philosophical outlook had been permanently revised—as Descartes himself might say—from the foundations.

The chronology of his major works is as follows:

1628–9 (?) *Rules for the Direction of the Mind*
            A methodological treatise, written in Latin and never completed; published posthumously.
1634 *The World*
       Scientific system; published posthumously.
1637 *Discourse on Method, Optics, Geometry, Meteorology*
       Published in French. The *Discourse* contains a sketch of Descartes's life and education, together with a sort of summary of his philosophical and scientific position. The

scientific essays are presented as samples of what his method can accomplish.

1641 *Meditations Concerning First Philosophy* and *Objections and Replies*
Published in Latin; the Objections were collected by Mersenne from various philosophers and theologians at Descartes's request.

1644 *Principles of Philosophy*
Written in Latin. Part I expounds Descartes's general philosophical position; Parts II, III, and IV are largely concerned with explaining 'all the phenomena of nature.'

1647 *Notes Against a Certain Program*
Response to anti-Cartesian views published by a former disciple, Regius. While not really a 'major work,' the '*Notae*' contains important and frequently cited statements on the mind-body relation and other central topics.

1649 *The Passions of the Soul*
Written in French. Primarily concerned with the physiology of emotion, and the possibility of rational control of the passions.

Two additional important sources on Descartes's philosophy are *The Search for Truth* and the *Conversation with Burman*. The former is an unfinished dialogue in French, published posthumously. Scholars disagree on the probable date of its composition (a substantial portion of this work has been preserved only in Latin translation). The *Conversation* consists of Frans Burman's notes on his long philosophical interview with Descartes that took place in 1648.

Editions and Abbreviations

The standard edition of Descartes's work is:

AT   *Oeuvres de Descartes*, publiées par Ch. Adam et P. Tannery, Paris, Cerf, 1897–1913; reprinted Paris, J. Vrin, 1957– ; 12 vols.

For most Cartesian texts cited I follow convention and provide a reference to the widely used English edition:

HR   *The Philosophical Works of Descartes*, edited and translated by Elizabeth Haldane and G. R. T. Ross, Cambridge, Cambridge University Press, 1911; reprinted 1969; 2 vols.

Haldane and Ross translated hardly any of Descartes's immense correspondence, despite its philosophical importance. Fortunately, we now have Anthony Kenny's valuable edition.

PL   *Descartes: Philosophical Letters*, translated and edited by Anthony Kenny, Oxford, Clarendon Press, 1970.

Also omitted from HR are Burman's notes on his conversation with Descartes (originally published in Latin). These have now been translated also:

B   *Descartes' Conversation with Burman*, translated with introduction and commentary by John Cottingham, Oxford, Clarendon Press, 1976.

The English translation of the 'Optics' cited is by Paul Olscamp:

Ols. Descartes, *Discourse on Method, Optics, Geometry, and Meteorology*, translated with introduction by Paul J. Olscamp, Indianapolis, Bobbs-Merrill (Library of Liberal Arts), 1965.

The following abbreviations are employed in the notes for frequently cited secondary works:

CS   R. J. Butler, editor, *Cartesian Studies*, New York, Bobbs-Merrill, 1972.

DDM   Harry G. Frankfurt, *Demons, Dreamers, and Madmen: The defense of reason in Descartes's 'Meditations,'* Indianapolis, Bobbs-Merrill, 1970.

Doney Willis Doney, editor, *Descartes: A Collection of Critical Essays*, Garden City, N.Y., Doubleday (Anchor Books), 1967.

Kenny Anthony Kenny, *Descartes: A Study of His Philosophy*, New York, Random House, 1968.

Other editions, commentaries, etc., are listed in the Bibliography.

I

General Doubt

1 Cartesian doubt and Cartesian revolution

Meditation I is dedicated to the 'overthrow' of present opinions. The first sentence of the Meditation introduces this project as a necessary condition of establishing 'something firm and lasting in the sciences'—and seems to offer an explanation of why it *is* necessary:

> It has already been some years since I noticed how many false things I accepted as true when I was young, and how doubtful is whatever I erected afterwards on these, and thus that once in my life everything ought to be overturned completely, and begun again from the first foundations, if I desire to establish anything firm and enduring [*firmum et mansurum*] in the sciences. . . .
> (AT VII, 17; HR I, 144)

This enterprise, Descartes continues, had seemed to him 'enormous'; but circumstances of leisure and comfort, together with increased maturity, now make the time opportune to 'apply' himself 'seriously and freely to the general overthrow of my present opinions.' To do this, he says, it will be sufficient to find in them 'any reason for doubt,' since 'reason already persuades me, that assent should be withheld from those that are not completely certain and indubitable, no less carefully than from those that are obviously false' (AT VII, 18; HR I, 145). The foundations metaphor is carried on in the further remark that since 'if the foundations are undermined, whatever is built on top of them automatically collapses,' it is not necessary to consider our beliefs one by one, which would be 'an infinite task.' Rather, Descartes says, he will directly attack the principles on which all that he formerly believed is based: '*aggrediar statim ipsa principia, quibus illud omne quod olim credidi nitebatur*' (*ibid.*).

Subsequently, Descartes finds increasingly powerful 'reasons for doubting' his beliefs, in arguments based on the consideration of normal sensory illusion, on the experience of dreaming and on the possibility that God is a deceiver (who systematically causes his creature to make erroneous judgments even on such basic matters as that there exist physical objects or that $2 + 3 = 5$). By the end of the Meditation Descartes has concluded that he has 'nothing to reply' to these arguments,

> but at last I am compelled to admit there is nothing among those things that I formerly thought to be true which it is not possible to doubt, not through lack of consideration, or levity, but for sound and considered reasons. (AT VII, 21; HR I, 147–8)

In this chapter I will explore certain problems of interpretation of the First Meditation. Most of the problems I will discuss are connected with the question of how the work as a whole is to be understood. I believe that Descartes's arguments, in the first and in later Meditations, have very often been misunderstood and miscriticized, because we have given insufficient attention to the question of what the work as a whole was meant to accomplish, and to the interrelations of its various arguments.[1] In this connection, some preliminary comments are in order.

In the first sentence of the First Meditation Descartes gives, as the underlying motive for bringing in question his 'present opinions,' the desire to establish something 'firm and enduring in the sciences.' This remark should be read in connection with his famous statement in the introduction to the French translation of the *Principles of Philosophy* that metaphysics provides the roots for the tree of science.[2] (As already noted, the structure of the *Principles* exemplifies this notion: the scientific parts follow on the presentation of Descartes's metaphysics in Part I.) Even more illuminating in this connection is a letter to Mersenne of 28 January 1641, which is also rather frequently quoted. Descartes comments to Mersenne that the titles of individual Meditations should call attention to the points he particularly wants people to notice, and these have to do with the nature and knowledge of mind, its distinctness from body, the existence of God and the essence and existence of matter (AT III, 297; PL 94). But, he continues,

> I think I have put in many other things; and I will tell you, between ourselves, that these six Meditations contain all the foundations of my Physics. But please don't say so; because those who favor Aristotle would perhaps make more difficulty about approving them; and I hope those who read them will accustom

themselves insensibly to my principles, and recognize their truth, before noticing that they destroy those of Aristotle. (AT III, 297–8; PL 94)

Now, we do know, independently of the *Meditations*, that Descartes was one of the most original and successful mathematicians who had lived up to his time, and also a phenomenally dedicated and systematic physical scientist. We know too that Cartesian physics—for all the embarrassments of its particular formulations and accounts—*was* in fact highly instrumental in 'overthrowing the principles of Aristotle'—in establishing the concept of a universal science of matter that seeks to explain all phenomena in terms of basic quantifiable properties and simple laws governing change. There is, then, reason to take very seriously the idea that Descartes thinks his philosophy, as presented in the *Meditations*, is fundamentally connected with his projected revolution in science.

There is, on the other hand, no good reason to suppose that Descartes's *sole* concern in the *Meditations* is the introduction of a certain scientific perspective—at least as we understand the term 'scientific' today. With all due acknowledgment of Descartes's powers as an ironist, it would be extreme to doubt the sincerity of his repeated self-congratulation for having proved, in the *Meditations*, the immateriality of the soul and the existence of God—and that both are 'better known' than either the truths of geometry or the existence of matter.[3] (It is unlikely Descartes would have impugned his geometry by insisting his proofs of God's existence were 'more certain,' when he was in reality an agnostic or atheist.[4]) In correspondence and in other works, Descartes repeatedly insists on the great importance of establishing his own conception of God as strictly infinite and omnipotent; he implies that other, 'unworthy' conceptions are prevalent among his contemporaries.[5] And, while he eventually surrendered his original claim to have proved the 'immortality' of the soul,[6] his concern with proving its 'distinctness from matter' is already prominent in the Second Meditation (and is a dominant theme in the Replies to Objections). Descartes's treatments of God and the soul certainly have important *relevance* to his conceptions of universal science—as I shall argue repeatedly below. But this is no reason to deny that the proofs of God's existence and of the soul's immateriality have intrinsic importance in his thinking. The 'skeptical' arguments of the First Meditation, and also the assertion of the indubitability of the *cogito* which begins the Second, cannot be fully understood in isolation from such stated or indicated objectives of the work.

3

In a letter to Mersenne of 30 September 1640 (AT III, 192; PL 79), Descartes asserts: 'The principal aim of my metaphysics is to make clear which are the things that can be distinctly conceived.' Distinct conception provides the foundations at once of science, of theory of mind and of theology. The 'doubts' of the First Meditation lead ultimately to the conclusion that what we can distinctly conceive are, in reverse order, matter as represented by *Cartesian* science, the mind as an immaterial substance, and the omnipotence, existence, infinity and non-deceiving benevolence of God.

None of the points I have just stated is in the least novel. But I think contemporary Descartes criticism too often loses sight of them. For example, one still finds Descartes's arguments approached as if his concerns and attitudes were almost the same as classical (or Renaissance) skepticism, or of British academic philosophers of the mid-twentieth century. For example, the Dreaming Argument and the *cogito* have both been almost consistently 'interpreted' by English-speaking analytical philosophers, as if they were self-standing arguments, without place in a larger strategy. I hope to persuade the reader that a more systematic approach is preferable—beginning with the subject of Cartesian doubt.

2   The 'I' of the Meditations

First, a very preliminary, almost incidental point of interpretation should be considered. The first sentence of the *Meditations* has already made clear that Descartes's exposition of his mature philosophy will be presented in the style of colloquial autobiographical narrative. This style can lead to the assumption that Descartes is directly concerned in the *Meditations* with the facts of his own intellectual development, his private mental history. It seems to me, however, that we should guard against such an assumption. While perhaps the order cf arguments presented in the *Meditations* does reflect Descartes's own progress in philosophical inquiry, it is not obvious that this is so, and not in the least relevant to the philosophical purpose of the *Meditations* whether or not it is so.[7] In this connection, one should bear in mind that in works other than the *Meditations* Descartes uses different pronouns to set forth essentially the same ideas. In *The Search After Truth* he makes heavy use of the second person. In the general philosophical parts of the *Principles*, 'we' and 'it' (i.e., 'the mind') predominate. To note these points is not, of course, to deny that Descartes's system in some sense presupposes the availability of the concept of subject or self—or the form of the first person singular. (It does, in fact, make this presupposition, and for this very reason—a philosophical, not an historical reason—the first person form probably does provide the most effective mode of exposition.) The main point is just that the work must be read primarily as the presentation of a philosophical position having some claim to general relevance, and not as history or autobiography at all.

There is, I believe, a rhetorical, as well as a philosophical reason for Descartes's reliance on the first person in the most important exposition of his philosophy. As already noted, Descartes indicates in correspondence that the *Meditations* were intended to gain 'acceptance' for his physical theory—in other words to change people's minds, to overthrow preconceptions, though in a rather insidious manner. And elsewhere he implies that the work is intended as a set of Meditations in something like the traditional religious sense: the reader is supposed to 'give months, or at least weeks, to [thinking over the matter of which the First Meditation treats], before going further . . .' (AT VII, 130; HR II, 31).[8] Descartes's use of the first person, then, may very well be intended to promote *identification* on the part of the reader—thereby smoothing his transition from darkness and vain philosophy into the new light of modern, anti-Aristotelian, philosophy and science.

On the other hand, it is rather difficult to expound the argument of the *Meditations* without sliding into such improbable assertions as 'Descartes notes that he had little by little lost all faith in his senses by finding that towers which looked round from a distance looked square close-up.' I will not try to avoid this mode of expression completely, but will try to avoid what seem to me the more serious pitfalls associated with it.

3 Assumptions and aims of methodic doubt

The beginning of the First Meditation introduces, as well, some substantive problems in interpreting and evaluating Descartes's endeavor. In the first place, Descartes indicates very casually that he will attack his opinions by attacking the 'principles' on which they are based. He gives no explanation or justification of the notion that his beliefs are 'based on principles,' and no clarification of what he means by 'principle.' The initial remarks about the false things accepted in youth suggest a rather commonsensical conception of how our beliefs are founded on principles. Descartes at first seems to be implying that (a) opinions acquired later in life are, in general, 'founded on' opinions acquired earlier; and (b) all the 'many false opinions' acquired earlier are counted among the 'principles' on which later opinions may be founded. (In this way, it seems, my present opinion that your dog is dangerous might be founded on the opinion, acquired from my nurse in childhood, that all dogs are dangerous.) It immediately emerges, however, that Descartes has in mind something more special than this. For the statement that he will avoid an infinite task by attacking 'principles' seems to imply that the principles in question are few in number. But he doesn't explain this assumption. Nor does one find, as the argument proceeds, that any principles are stated explicitly. It does emerge that 'trust in the senses' figures basically in the early, suspect 'foundation' of our opinions. One possibility, then, is that the 'principles' in question should be construed as rules of sensory evidence. Later in the chapter I will discuss this proposal and offer what seems to me a better alternative.[9]

Second, the beginning of the *Meditations* raises in a quite clear-cut way the question of the *point* or *objective* of Cartesian doubt. Taken literally, Descartes seems to be saying that science must be established on a base of certainty, that presently formed opinions are 'founded' on opinions acquired earlier, and that merely because he has discovered that some beliefs acquired in his early years are false, he must get rid of *all* his earlier beliefs in order to make sure that only true opinions will be included among the foundations to be provided for his science. It is almost as if, having come to acknowledge the utter innocuousness of most of my friends' dogs, and having found myself in the wrong on a number of other points as well, I make up my mind to get rid of *all* my beliefs, and 'reinstate' only those that are in some sense completely beyond question. When Descartes's project is thus interpreted in terms of his initial statement, certain objections fairly naturally arise. It has, for example, been objected that there is no justification offered (or available) for throwing out *all* one's former beliefs, even in pursuit of certainty: the rational procedure is to examine them one by one and discard the bad ones only.[10] And it has been objected that in any case the only possible path to intellectual progress is to criticize one's opinions in piecemeal fashion, using other opinions as a basis while doing so (i.e., Descartes has failed to grasp the nature of criticism and the growth of knowledge).[11]

I believe that these objections are basically quite misguided. Roughly, the problem is this. The first sentence, or first paragraph, of Meditation I provides a picture of Descartes's undertaking which, while it may invite such objections, does not in fact represent his intentions adequately. This colloquial beginning seems to imply that the *Meditations* are generated by a rather commonsensical desire to

6

bring one's beliefs into accord with the facts—or more precisely by a scientist's desire to assure himself, so far as possible, that he has avoided false presuppositions, in the ordinary sense. Viewed from this perspective, the rest of the First Meditation, from the announcement that opinions in the most tenuous sense doubtful must be rejected as false, to the final preoccupation with the hypothesis of an all-powerful deceiver, may well take on the aspect of a baffling *tour de force*. But the beginning of the Meditation does not need to be read so literally. It can and should be viewed as principally a device for initiating a constructive philosophical inquiry—one that will conclude by enunciating a rationalist epistemology and a non-commonsensical theory of mind and nature—at a point as close as possible to common sense assumptions.

In the 'Synopsis' to the *Meditations* Descartes had provided a more complete and more suggestive explanation of methodic doubt:[12]

> In the first [Meditation], I put forward the reasons for which we
> can doubt generally of all things, and particularly of material
> things, at least as long as we have no other foundations in the
> sciences than those which we have had up to now. And, although
> the utility of a doubt so general may not at first be apparent, it is
> nevertheless very great, in that [such doubt] delivers us from all
> sorts of prejudices, and prepares for us a very easy way of
> accustoming our mind to detaching itself from the senses, and
> finally, in that it brings it about that it is no longer possible that
> we can have any doubt about that which we afterwards discover to
> be true. (AT VII, 12; HR I, 140)

The First Meditation is concerned to set forth some skeptical arguments relating, especially, to sense experience—and also, ultimately, to issues about mathematical knowledge. As Descartes says in the passage just cited, the aim of these arguments is, in large degree, to promote 'detachment from sense.' In addition, the views that emerge as unshaken in the face of these arguments will be such that we can have no doubts about them.

But why 'detachment from sense'? Because from the point of view of Descartes as scientist, the beliefs imposed on all of us by uncriticized sense experience, together with the claims of the relatively empiricistic Aristotelian tradition, are nothing but false though very deeply implanted 'prejudices.' These prejudices can only interfere with our acceptance of the true scientific and philosophic image of reality.

Descartes's concern with 'certainty' in the early parts of the *Meditations* must partly be understood in light of this objective.

What he will first note against sense-dependent beliefs about the world and about the mind is that they are not incorrigible and hence as a class they are not 'certain' beyond the shadow of a doubt. But in the course of the *Meditations* the (apparently marginal) unreliability of the senses with respect to particular states of affairs (over there is a round tower; I am sitting by the fire) becomes gradually converted into a doctrine of the mere subjectivity of much of the sensory image of reality. While Descartes is, no doubt, concerned with the problem of certainty—of traditional skepticism—in its own right, he is also concerned to *use* this problem to present convincingly an anti-empiricist metaphysics, a form of (rationalist) 'scientific realism.'[13] Thus, in seeking to produce 'detachment from sense' Descartes is making way for a doctrine of physical reality that depends on supposedly innate, partly mathematical concepts, and a doctrine of mind that is both anti-materialistic and anti-empiricistic. The 'quest for certainty' is not sharply distinguished within Descartes's framework from the mere quest for philosophical and scientific truth. And 'methodic doubt' is not a barren exercise, which ultimately results in adding some fastidious bit of super-certainty to the normal assurance one already had about things seen, felt or calculated. Nor is it a bizarrely misguided way of speedily recategorizing the commonsensical beliefs and scientific hypotheses of a pre-philosophical mind as true or false. It is nothing less than a strategy for shaking and ultimately revising nearly universal conceptions of the true image of reality.

There is, then, a danger of confusion when gradualist or holistic conceptions of scientific progress are brought against Descartes's enterprise of categorical doubt, as in the objections mentioned above. Consider for instance the following:

> Since one can only criticize one's opinions in piecemeal fashion, using other opinions as a base while doing so, Descartes's plan of doubting all his opinions and 'starting over again from the foundations' is thoroughly misconceived.

Up to a point, this objection depends on taking Descartes too much at his word in the first statements of the *Meditations*. For the objection assumes that Descartes's objective is to bring his own particular beliefs into accord with the facts as much as possible—to determine, for example, whether or not all dogs are really dangerous. Once we consider that Descartes is really playing a deeper game—is in effect trying to *overthrow* prevailing conceptions and opinions—the objection emerges as rather naïve. Whether or not there really is a cogent way of philosophically criticizing commonsense assumptions

8

about reality—or the 'deliverances of the senses' in general—it seems clear enough that piecemeal criticism of particular commonsense or 'scientific' beliefs, on the grounds of other things one happens to think, commonsensically or scientifically, would not be a very promising approach to the problem. Similarly, it is misguided to announce that Descartes is unjustified in 'overthrowing' all opinions in order to get rid of the bad ones (he should just get rid of the bad ones); or that he is unjustified in 'discarding' all opinions in which he finds 'the least reason for doubt' (he should just discard those that he finds, on reflection, to be inadequately supported according to reasonable standards of evidence). The 'prejudices of our youth' have a strong hold, both psychologically and epistemically. A concerted onslaught is the *only* justifiable approach for the sort of intellectual revolution Descartes intends to bring about.

But, I suppose, we cannot quite leave the matter here. There is, after all, an element of truth in the objections I have just been disputing. It does seem, at times, as if Descartes regards his system as springing forth from the bed-rock of Truth, independently of *any* preconception or historically conditioned commitment. Similarly, Descartes does seem to be concerned with presenting the metaphysical foundations of his science, and its basic concepts, as intrinsically and completely beyond reasonable doubt—as incorrigible deliverances of 'the light of nature.' Thus, to the deceptiveness of the senses will ultimately be opposed the absolute *data* of certain deliverances of reason. Such notions are, of course, subject to criticism on logical grounds (how could one ever get started philosophically, if he seriously resolved to accept *no* uncriticized assumptions?). In addition, they appear naïvely absolutistic in several senses, from the point of view of the historical relativism characteristic of our century. (As will emerge later, Descartes goes so far as to hold that the laws of nature and the true concept of matter, as well as of mind and God, are innate in the human mind, where they can be 'discovered' once the prejudices of the senses have been set behind us.) However, these concessions must not obscure the primary point: that through methodic doubt Descartes is attempting to bring about a radical and systematic revision in the contemporary world view. His procedure cannot be comprehended or criticized in abstraction from this goal.

A similar misunderstanding is reflected in another critic's claim that the first sentence of the *Meditations* already provides Descartes with a reason for regarding all his opinions as suspect, and hence the 'reasons for doubt' that he will spend the rest of the Meditation expounding are in an important respect gratuitous.[14] (This claim is

9

backed up by the observation that since Descartes regards belief as dependent on the will (as he explains in Meditation IV), a bare act of will should be sufficient to suspend all beliefs on the basis of the observation, contained in the first sentence, that it is important that he do so.[15]) In other words, the initial observation that his beliefs have been acquired uncritically 'from an early age,' should be all the cause or reason needed 'to doubt of all things.' But, in the first place, Descartes does not say at the outset that all his beliefs are suspect, but only that *whatever* is founded on possibly false beliefs acquired in childhood is uncertain. The enterprise of achieving 'general doubt' is the enterprise of demonstrating to himself (or, more realistically, to the reader) that there is no class of his beliefs, as they are presently structured, that can hold out against skeptical attack. And there is good reason for proceeding in this way, given Descartes's objectives as we have sketched them above. There is nothing potentially revolutionary in the observation that one has from youth accepted certain false things as true. I presume that anyone would agree that he has over the years believed many false propositions: e.g., that Santa Claus brings Christmas presents and that storks bring babies. But few would conclude from such an admission that all their present beliefs should be regarded as uncertain. Even if it were agreed that the consideration of past error is sufficient to raise the question whether I might not always be unable to distinguish truth from error with certainty, some kind of 'skeptical' arguments are needed to forestall an immediate negative *answer* to this question. For surely anyone who hadn't heard yet of such arguments would be likely to respond: 'Of course I can distinguish truth from falsity in some cases—for example, when it is a matter of something I see right before me with my own eyes, or of very simple arithmetical propositions!' But these are precisely the 'opinions' that Descartes is most concerned to distance himself and the reader from in the early parts of the *Meditations*.

The conception of the *Meditations* as having revolutionary intent also has some implications for another question that is frequently raised in connection with the enterprise of 'methodic doubt': namely, in what sense, if at all, should the 'doubts' generated by Descartes's use of skeptical arguments be considered *genuine doubts*? Kenny puts the question this way:[16]

> Does [Descartes] ever *really* doubt the existence of God and the world?

Descartes himself, in different places, characterized the doubts generated in the First Meditation as 'hyperbolical,' 'metaphysical,' 'laughable' and 'ridiculous.' Yet on the conception of the *Meditations* as intended to bring about a sweeping *revision* of one's conceptual scheme, and the *abandonment* of long-standing 'prejudices,' it seems that these 'doubts' can hardly be construed as completely nugatory. (As Descartes might put it, the cause must have as much reality as the effect!) I prefer to delay consideration of this complex issue, together with the question raised above about the nature of the 'principles' supposedly under attack, until the actual skeptical arguments that Descartes employs have been examined and analyzed.

4 Attacking the foundations: 'these familiar things'

Having announced his intention of attacking the foundations of his 'present beliefs,' Descartes proceeds:

> All that I have up to now accepted as most true, I have received either from the senses or through the senses; these however I have sometimes found to deceive [*fallere deprehendi*], and it is prudent never to trust completely those which have once deceived us. (AT VII, 18; HR I, 145)

This truistic observation is followed by consideration of the much more significant proposal that the senses are reliable at least in circumstances that commonsense would regard as unproblematic:

> But, although the senses sometimes deceive us about things that are very small and very distant, perhaps nevertheless there are many others about which it is completely impossible to doubt, although they are derived from the senses: such as that I am now here, seated by the fire, clothed in a winter robe, holding this paper in my hands, and similar things. For by what reason could the being of these hands themselves, and this whole body, be denied? [*Manus vero has ipsas, totumque hoc corpus meum esse, quā ratione posset negari?*] (*Ibid.*)

In calling into question this proposition Descartes considers first the fantasies of madness and then the experience of dreaming. In the condition of madness, he observes, people imagine they have an earthenware head, or are pumpkins, or are made of glass. However, this does not seem to him to provide a fully satisfactory 'reason for doubt' since 'these people are insane and I would myself seem not less insane if I should transfer this case from them to myself' (AT VII, 18–19; HR I, 145). At this point, however, the so-called Dreaming Argument is introduced as an *acceptable* reason for doubting these

11

things. The phenomenon of dreaming can be used to make a point similar to that first attempted by the consideration of madness, without going outside the experiences of a normal person. Having noted that, as a man, he is accustomed to dream, Descartes continues:

> How often indeed during repose at night am I persuaded of these familiar things, that I am here, clothed in a robe, seated near the fire, when I am nevertheless lying without clothes between the sheets! But now surely I view this paper with waking eyes, the head which I move is not somnolent, I extend and perceive this hand carefully and knowingly; things would not happen so distinctly to one asleep. As if I did not remember having been deceived on other occasions by similar thoughts in sleep; so that when I think of this more attentively, I see so clearly that it is never possible to distinguish waking from sleeping by certain marks, that I am amazed, and this amazement almost confirms me in the supposition of sleep. (AT VII, 19; HR I, 145–6)

Descartes suggests, then, that the alleged impossibility of distinguishing waking from sleeping by certain marks provides some reason for doubting even those sense-based beliefs that concern the most obvious aspects of his current personal circumstances and surroundings.

What exactly is the structure of the Dreaming Argument, and what exactly is it intended to establish? According to the most common interpretation—that assumed for example in the well-known critical discussions of Moore and Malcolm[17]—the argument is intended to show that I cannot be certain of particular sense-based judgments such as 'I am sitting by the fire,' 'I am standing up,' or 'here are two human hands.' And it is supposed to reach this conclusion via the premiss, 'I cannot know for certain that I am now awake, rather than asleep and dreaming.' Moore, for instance, states the argument as follows:[18]

> 'You do not know for certain that you are not dreaming; it is not absolutely certain that you are not; there is *some* chance, though perhaps only a very small one, that you are.' And from this, that I do not know for certain that I am not dreaming, it is supposed to follow that I do not know for certain that I am standing up.

Harry Frankfurt has recently endorsed a similar interpretation, but with an added embellishment: Frankfurt thinks Descartes's point is that there are no purely sensory characteristics to distinguish waking experience from dreams, and that hence we cannot tell 'on the basis of sensory data alone' that we are not presently dreaming.[19]

The interpretations of Moore, Malcolm and Frankfurt agree in viewing the Dreaming Argument as directed against the certainty of any particular sense-based judgment at any particular moment. An alternative interpretation, advanced by W. H. Walsh, holds on the contrary that Descartes's conclusion is that we might be *dreaming all the time*.[20] While Frankfurt dismisses Walsh's account as involving 'rather typical misconceptions,'[21] I believe that Walsh is in fact much closer to the truth than the others. This becomes clear as soon as one considers what exactly it is that the Dreaming Argument is meant to accomplish in the over-all structure of Descartes's argument. However, I will propose an interpretation that differs from all of the above.

Unfortunately for my interpretation, and also for those already stated, Frankfurt is flatly wrong in his assertion that 'there is no ambiguity in Descartes's treatment of dreaming in the *Meditations*.'[22] I will not claim that my reading accords well with all the texts—only that it receives strong support from *some* texts, in the *Meditations* and elsewhere, that do not fit well with the other readings. And I think that my interpretation of the argument has philosophical, as well as strategic advantages. But before presenting it I must first show how Descartes's reasoning proceeds *after* he has presented the Dreaming Argument. For this sequel provides, on my view, a crucial key to the interpretation of the argument itself.

5   Attacking the foundations: 'simple and universal things'

Retrenchment after the Dreaming Argument takes place in two phases—that is, two different assumptions are implicitly advanced (in succession) as unimpugned by it. First Descartes suggests that the argument is effective only against certain 'particulars':

> Suppose therefore that we are asleep, and that these particulars are not true, that we open our eyes, move our head, extend our hands, and that perhaps we don't even have such hands, nor such a whole body; nevertheless it at least must be admitted that things seen in sleep [*visa per quietem*] are like some sort of painted images [*veluti quasdam pictas imagines*], which cannot be formed except on resemblance to real things [*nisi ad similitudinem rerum verarum*]; and that thus at least these general [things], eyes, head, hands, and the whole body are not imaginary things, but really existing ones [*res quasdam non imaginarias, sed veras existere*].
> (AT VII, 19; HR I, 146)

If we do admit what Descartes here says we must admit, we would hold that only some such assumption as the following can survive the Dreaming Argument:

Beliefs that certain *sorts* of experienced physical objects exist are true beliefs, as long as the things in question aren't specified at all particularly.

One might perhaps expect this claim to be based on the grounds that only those *types* of propositions that we believe we have in fact been deceived about in dreams can be called into question by the Dreaming Argument. For example, while we have had the experience of waking up to discover we were not, after all, sitting by the fire, or examining a piece of wax at close range, or in some other particular circumstance, we have not had the experience of waking up to find there aren't really any heads, hands or bodies. In fact, Descartes's reasoning takes a different form: it proceeds from the apparently *a priori* assumption that 'things that we see in sleep . . . cannot be imagined except on resemblance to real things . . .'' (*ibid.*). (This assumption is a condition on the causal basis of dream images—a point of some importance as I will indicate later.) But this assumption is immediately abandoned in favor of one that Descartes evidently considers more plausible. Having noted, in line with the previous considerations, that painters who make up fantastic animals 'do so by making a mixture of the members of different [real] animals,' he continues:

or if perhaps they invent something completely new, such that nothing at all similar to it has been seen, and that is therefore completely fictitious and false, certainly nevertheless at least the colors of which it is composed must be real [*veri*]. And for the same reason, although even these general things, eyes, head, hands, and the like, can be imaginary, still it is at least necessary to admit that certain others even more simple and universal are real [*vera*], from which as if from real colors all these images of things, whether true or false, which are in our thought [*in cogitatione nostra sunt*] are made [*effinguntur*]. (AT VII, 20; HR I, 146)

Descartes then specifies (without argument or clarification) what some of these simple and universal things are:

Corporeal nature in general and its extension seems to be of this sort; also the figure of extended things; also their quantity, or magnitude and number; also the place in which they exist, and the time through which they endure, and the like. (AT VII, 20; HR I, 146)

14

Some sciences, indeed, treat of just such things 'without taking much trouble whether they are in nature [*in rerum natura*] or not.' Perhaps we would be right to conclude, Descartes says, that these sciences—he mentions arithmetic and geometry as examples—'contain something certain and indubitable,' while 'physics, astronomy, medicine, and all other sciences that depend on the consideration of composite things are indeed doubtful' (AT VII, 20; HR I, 147). Descartes concludes these remarks, intended (in part) to exhibit the limitations of the Dreaming Argument as an initiator of universal doubt, with the following (rather notorious) observation:

> For whether I am awake or asleep, two and three joined together are five, and the square does not have more than four sides, and it does not seem possible that such perspicuous truths should incur the suspicion of falsehood. (*Ibid*)

It seems, then, that beliefs in the reality of 'simple and universal things,' and sciences that 'treat' only of these most simple and general things are not supposed to be brought into question by the Dreaming Argument.

But what sort of beliefs are 'beliefs in the reality of simple natures'? Are these beliefs about existence in nature, or are they not? That is, should we take Descartes to be saying in this transitional passage that

(1) We cannot doubt (on the basis of the Dreaming Argument) that there exists a physical world with certain categorial features (extension, figure, duration) though more determinate existential judgments are uncertain (e.g. there exists here before me a physical object of such and such shape and size that has existed for such and such length of time, etc.)?

Or only that

(2) We cannot doubt that the fundamental constitutive ingredients of our ideas or experiences represent things that are *in some sense* real, and these include extension, figure, etc.?

On the first view, we could say that claims about the veridical nature of our thoughts *qua* representings of a real world in space are being upheld: the world is still supposed to be 'out there,' but can confidently be characterized only in the most general and non-determinate ways. This reading seems natural if one concentrates on the *pattern* that the extension of doubt seems to follow, from the Dreaming Argument on: first very specific judgments about what is

15

known to exist are questioned (this human body as I perceive it, of a certain size and in a certain position, wearing a robe of a certain sort, etc.); then (it seems) the final bulwark is set up for assault: there is a physical nature, which is extended, endures, manifests figure, and so forth (things more simple and more general). Read this way, the definiteness of the description of what we are committed to changes but the sort of commitment does not: namely, physical existence, or 'rerum natura.'

The continuation of the argument of the First Meditation seems to support the view that the question of the reality of simple natures does involve the question of the existence of a physical world. To bring into question beliefs about simple and universal things, Descartes introduces the hypothesis of a God 'who can do everything.' And he writes:

> Still for a long time I have had impressed in my mind the opinion
> that there is a God who can do everything, and by whom I have
> been created such as I exist. Now how can I know that this God has
> not made it the case that there is no earth at all, no sky, no
> extended thing, no figure, no magnitude, no place, and that
> nevertheless all these seem to me to exist just as they do now? And
> even, just as I sometimes judge others to err concerning those
> things that they think they know most perfectly, [he can have
> made] me such that I err as often as I add two and three together,
> or count the sides of a square, or [do] whatever might be easier?
> (AT VII, 21; HR I, 147)

However, there are reasons to be cautious on this point. First, it becomes clear later in the *Meditations* that Descartes does not think the question whether an idea is of 'something real' is the same as the question whether it is of something existent. One can, that is, commit oneself to the 'reality' of what is represented by an idea, without committing oneself to the existence of what is represented by that idea.[23] Second, it becomes clear in the Fifth Meditation that Descartes thinks there is a problem about mathematical truth that *precedes* the question of the existence in nature of things answering to mathematical concepts.[24] Further, this position is foreshadowed in the First Meditation, by Descartes's statement that sciences like arithmetic and geometry, which 'treat' of simple and universal things, do not 'take much trouble whether [these things] are in nature or not.' For there is a clear suggestion that the superior certainty of these sciences is to some degree a result of this relative indifference to existence in nature.

Thus, on the one hand, it seems reasonable to suppose that

Descartes intended for certain minimal beliefs in external existence to survive the Dreaming Argument. On the other hand, the deceiving God hypothesis that is next introduced is probably supposed to do more than *just* provide a reason for doubting these residual existential beliefs. For beliefs about simple mathematical truths, which survive the Dreaming Argument, *are* finally brought into question by the last skeptical argument. And evidence from both the First and the Fifth Meditations indicates that Descartes did not regard these sciences as dependent for their truth on physical existence.

But *what* more? What more is there to doubt, once we have embarked upon a total questioning of the existence of a physical world? Well, perhaps something like the reality of essences, or the objectivity of the relations that our thought seems to reveal as obtaining among the various mathematical natures.[25]

According to our exposition, then, Descartes's first 'skeptical' observation is intended to underscore the fact that 'appeal to the senses' is not sufficient foundation for claims to certainty. The second piece of 'skeptical' reasoning—the Dreaming Argument—is intended to show there is some element of uncertainty about even the most obvious and certain sense-based beliefs. At first Descartes suggests that the implications of this argument may extend only to 'particulars' or very determinate judgments about the existence of physical objects. Immediately, however, he draws from the consideration of dreaming the conclusion that *all* real existence except that of simple natures is 'uncertain.' The third main piece of skeptical reasoning—the appeal to the possibility of a powerful deceiving God—is then presented as a 'reason for doubting' even these most minimal beliefs about real existence, together with beliefs about the most basic conceptual relations that the mathematical sciences find among their constituents, conceived very abstractly.

6 The Dreaming Argument: a reconstruction

We may now return to the analysis of the Dreaming Argument itself. As we have seen above, a number of philosophers interested in Descartes's argument have taken him to be arguing along something like the following lines:

(1) It seems to me that I am now sitting in a chair (viewing a human hand at close range, etc.).

(2) I have in the past dreamed I was sitting in a chair (or whatever), when it was false that I was.

17

(3) Thus, if I have reason to think it is possible I am dreaming I am sitting in a chair, I have reason to believe that it may be false that I am.

(4) I can be absolutely certain that p only if I do not have any reason to believe that p may be false.

(5) Therefore I can be absolutely certain that I am now sitting in a chair (or whatever) only if I do not have reason to think it is possible I am dreaming.

(6) Unless there are certain marks to distinguish dreaming from waking, it is not the case that I do not have reason to think it is possible that I am dreaming.

(7) But I see (on reflection) that there are no certain marks to distinguish dreaming from waking.

(8) Hence, I cannot be absolutely certain that I am now sitting in a chair (or whatever).

(Some commentators do not phrase the argument in a way that places weight on the problem of finding 'distinguishing marks': see the passage cited from Moore above. However, Descartes does place weight on this problem—both in stating the argument and (as we will see) in subsequently replying to it. For present purposes, therefore, I will take the claim that there are 'no certain marks to distinguish dreaming from waking' as essential to the Dreaming Argument.)

The major objection to this interpretation of the argument is that it simply does not lead to the conclusion that, I would hold, Descartes clearly desires. As I hope to have shown above, Descartes takes the Dreaming Argument to establish that there is reason to doubt the world is *anything like* what the senses seem to reveal. In other words, the argument calls into question the existence of *all* 'composites' or ordinary physical objects—not just any particular one that I happen to be 'viewing' at a given time. The question Descartes wishes to raise is not whether I can know that this or that sense experience is veridical, but whether I can know with certainty that the senses ever afford us truth at all (apart from the reality of simples).

Should we then accept Walsh's interpretation, according to which Descartes is raising the possibility that he might be *always* dreaming? While I believe this is a much better reading (for the reasons just given), there is a second important problem that arises equally in connection with Walsh's interpretation and the one I have already rejected.

According to all the interpretations considered so far, the problem Descartes sets himself in the First Meditation is to find 'certain marks to distinguish dreaming from waking,' where this is understood to mean 'marks by which one may certainly *tell* on a given occasion *whether* one is, on that occasion, dreaming or waking.' It is because he doesn't 'see' any such marks in the First Meditation that he is said to conclude that he can't know for certain that he isn't dreaming. Now suppose (as seems obvious) that to seek marks by which one may certainly *tell whether* one is dreaming or waking is to seek criteria, satisfied by waking experience but not by dreams, which one may *apply* to one's current experience to determine whether or not one is dreaming. Unfortunately, this seems to describe a nonsensical quest. For first, the description of the objective implies that it is possible to apply a criterion to dreaming experience while one is dreaming. But in fact (one common objection runs) under such circumstances one can only *dream* one applies a criterion.[26] And, second (waiving this objection), suppose such an alleged criterion *is produced*, is applied to one's experience, and deemed to be satisfied—i.e., one 'determines that one is awake.' Still it seems we have accomplished nothing. For we can adapt Descartes's own reasoning and argue: How many times in the past have I concluded my experience satisfied the criterion of waking experience, only to decide subsequently that I was only dreaming that it did![27]

Now it is certain, as noted above, that Descartes sees *a* problem about 'marks to distinguish waking from dreaming' as central to the Dreaming Argument. He believes it makes *sense* to search for such marks, and he believes the Dreaming Argument can be dismissed when he ultimately 'finds' some. Thus, in the First Meditation he inspects his experience, past and present, and concludes there are no such marks. But, as is by now well enough known, he comes to *retract* the denial at the end of the last (Sixth) Meditation. That is, he comes to affirm that there *are* certain marks to distinguish waking from dreaming.[28] He writes:

And I must reject all the doubts of these past days, as hyperbolic and ridiculous, particularly that one about sleep, which I could not distinguish from waking; for now I notice that there is a very great distinction between them, in as much as the things of sleep are never joined together with all the other actions of life by memory, like those which occur when awake. . . . (AT VII, 89; HR I, 198–9)

As the sequel makes clear, the joining together of waking actions is closely connected in Descartes's mind with the idea of spatio-temporal unity in what is observed:

For indeed, if someone, while I am awake, should appear to me abruptly and later disappear in the same way, as happens in sleep, so that it was not clear to me whence he came nor where he went, I would not without reason judge him to be a specter, or a phantom produced by my brain, rather than a real man. But when these things occur, of which I notice distinctly whence, where, and when they appear to me, and the perception of which I connect without any interruption with the whole rest of my life, I am fully certain that they occur not in sleep but in waking. (AT VII, 89–90; HR I, 199)

If 'marks to distinguish dreaming from waking' mean 'marks by which to *tell whether* one is dreaming' Descartes's whole approach is vulnerable to the objection of absurdity and incoherence.

Of course, for all we have said so far, we may have only been developing an objection to *Descartes* rather than (as I implied) to particular interpretations of Descartes. (Walsh, for example, is the first to deny that the argument as he construes it is sound.) There are, however, grounds for considering a different reading of both the initial argument and the reply of the Sixth Meditation. On this reading the 'marks' Descartes seeks are *not* criteria to determine whether he is on a given occasion dreaming.

An objection of the sort we have just been considering was raised by Hobbes at the end of the Third Objections. Hobbes pointed out the possibility that a person, 'dreaming that he doubted whether he dreamed or not,' could go on to dream that 'his dream is joined and connected with the ideas of a long course of past things' (AT VII, 195; HR II, 78). Descartes's reply, which is not often seriously regarded, is actually rather interesting:

Someone who sleeps and dreams, cannot join and assemble, perfectly and with truth, his dreams with the ideas of past things, even if he can dream that he assembles them. For who denies that one who sleeps can deceive himself? But after, when awake, he will easily know his error. (AT VII, 196; HR II, 78)

Now the first part of this reply, read as merely a reaffirmation that connectability with past experience is a sufficient mark of waking experience, is clearly open to question—even *apart from* the contention that one might merely be dreaming that this is the case. It is surely easy to imagine falling asleep in the middle of this discussion and dreaming a 'logical' continuation of the discussion. On the other hand, it is worth noting that this initial part of Descartes's reply seemingly *could* be read as an attempt to make a Malcolmian point—that to dream one joins and assembles is not to join and assemble. However, I want to set this question aside and focus rather on the second half of Descartes's reply to Hobbes. The question it invites is obvious: what point could there be in searching for a mark not found in dreams, if for any such mark, there is no denying the possibility that one might (merely) dream that one's experience did have that mark?

Here someone might rejoin, on Descartes's behalf, that if there *is* (for all dreams) a mark to distinguish them from waking, there is *a fortiori* a mark to distinguish dreaming one's experience satisfies that mark from observing that it does. But, first, if this means that we must be able to say things like 'my current judgment that my current experience coheres with the past course of my life, coheres with the past course of my life,' it is not clear we will be attributing to Descartes a position that is readily intelligible. More important, perhaps, we seem to be embarked on a rather uncomfortable regress.

But let us look again at Descartes's reply to Hobbes. The striking thing, surely, is that he does not maintain, in response to Hobbes's objection, that he has solved the problem of distinguishing dreaming from waking *in such a way that one no longer need be deceived by dreams. In particular* he does not deny that one may be deceived in dreams in respect of dreaming that one's experience satisfies the criteria of waking. So let us put our question in this way: is there any *other* problem that he might think he *has* solved? That is, is there any other way, besides the one we have considered, in which the 'mark' of connectability with past experience might seem to answer the Dreaming Argument and refute the conclusion that we have some good reason to doubt even the most apparently obvious sorts of sense experience?

At first glance, the chances for an affirmative answer to this question do not seem very bright. For the point of the Dreaming Argument does seem to be that one can be certain the senses provide veridical experience only if one can 'distinguish' waking experience from dreams. And what this seems to demand is precisely a way of proving with certainty that one is awake when one is awake. But if, as Descartes seems to concede, one can also merely dream that the 'connection' criterion he finally offers is satisfied, the problem seems to be left exactly where it was. One might be tempted to conclude, then, that Descartes simply missed Hobbes's point—or else pretended to miss it.

But suppose for a moment we take seriously Descartes's implication that the conclusion of Meditation VI is not meant to be that (as a result of the discovered 'mark') we can now infallibly 'tell' we are

21

dreaming when we are dreaming. If this is so, it seems that the conclusion can neither be that, as a result of the discovered mark, we can now infallibly *ascertain* we are awake when we are awake.

According to the interpretations mentioned above, the Dreaming Argument proceeds to the conclusion that sense-based beliefs are 'doubtful,' either via the subconclusion (Moore, Malcolm, Frankfurt) 'I cannot be certain I am not now dreaming,' or via the subconclusion (Walsh) 'I cannot be certain it is ever the case that I am awake and not dreaming.' In either case, it seems, the end of Meditation VI must be construed as an attempt to refute the subconclusion (and hence avoid the conclusion) by claiming that there are after all certain marks by which we may determine that we are not now dreaming. Now I would like to propose an interpretation of the Dreaming Argument that seems, at least, to reach the desired conclusion without benefit of the subconclusion that I cannot be certain I am not now dreaming. It goes as follows:

(1) I believe I have in the past dreamed that, for example, I was sitting in a chair (with no feeling of sensory limitation, etc.), when it was false that I was sitting in a chair.

(2) If I see no certain marks to distinguish the present occasion from past occasions when I believe I was deceived, I have reason to believe I may be on the present occasion deceived.

(3) I see no certain marks to distinguish the present occasion from such past occasions.

(4) I have reason to suppose I may be deceived in my present belief that I am sitting in a chair.

Here the third premiss should be read in the following way: I see no marks that would justify construing waking experience of physical objects as veridical, when I construe dream experience of physical objects as deceptive. In fact, the argument can now be generalized to reach the actual final conclusion Descartes wants:

(1') I believe in the past I have dreamed that I was perceiving various physical objects at close range when it was false that I was really perceiving any such objects (when my experience was thoroughly delusory).

(2') If I see no certain marks to distinguish waking experience of physical objects from dream experience when, I believe, I was deceived, I have reason to believe my waking experience too may be deceptive.

(3') I see no such certain marks to distinguish waking experience from dreams.

22

(4′) Therefore, I have reason to suppose that waking experience too may be deceptive (thoroughly delusory).

(5′) But if I have reason to suppose my waking experience may be deceptive (thoroughly delusory), I have reason to doubt the existence of physical objects (for at present we are supposing this experience to be the best foundation for our belief in physical objects).

Here the source of doubt is not located in the problem of knowing one is awake; it is rather expressed in the claim that I cannot say *why I should unquestioningly regard waking experience of physical objects as real or veridical, when there are no marks to distinguish it from the 'illusions of dreams.'*[29]

On this reading, the point of the observations about connectability in Meditation VI is that there are after all marks present in waking experience that explain why we should rationally regard it as different from the illusions of dreams—i.e. as having some claims to veridicality. The fact one has falsely dreamed he is perceiving physical objects no longer provides a ground for doubt of one's present (waking) belief that one is perceiving physical objects. For one notices that his waking experience has a characteristic one finds to be lacking in the dream experience he dismisses as unreal: it fits into the whole course of his life (and is subsumable in appropriate ways under categories of causation and spatio-temporal continuity).

As I mentioned at the beginning, I don't want to claim that this alternative reading of Descartes's argument fits naturally with everything he says in stating the Dreaming Argument or replying to it. Sometimes he certainly does seem to be saying that the problem posed by the argument is how one can determine with certainty whether one is awake or dreaming. However, there is both indirect and direct textual support for the alternative reading.

Descartes's treatment of the question of sanity provides a minor point of indirect support. As we saw, he does not see any reason to doubt that he is sane. But this assurance appears rather arbitrary if he *is* prepared to doubt that he's awake: it simply isn't clear why one of these propositions should be taken for granted if the other is to be questioned. It is also quite significant that the criterion of connectability is treated more as a mark of reality or veridicality than as a mark of waking experience *per se*:

For indeed, if someone, while I am awake, should appear to me abruptly, and later disappear in the same way, as happens in sleep, so that it was not clear to me whence he came nor where he went, I would not without reason judge him to be a specter, or a phantom

23

produced by my brain, rather than a real man. (AT VII, 89–90; HR I, 199)

But towards the middle of the Sixth Meditation one finds much more direct support for my proposed interpretation of the Dreaming Argument. There Descartes writes:

To those [considerations of sensory illusion] I have recently added two other grounds of doubt of the highest generality: the first is that I believed that I never experienced [*sentire*] anything while awake that I could not think that I sometimes also experienced in sleep; and since I do not believe that those things which I seem to experience in sleep come to me from objects outside me, I do not see why I should any more believe this of those that I seem to experience while awake. (AT VII, 77; HR I, 189)

Descartes's statements of the Dreaming Argument in the 'Discourse on Method' and in the French version of the *Principles of Philosophy* also indicate that the question to be raised is not whether he is awake, but rather whether the objects experienced when awake are real. For example, in Part IV of the *Discourse* Descartes writes that, when it is a question of metaphysical certainty, there are grounds for doubting that one has a body, that there are stars and an earth and so on, since

one can . . . imagine, being asleep, that one has another body, and that one sees other stars, and another earth, without any of this being the case. For how does one know that the thoughts that come in dreams are false rather than the others [*plustost fausses que les autres*], given that often they are not less vivid and definite?

But, once the criterion of clear and distinct perception has been established (through the demonstration of God's existence and veracity),

it is quite easy to know that the reveries that we imagine while asleep, should not at all make us doubt about the truth of the thoughts that we have while awake [*ne doiuent aucunement nous faire douter de la verité des pensées que nous auons estant esueillez*]. (AT VI, 38–9; HR I, 104–5; cf. AT VIII–1, 6 and IX–2, 26 (the French version of *Principles* I, iv is closer to the *Discourse* than the Latin); HR I, 220)

Now I would like to consider some objections, other than purely textual ones, to this reading of the argument and its implications.

First, someone might claim that the apparent difference between my interpretation and Walsh's is merely specious. For what distinction remains between waking experience and dreams, if it is not the distinction between veridical experiences on the one hand, and delusive experiences on the other hand? Surely, it will be argued, if I say 'of course I'm awake,' and then go on to say, 'but the objects of my experience, my beliefs about what is in front of me, might be no more real and true than the phantoms and illusions of dreams,' then I have simply taken back with one human hand what I have given with the other. And, obviously, we cannot here resort to the ordinary criteria of sleep and waking—such as whether one is breathing quickly or slowly, whether one's eyes are open and responding to environmental stimuli, or closed and engaging in REM, etc.—to explain what one presently means in asserting one is awake. For such physical states are just what the argument is supposed to be calling in question.

This objection can, I think, be answered in the following way. To say the Dreaming Argument is not meant to call into question the proposition that I can know I'm awake, is to say it is not meant to imply that for all I know I may soon undergo something like the ordinary experience of 'waking up.' The idea is not that in the ordinary course of things I may come to realize this is all a dream; it is rather that the ordinary way of coming to think one was dreaming may not reflect a genuine distinction between what is merely imagined or dreamed, and what is really perceived.

A related objection derives from Walsh's criticism of the argument as *he* interprets it. Walsh holds that the conclusion 'we might for all we know be always dreaming' is inconsistent with an indispensable premiss of the argument: that we have in the past found out that we were only dreaming that p, that our 'perceptual experiences' had been deceptive, that the 'objects experienced' didn't really exist. Walsh writes:[30]

> In order to decide that we were mistaken on a particular occasion
> we need to be able to contrast the experience we had then with
> others which we take to be non-deceptive; if no sense-experience
> can be taken as being in order the contrast cannot be made.
> Similarly with dreaming.

This objection is, it seems, relevant to my interpretation too. For on my interpretation, as well as on Walsh's, the argument apparently begins with the premiss that I have in the past found certain experiences to be illusory and deceptive, and proceeds to the conclusion that I have reason to suppose all experiences may be deceptive. But the initial allegation that some experiences are deceptive can be made only so long as I suppose a standpoint of veridical experiences from which the 'delusive' ones can be criticized.

Now I have already tacitly made one step toward meeting this objection. For I have phrased my account of the argument in terms of the claim 'it seems to me (I believe) I have in the past been deceived by dreams,' rather than the simple affirmation, 'I have in the past been deceived by dreams.' The point, intuitively, is that one doesn't need to *know* one has ever been deceived with respect to p in order to have reason to doubt one's present belief that p (where one's 'evidence' is similar to what one had in the past). It is sufficient that one is *inclined to believe or to affirm* that one has in the past been 'taken in.'

But actually this move by itself doesn't amount to much. For it seems we are still committed to something like the following: I have in the past come to believe that certain experiences, namely dreaming experiences, are delusive, *in contrast to waking experiences which I took to be veridical*. In other words, the supposition that dreaming experiences are delusive is still correlative to the supposition that waking experiences are veridical—even though we are not now claiming to *know* that these experiences are delusory, these veridical. We are still left with the question whether there is an indissolvable connection between the notion that dreams are illusions and the notion that waking experience is (with circumscribed exceptions) not.

The simplest answer to all this is that it doesn't really matter for Descartes's purposes what the ultimate philosophical resolution of 'bounds of sense' issues may be.[31] The First Meditation arguments are not meant to set forth an ultimate philosophical position, but merely to leave us, provisionally, with a shadow of doubt or unease, particularly with reference to sense experience. And if they didn't at least do *that*, it is very unlikely that they would over the years have received as much philosophical attention as they have. While the data of sense are *initially* brought in question by the Dreaming Argument, Descartes does not ultimately base his rejection of the manifest image on this argument. The rejection is ultimately based on a standard of veridicality which sense data do not meet: the standard of clear and distinct perception.

But it's perhaps worth asking briefly how the Dream Argument in particular does work to bring about 'detachment from sense.' To ask this is not necessarily to request a defensible philosophical position, but merely to ask what possible pre-philosophical assumptions about veridical sense experience might be called into question by the Argument. I would suggest the following assumption as a candidate:

There is no sharp qualitative difference between the cause and the content of our experiences.

Or, in grand metaphysical terms:

> Things in themselves that cause our perceptions are qualitatively similar to the content of the perceptions caused.

As Descartes stresses in the *Optics* and elsewhere this is an assumption behind part of the Aristotelian-Scholastic theory that he particularly wants to reject: the doctrine of 'sensible species.'[32] The Dreaming Argument brings out the fact that we do not accept this assumption universally (we don't accept it in the case of dreams). It raises the question whether we are then entitled to accept the assumption ('with certainty') in any case at all. One response to the argument would be to show that the assumption is nevertheless justifiable in the case of waking experience. Another would be to argue that any concept of veridical experience that relies on this assumption is mistaken. But even in the latter case, a good deal of reasoning would be required to make plausible the position that the argument itself is 'incoherent.'

One advantage of the interpretation I have suggested is that it does not saddle Descartes with the improbable quest for 'marks by which to determine whether one is dreaming'—as Walsh's reading as well as the others do. For I have suggested that Descartes should be read as trying to find reasons to regard his waking experience as veridical—rather than as trying to determine whether or not he is awake. There does not seem to be anything wrong with looking for marks to distinguish veridical experience from the non-veridical. In fact, as the Sixth Meditation passage suggests, we do acknowledge such 'marks' in ordinary experience—when, for example we distinguish real men from 'phantoms.'

Nevertheless, there is still a related problem to consider—one having to do with the scope of the Dreaming Argument. Given that the Dreaming Argument is enough to render suspect our ordinary sensory judgments, prior to discovery of the 'coherence' criteria, why is it not sufficient to render suspect any appeal to the coherence criteria themselves? If waking experience of examining one's hands at close range is at all questionable, on the grounds that one thinks one sometimes only dreams he is examining his hands, why should not the waking belief that one's current experience is connectable in certain ways with 'the whole course of one's life,' be questionable on the grounds that one can 'only dream' that *this* is so?

The full answer to this question is more complicated than one might suppose—especially since Descartes seems to have changed his position slightly between the *Discourse* and the later works. Let us first consider the question why the marks 'discovered' in the Sixth

27

Meditation could not already be 'discovered' in the First. Here I think Frankfurt is basically right in holding that the marks stated in the Sixth were not available in the First because they involve explicit recognition of faculties other than sense.[33] (Although, as I will explain later, I do not fully accept Frankfurt's claims concerning the *degree* to which the 'protagonist' of the First Meditation is 'immersed in sense.') Thus, after discussion of certain systematic 'errors of sense' towards the end of the Sixth Meditation, Descartes introduces the final 'refutation' of the Dreaming Argument with the following words:

> Since I [now] know that all the senses more frequently indicate truth than falsity, concerning those things which have to do with the well-being of the body, and [since] I can always use several of them to examine the same thing [*eandem rem*], and memory as well, which connects present things with preceding ones, and intellect, which now has considered all causes of error; I should no more fear that those things which are exhibited to me everyday by the senses are false, but the hyperbolical doubts of earlier days, worthy of laughter, are exploded. Above all the one concerning sleep, which I could not distinguish from waking. . . . (AT VII, 89; HR I, 198–9)

As Frankfurt might put it, the Dreaming Argument cannot be met by one relying on more or less naïve use of the senses, and that is all that the protagonist of the First Meditation so far has available to him. In addition the 'validation' of clear and distinct perceptions of intellect developed in the central sections of the *Meditations* is presumably a condition, in Descartes's mind, of the solution he ultimately offers to the Dreaming Argument.[34]

But these observations do not take us very far in answering the original objection. For since Descartes admits (to Hobbes) that one can merely dream the connection of one's present experience with one's past, why are not the uses of memory and intellect themselves suspect by virtue of the consideration of dreaming?

It seems that Descartes's thinking on this issue can only be explained with reference to the notion of clear and distinct perceptions, which, in the *Meditations*, is not explicitly introduced till the Second and Third. For a perception to be clear and distinct it is not sufficient that the understanding be involved in the perception: the perception must be perfectly understood. To avoid error, he will argue (in the Fourth Meditation) we need only restrict our perception to matters clearly and distinctly perceived.[35] And Descartes holds explicitly in the *Discourse*, the *Principles* (I, 30), and

28

So what? What's true can't fail to be true even if I dream it ...?

the VII Replies that a clear and distinct perception cannot fail to be true, even in a dream. It is for this reason that the Dreaming Argument is not supposed to be sufficient to call in doubt mathematical knowledge.[36] Now Descartes presumably thinks that our perceptions of the connection and coherence of our experience can be clear and distinct, when we are awake. If so, such perceptions will also fall outside the scope of the Dreaming Argument. (He would, of course, deny that I can ever clearly and distinctly perceive in a dream that my present experience has the proper 'waking' connections. In the same way, while I might dream that $2 + 3 = 7$, I could never clearly and distinctly perceive this—even in a dream.)

But suppose I not only dream my current experience satisfies the criterion of waking but also dream that I clearly and distinctly perceive that it does. Doesn't this possibility (and surely it is possible) give us grounds for doubting any purported use of the criterion of clear and distinct perception?[37] Granted, however, that Descartes isn't trying to 'prove he's awake,' the following reply may be available. To the waking mind ordinary sense experience appears (initially) similar to the 'experiences of dreams.' However, a philosopher who discovers the criterion of clear and distinct perceptions sees at once that the genuine item is very different from what might erroneously be taken for such in a dream. As far as I can see this is a logically coherent defense (although, as will emerge later, I am unable to defend in any detail the notion of clear and distinct perception itself).

In the *Discourse* Descartes holds (or at least strongly implies) that the criterion of clear and distinct perception is sufficient to enable one to avoid error even in dreams. He writes:

> After knowledge of God and of the soul has made us certain of this rule [that clear and distinct ideas are true] it is very easy to know that the reveries we imagine while asleep can not at all make us doubt the truth of the thoughts that we have while awake. For, if it happens, even in sleep, that one has some very distinct idea, as, for instance, that a geometer invents some new demonstration, his sleep does not prevent it from being true. . . . Whether we are awake or we are asleep, we should never allow ourselves to be persuaded except by the evidence of our reason. (AT VI, 40; HR I, 105–6)

And this rather bizarre passage has an implication that is somewhat awkward from my point of view. For if Descartes does continue (after the *Discourse*) to hold that the clarity and distinctness criterion can enable us to avoid error even in dreams, and if he believes that the 'connectability' criterion is a function of clear and distinct perception, it would follow that he is *after all* committed to the legitimacy of talk about 'marks for telling whether or not one is dreaming.' That is, he would be committed to the view that we can determine that we are not dreaming if we clearly and distinctly perceive that our present experience coheres with our past, etc. Since dreams are not—by (dubious) hypothesis—ever connected in this way, it will never be the case that we *can* clearly and distinctly perceive that such a connection obtains while we are dreaming! My efforts to save him from this commitment would be in vain.

However, I want to suggest that Descartes's reply to Hobbes indicates he gave up the idea of the *Discourse*, that one can avoid being 'deceived in dreams' by a policy of adhering to the criterion of clear and distinct perception. If so, his later position may be described in the following terms. *If* it were possible to restrict oneself to affirming only clear and distinct perceptions in dreams as well as while awake, there would be nothing paradoxical or futile in applying marks to determine whether one is awake. For if one were in fact asleep and dreaming when one sought to apply the test, one would necessarily fail to have the requisite clear and distinct perception of connectedness. However, since (we are supposing Descartes eventually to concede) we cannot rely on our ability to follow this policy in dreams, we cannot rule out the possibility that we will be 'deceived in dreams' into supposing our criteria of waking are satisfied. For this reason we cannot say that the 'marks' in question are used to 'determine whether we are awake.'

Apart from the reply to Hobbes, certain letters provide some evidence for the postulated change in Descartes's position concerning our ability to adhere to reason in dreams. For example, he remarks to Princess Elizabeth in a letter of 1 September 1645:[38]

> I spoke of a happiness which depends entirely on our free will, and
> which all men can acquire without any assistance from without.
> You observe very well that there are diseases which, taking away
> the power of reasoning, take also that of enjoying the satisfaction
> of a rational mind; and that teaches me that what I said generally
> about all men, should be understood only of those who have the
> free use of their reason. . . . For there is no one who doesn't want
> to be happy; but . . . often the indisposition which is in the body
> prevents the will from being free. This happens too when we sleep;
> for the most philosophical person in the world cannot prevent
> himself from having bad dreams when his temperament so
> disposes him. (AT IV, 281–2; PL 167–8)

The implication of this passage is, clearly, that one does not have 'free use of one's reason,' or the use of free will, in controlling one's thoughts when asleep—no matter how 'philosophical' one may be. This would entail not only our vulnerability to bad dreams, but also, perhaps, the inability to adhere to the *Discourse*'s policy, and hence to avoid 'deception' even in sleep.[39]

I certainly do not claim to have provided in this section a complete defense of Descartes's use and presentation of the Dreaming Argument against all the objections set forth in the critical literature. (That would be, in the words of the master, an infinite task.) What I hope to have shown is that Descartes's reasoning is not, after all, obviously vulnerable to some of the most popular and important criticisms. Also, I have tried to call attention to a few significant and neglected passages and points of emphasis.

7   *The opinion of a God who can do anything*

As we have already seen, at any rate, Descartes does regard the Dreaming Argument as insufficient to cast doubt on the reality of simples, and his elementary mathematical judgments. These have a higher degree of certainty than the particular judgments of sense. However, the opinion he finds in himself of a God who can do anything 'and by whom I have been created such as I exist' (AT VII, 21; HR I, 147), supplies a reason for doubting even these most basic and simple beliefs. Descartes conceives himself as the dependent creature of some powerful cause. 'How do I know' that this cause has not created me so as to be *always* in error?

This philosophical show-stopper may be characterized without too much hyperbole as the most fundamental Cartesian problem. After briefly considering Descartes's further development of the idea in Meditation I, I will comment on some implications and difficulties of the Deceiver Hypothesis. But some related issues will not be discussed in detail until Chapter III.

In the First Meditation Descartes already considers the response— to be developed in the Third Meditation—that since the idea of God includes goodness as well as omnipotence, it is perhaps unnecessary to worry about the possibility of deception (AT VII, 21; HR I, 147). But then, rehearsing the dialectical transition from the Third to Fourth Meditation, he replies that after all we do sometimes err—and this seems equally incompatible with the idea of God's goodness as constant deception (*ibid.*).

Descartes also considers another, rather interesting, response to the

Deceiver Hypothesis. Perhaps it might just be better to give up the idea of omnipotence, if it seems to have such an untoward consequence (that I might always be deceived) (*ibid.*)? But he then points out, in effect, that this option isn't really available. For doubt of all things can be generated from *whatever* hypothesis may be proposed concerning the origins of my being. Thus, if I have come into being in some other way—e.g., by chance—the *very deficiency* of power or perfection in the source of my being would render it possible 'that I am so imperfect that I am always deceived':

> Since to be mistaken and to err seem to be a sort of imperfection, the less power [is assigned] the author of my being, the more probable it will be that I am so imperfect as to be always mistaken. (*Ibid.*)

Thus, given either side of an exhaustive dichotomy—that I am or am not the creature of an omnipotent being—I have reason to suppose I may be always deceived. It is more likely I am deceived if I lack a perfect cause. (Here Descartes invokes in a muted way a principle explicitly relied on later in the *Meditations* for the demonstration of God's existence: an effect cannot be more perfect (though it can be less perfect) than its cause.) On the other hand, an omnipotent being would have the power, and for all I know the will, also to cause me constantly to err.

There is then no way, it seems, to avoid the conclusion that all our opinions are doubtful:

> To which arguments I certainly have no response, but at last I am compelled to admit that there is nothing among those things that I formerly thought to be true, which it is not possible to doubt, not through lack of consideration, or levity, but for sound and considered reasons; and indeed even from these, not less than from those that are obviously false, my assent should from now on be carefully withheld, if I wish to discover anything certain. (*Ibid.*)

At the end of the First Meditation, however, Descartes sets aside the hypothesis that God is a deceiver, and postulates instead a 'certain malign spirit.' The issue of this being's claim to perfection is not explicitly resolved:

> I will suppose, therefore, not the optimum God, the fountain of truth, but a certain malign spirit, maximally powerful and clever, has employed all his industry so that I am deceived: I will think that sky, air, earth, colors, figures, sounds, and all external things are nothing else but the delusions of dreams (*ludificationes*

somniorum), by which he tries to ambush my credulity: I will consider myself as not having hands, nor eyes, nor flesh, nor blood, nor any senses, but falsely believing myself to have all these things; I will remain firmly fixed in this meditation, and thus, even if it is not in my power to know any truth, certainly [the power] is in me, not to assent to the false, and so that this deceiver, however powerful, however clever, cannot impose anything on me, I will beware with a determined mind. (AT VII, 22–3; HR I, 148)

As Gouhier has shown, the hypothesis of the malign spirit takes over from that of the Deceiving God from the end of the First Meditation to the beginning of the Third—where the latter figure is resubstituted without comment or explanation.[40] As Gouhier has also noted, the summary of 'doubts' in the concluding passage just quoted does not include mention of mathematical propositions— which are not again brought into discussion until the Third Meditation. It seems likely, then, that Descartes wishes to divide the doubts engendered in the First Meditation into two classes: doubts about external existence, and doubts about mathematics and other questions of essence (the so-called 'eternal truths'). The idea of a 'certain malign spirit, maximally powerful and clever' is used to undermine my initial certainties about real existence. This idea is confronted, and in some sense banished, by the *Cogito* argument at the beginning of Meditation II. The question whether *optimus Deus* himself may be supposed a deceiver is not, then, really addressed till the Third Meditation, when it is reintroduced in connection with the problem of the certainty of (apparent) eternal truths.[41]

Superficially, the conclusion of the First Meditation leaves Descartes in the position, not of suspending judgment, but of affirming the probably false: that he has no hands, etc. But, clearly he means to 'affirm' these improbable things only as a sort of mental play-acting (to borrow a phrase),[42] where the strategy is merely to fight off the overwhelming inclination to give assent to the 'obvious.' (We will touch on this issue again briefly below.)

I will argue in Chapter III that there are important connections between the Deceiving God Hypothesis and Descartes's doctrine that the eternal truths are created by God and depend on His will. This is not to say that there is some kind of strict logical entailment from one supposition to the other. I could, it seems, consistently suppose that while the eternal truths are *not* dependent on God's power, nevertheless *my mind is* so dependent, and thus come up with the Deceiving God Hypothesis while rejecting the doctrine of the creation of the eternal truths. That is, I could suppose that God makes me *think* the eternal truths are other than they are, without its being in His power to make them other than they are. Conversely, there doesn't seem to be any strictly logical path (or at least any direct and obvious one) from the doctrine that the eternal truths depend on God's power, to the supposition that I might be deceived even in my simplest mathematical judgments. (I believe my existence is dependent on God's power; it doesn't follow that I think I could be wrong in believing I exist.) Besides, the Deceiving God Hypothesis is presented, discussed, and ultimately (in the Third Meditation) dismissed, without any direct consideration of the question of whether the eternal truths are or are not dependent on the Creative power.

For now I wish only to make two further observations concerning the relation of these two ideas. First, the Deceiving God Hypothesis carries the implication that 'my mind' is *as a whole* a dependent being, and hence that the problem of dependence must be confronted in connection with *any claim at all* I make to knowledge of the truth. That is, my thoughts can never be viewed as guides to the reality and truth of things without mediation: as dependent on God's will or power, they are opaquely rather than transparently related to the truth. Now suppose among my thoughts is the judgment that $2 + 3 = 5$ is not merely true, but necessarily true. *This* thought cannot be regarded as any more transparently connected to the truth of things than the others. Thus, the Deceiving God Hypothesis would at least provide grounds for calling in question whatever assurance I might initially feel that the eternal truths *are beyond* God's power. Second, the idea of God's omnipotence that introduces the Deceiver Hypothesis, is at least closely allied to the idea of omnipotence that gives rise to the 'creation' doctrine. In both cases it is ultimately a question of putting God in some sense above 'reason' as traditionally conceived.

It followed from my interpretation of Descartes's position and objectives that the Dreaming Argument is not a mere fiction or pretext, despite the fact that it receives a sort of 'answer' at the end of Meditation VI. It is part of Descartes's considered position that our waking experience is never through and through veridical, is always partly dream-like—though we can learn to avoid being taken in by adhering to the God-given standard of clear and distinct perception. I want now to suggest that the Deceiving God Hypothesis also has a sort of reality in Descartes's thought, although in a different sense. First, it is part of Descartes's view of the world that the senses do tend to 'deceive' very systematically, and this does pose a problem about the nature and good intentions of our creator. I believe that this concern actually permeates Descartes's philosophical thought—as I will explain in more detail later. Second, since the idea that God can do anything is stressed by Descartes himself (in works other than the *Meditations*) as an important *positive* tenet of his philosophy, it would be wrong to dismiss the Deceiver Hypothesis as mere philosophical play. For it has, I want to hold, obvious affinities, if not logical connections, with the positive doctrine.

In Chapter III I will also relate Descartes's eternal truths doctrine to the well-known problem of 'Cartesian circularity.' The latter constitutes, of course, the most serious and interesting objection to his use of the Deceiving God Hypothesis. There are one or two points about it that can usefully be noted now.

By the end of the First Meditation Descartes is holding that all his beliefs are rendered 'uncertain' by his uncertainty about the nature and inclinations of his—or their—cause.[43] He will ultimately attempt to remove the Deceiver Hypothesis by proving that he is in the hands of an omnipotent, benevolent being, who would not permit him to be deceived in what seems to him most certain. But, according to the most common form of the circularity objection, one cannot know the premisses of such a proof to be true, unless one already knows that one is not subject to systematic deception. The problem, then, is just this: if we find it coherent to suppose that all our beliefs are the function of a non-truth-conferring mechanism, then we seem permanently to be stuck with the possibility that they might well be. For any attempt to reason oneself out of the position will require giving more credence to 'what seems to me to be true' than the hypothesis to be defeated would allow as legitimate.

However, I want to suggest that even the attempt to show by argument that the hypothesis is (really) *not coherent* is subject to this objection. (This approach has been tried, for instance, by O.K. Bouwsma, in a rather well-known article.[44]) For once one tentatively accepts for discussion the hypothesis of the Deceiver, one is obligated to suppose that any premisses employed in an argument to show that the hypothesis is incoherent were themselves introduced as plausible by the Deceiver and are false.

This line of reasoning leads to an interesting conclusion. Since the Deceiver Argument itself involves premisses, it is in a certain sense self-annihilating. Of course, the supposition that there could be a Deceiver is not directly self-refuting if formulated with reasonable care. That there may be a Deceiver is one of the few things that such a being could not be supposed *fallaciously* to cause me to believe (though he might decide when to put the idea into my mind). This shows I cannot consistently believe that there may be a being who causes *all* my beliefs to be false. But for Descartes's purposes one can manage just as well with a slightly weaker supposition. (The bare belief that it is possible that all my beliefs are false is similarly self-refuting; but one need only judiciously insert the word 'other' to retain the impact while avoiding self-contradiction.) But suppose we raise the following question: could not an unknown being with power over my mind deceive me into falsely believing there are trans-cendental causal conditions on the truth of my beliefs? Or, to put it a little more simply, could not an unknown being deceive me into falsely believing the following: it makes sense to suppose that nearly all my beliefs are false, though I can never tell that they are? If the answer is yes, then, it seems, the very question that the Deceiver Argument attempts to pose is undermined by that argument. If we try to advance a negative answer, we are still faced with the question: how do you know the Deceiver isn't causing you falsely to believe that the answer is 'no'?

There is, perhaps, one possible way of answering this objection within the Cartesian framework. For someone might suggest that this sort of doubt is really a doubt about whether I might have misconceptions about the meaning of 'true' and 'false.' And Descartes, under questioning, exempts our understanding of the meanings of words from the scope of general doubt. The authors of the Sixth Objections to the *Meditations* thought Descartes's argu-ment required him to hold that he was ignorant of what thought is and what existence is, of 'the meaning of what you say,' when he began (in the Second Meditation) to talk about thought and existence (AT VII, 413; HR II, 234). To this Descartes replies that one knows non-reflexively what thought and existence are, since these ideas are innate (AT VII, 422; HR II, 241). And presumably he might wish to hold also that the meanings of 'true' and 'false' are innate.

However, it really isn't clear that this observation will suffice to meet the objection. Even if Descartes does wish to hold that we certainly know the meaning of 'true' and 'false,' the reasoning sketched above may still go through. For we do not need to suppose for the purposes of this objection that the Deceiver could cause him to be totally ignorant of the meaning of his words—might cause him to 'reason' without 'knowing what he's saying.' To have a *theory* of what truth is one must first in some sense know what the word 'true' means. It seems reasonable to suppose that the Deceiver Hypothesis rests on a theoretical conception of truth which might be false without it being the case that the meaning of a word is unknown. Thus, Descartes's reply to the Sixth Objectors does not clearly meet the problem I have pointed out in the Deceiver Argument.

36

Even someone who concedes that the traditional 'circularity' objection is unanswerable—that it's impossible non-fallaciously to demonstrate that the cause of one's beliefs is truth-generating—might still be tempted by a quasi-Cartesian position such as the following:

> Only if I could be sure that the cause(s) of my beliefs is (are) on the whole truth-conveying could I be sure that I am not almost always in error even in what seems to me most certain. But I cannot assure myself by valid argument that the cause(s) of my beliefs is (are) truth generating; therefore, I cannot be sure, etc.

I have been suggesting that to introduce the Deceiver Hypothesis is to introduce the possibility that this line of reasoning—like any other—only *seems* cogent.[45]

As is now fairly widely acknowledged, Descartes seeks to limit the scope of the Deceiver Hypothesis, in the *Replies* and even in later parts of the *Meditations*, to, in effect, non-self-evident 'conclusions.' He suggests, that is, that the Deceiver Hypothesis generates doubt only of those propositions that can come before the mind without being immediately clearly and distinctly perceived. There remain, then, a class of propositions—those which *cannot* come before the mind without being clearly and distinctly perceived—that evade the force even of the Deceiver Argument, and provide the basis for a non-circular defense, in the face of the Deceiver, of our (merely) demonstrative knowledge.

This defense against the Circularity objection will be considered in somewhat more detail in Chapter III. For now, I want only to stress that in connection with this general problem we must distinguish two questions:

(1) Does Descartes lay himself open to the Circularity objection by seeming sometimes to allow the Deceiver Hypothesis unlimited scope?

(2) Does Descartes have a *philosophically defensible and consistent way* of limiting the Deceiver Hypothesis, so as to avoid the objection that it cannot be non-circularly refuted?

The answer to the first question is surely 'yes.' But this would be of little significance if the answer to the second were too. Later I will argue, though, that Descartes's own best solution to the Circularity objection involves him in philosophical inconsistency. (Another reply he could *consistently* have made is dubious on other grounds.)

37

8 'Principles'

I will now try to clarify the 'foundationalist' conceptions of the First Meditation by returning to the question, in what sense are the successive skeptical arguments to be construed as 'attacks on principles'? Harry Frankfurt has maintained that the 'principles' in question are rules of (sensory) evidence. His systematic development of this view deserves consideration. I will argue that Frankfurt's account is deficient in several respects, and propose an alternative.

Frankfurt holds that the principles Descartes attacks are attempts to 'define policies to be followed in determining whether or not to accept a belief,' by specifying types of evidence that may be regarded as adequate support for beliefs.[46]. Since in each case the evidence is a type of *sensory* evidence, the different principles can actually be considered 'versions of the same principle.' Descartes 'begins with the most naively uncritical of all policies regarding sense perception'—namely, 'that the senses are *always* reliable.' After quickly showing that the 'policy' of complete trust in the senses is 'unsatisfactory,'[47]

> Descartes proposes a revised principle . . . which may be understood as affirming that the senses are trustworthy whenever they operate under external conditions that are uniformly favorable, that is, whenever there is no basis in the particular external circumstances of their operation for mistrusting them.

But what about 'internal' conditions—the state of the perceiver himself? Frankfurt thinks (his reasoning here is not clear to me) that Descartes's mention of the problem of madness is meant to narrow down acceptable sensory evidence to the 'perceptions . . . of an ideally qualified perceiver under ideal external conditions.'[48] Therefore, according to Frankfurt, the 'third version' of the principle Descartes considers is the following:[49]

> Whatever is perceived under ideal external conditions by an ideally qualified perceiver certainly exists.

Or more precisely, as Frankfurt's further discussion indicates:[50]

> Whatever is perceived under circumstances such that the senses provide no reliable indication that conditions are not ideal, exists.

But 'if someone's policy is to accept the testimony of whatever bears the sensory marks of privileged perceptions, he may be led to accept some dream perceptions.' This observation discredits the third version of the sensory principle.[51] In attacking the first three versions of his 'principle' then, Descartes shows 'that the evidence the principle presumes to be sufficient for establishing the existence of something is in fact consistent with its non-existence.'[52]

Up to this point Frankfurt's account is plausible; it runs into conspicuous difficulties only with the sequel to the Dreaming Argument. However, on my interpretation of the objectives of the Meditation, his account even of the Dreaming Argument will not quite do. For it understates the extent to which that argument is supposed to result in 'detachment from sense.'

As I understand him, Frankfurt takes the main point of the First Meditation to be that the senses by themselves do not provide adequate 'evidence' for a firm 'foundation for the sciences.' In particular, the Dreaming Argument, and the 'answer' to it in the Sixth Meditation, are meant to show that intellect as well as sense is required to distinguish veridical from non-veridical perceptions. In my view, however, the Dreaming Argument is intended to make it possible for us to 'doubt the senses' in a much more sweeping way than this. It is to prepare us for the idea that there is much falsity in the ordinary sensory image of reality—even in the case of 'veridical' waking experiences. Descartes's view is not merely that sensations provide us with an inadequate basis for distinguishing true perceptions from false. Rather, Descartes thinks the senses actually *mislead* us concerning what the world is really like. We can free ourselves from the false sensory image, and move on to the correct rationalist conception, only after *distancing* ourselves from the senses in the way encouraged by the criticism of the First Meditation. (I will develop this point in more detail in later chapters.)

The material Descartes introduces after the Dreaming Argument lends itself much less readily to the 'rules of sensory evidence' interpretation. Frankfurt, in fact, both fails to make clear in what sense the Deceiver Argument can be construed as attacking a 'rule of evidence,' and also fails to make a convincing case for the claim that the Deceiver Argument too is directed (in the First Meditation) against empiricist preconceptions. His account of the final version of the 'sensory principle' allegedly under attack is not well defined. It seems, however, that he sees Descartes as implicitly formulating, in the wake of the Dreaming Argument, a principle that would specify the reliability of 'what can be learned from *any* sensory experience at all'—as opposed to a principle purporting to distinguish veridical from non-veridical sensory experiences.[53] At first this seems to mean that all simple natures must be 'given' in every sensory experience. Subsequent discussion, however, suggests the more plausible[54] notion that the senses must provide us—'veridically'—with the simple natures out of which all our visions—whether dreaming or waking—are constructed. The Deceiver Argument is then introduced to demonstrate that conceivably the ideas of simple natures are themselves not 'derived from reality,' and may after all be 'fictitious.'[55] This in turn leads to the conclusion that mathematical knowledge is doubtful, since the protagonist of the First Meditation is still thinking of mathematics in the concrete empiricist manner—as depénding on the existence in nature of the simple natures of which it treats.

I do not, in fact, see how the Deceiver Argument can soundly be construed as an attack on a rule of evidence; certainly Frankfurt does not show us how this can be done. Since these rules are supposed to 'define policies to be followed in determining whether or not to accept a belief,' by specifying types of evidence adequate to support a belief, the principle ultimately attacked would presumably have to be something specifying evidence adequate for supporting beliefs concerned exclusively with simple natures. It is not at all clear what such a rule would look like—or how the 'evidence' would be specified.

Further, contrary to what Frankfurt repeatedly implies,[56] there is no clear indication in the text that the simples are regarded, if only provisionally, as derived from sense. (This is not to say they are presented as *not* derived from sense.) Also there is no clear indication that mathematical truths are being construed as dependent on existence in nature—nor mathematical knowledge as dependent on sensory evidence about real existence. (This is not to say that mathematics is explicitly presented as a purely rational or *a priori* science.) Descartes simply does not commit himself—or his protagonist—on these matters at this point. He does not tell us where the ideas of simple natures come from, or what it would be for them to be 'false,' or whether or not mathematical truth depends on existence 'in nature.' On the one hand, then, Frankfurt is right in his claim (against many other commentators) that the Deceiver Argument is not presented in the First Meditation as an attack on 'reason' or clear and distinct perceptions (though it will be presented in this way later). On the other hand he is wrong in his position that the Deceiver Argument in the First Meditation is to be explicitly understood as an attack on the evidence of the senses.

It is worth noting that the list Descartes offers of simple natures in the First Meditation is a very non-empiricist list. As a matter of fact, it includes no examples that are not on his own canonical rationalist list of simples.[57] While someone 'mired in sense' would presumably think of colors, sounds, pains and so forth as among the basic elements out of which both waking and dreaming experiences are built, Descartes lists only extension, figure, situation and the other basic concepts of his science. It is only later, in the Third Meditation, that Descartes discusses such empiricist simples as heat and pain—holding that they are unreal, or represent no thing.

I conclude that it is unhelpful and unwarranted to suppose that the Deceiver Argument is directed against a 'rule of sensory evidence.' The underlying source of doubt about the reality of simple natures and about mathematics must be located elsewhere, even in Meditation I.

Is there, then, any way of understanding the First Meditation as a set of attacks on 'principles' or 'foundations' that *would* easily encompass the Deceiver Argument as well as the preceding material? I want to propose a *causal*, rather than an evidential, interpretation.—— The successive arguments are meant to undermine the confident assumption that the causes of our perceptions and beliefs are truth-conferring. Thus, the example of ordinary sensory illusion reminds us that a perception supporting our belief in a proposition like 'there is a round tower' is sometimes generated under circumstances independent of the truth of the proposition; in these cases, the causal chain involved in normal perception suffers more or less minor and local distortion. The Dreaming Argument purports to remind us how *radically* delusive experience can be—that a global and not merely local disruption is possible. In other words, it reminds us that the causal chain generating a particular belief-complex can be quite different from one which, we suppose, under normal waking circumstances results in our beliefs being true. This is enough to insinuate some doubt about the generation of perceptual beliefs under normal waking circumstances. It does not, however, bring into question the assumption that there is *some* truth-bestowing connection between the causes of our experiences or beliefs and their content, if we restrict ourselves to very minimal commitments about the nature of reality. Finally, the Deceiver Hypothesis is introduced to sever *all* truth-conveying connection between perceptions or beliefs and their causes, and to give color to the supposition that beliefs are generated in such a way as to guarantee their falsity. (It is worth noting, in this connection, that the 'reasons for doubt' that Descartes offers take us further and further away from the ordinary and natural; they reflect as well as produce the process of 'withdrawal from sense.')

If this perspective is valid, the arguments of Meditation I are indeed directed against different versions of one principle, but the 'foundation' attacked is not, as Frankfurt holds, faith in the senses specifically; it is rather faith in the truth-conferring nature of the immediate causes of our beliefs. Ordinary sense-perception provides the most obvious example of situations where beliefs are generated in what we take to be truth-conferring ways. Thus, we take it that to see a pencil in front of us is to be caused to believe there is a pencil in front of us through stimulation of our visual apparatus as the result of the presence of a pencil in front of us. Or, to put it a little differently, we suppose that its looking to us as if there is a pencil in front of us is caused by the presence, in front of us, of a pencil. But we may in some sense take it for granted that our beliefs are caused in truth-conferring ways, without having a specific conception of the causal mechanism in mind. Descartes does not need specifically to suppose that the cause of the belief in simple natures or mathematical propositions is *sensory* in order to question that they are founded on a truth-conferring causal process. (Incidentally, the present interpretation has the advantage of serving to enhance, rather than to diminish continuity between the First Meditation and later parts of the work, where the hypothesis of the Deceiving God is explicitly extended to the distinct perceptions of philosophical maturity.)

9   Real doubts

Finally, I return to the peculiar and perplexing question of how Cartesian skepticism relates to real doubt—or whether, in Kenny's terminology 'Descartes ever really doubts' his most basic philosophical and commonsense opinions. Now, of course, as Descartes points out to Regius,

> What could be more foolish than to suppose that, at least at the time at which these false opinions [that God is to be denied, that all credibility is to be denied to the senses, etc.] are being propounded and are not yet refuted, they are being taught, and that, accordingly, the man who states the arguments of the Atheists is *temporarily an Atheist*? What more puerile than to say that, if he were to die meantime, before writing or discovering the *hoped for demonstration* he would die an atheist. . .? . . . Is there anyone obtuse enough to think that the man who composed such a book [as the *Meditations*] was ignorant, while he was writing its first pages, of what he had undertaken to demonstrate in the following? (AT VIII-2, 367; HR I, 448-9)

But in fact it is not very relevant (at least to our concern) whether Descartes knew how he would 'answer' his 'doubts' when he started writing the *Meditations*. What we want to know is whether the 'doubts' did precede their 'answer,' in Descartes's mind, and whether someone who *has* gotten no further than Meditation I should really be said to be in *doubt*.

The continuation of this ill-tempered passage is more apposite, however. Descartes virtually tells Regius that there was never a time when he was occupied with doubts, other than in a purely rhetorical sense. For he goes on to indicate that skeptical and atheistical objections had been 'proposed as if they were mine,' merely because this was required by 'the style of meditations, which I judged most apt for expounding arguments' (*quem rationibus explicandis aptissimum judicavi*) (AT VIII-2, 368; HR I, 449).

Other statements of Descartes's seem to tend in the same direction. His characterizations of the doubts as 'hyperbolical,' 'exaggerated,' and so forth, might be held ambiguous: can they not be taken as connoting a perfectly genuine, if strained and unusual, scrupulosity? But further, Descartes also comments, in the Synopsis of the *Meditations*, that the reasons he employs to resolve the doubts about the external world are not

> very useful for proving that which they prove, namely, that really there is a certain world, that men have bodies, and the like, *which no one of sane mind has ever seriously doubted*. (AT VII, 15–16; HR I, 142–3; emphasis added)

(We are reminded of the dismissal of the beliefs, or doubts, of the insane as a relevant consideration in the First Meditation.) In addition, Descartes frequently stresses that the doubts are in some sense *isolated from questions of action*. For example, in a passage from the *Principles* he writes:

> Meanwhile this doubt is to be restricted only to the contemplation of truth. For as to the practice of life, because often an occasion for matters of action goes by, before we are able to resolve our doubts, frequently I am compelled to embrace what is only probable; or even sometimes, even if of two one does not appear more probable than the other, nevertheless one or the other must be chosen. (AT VIII-1, 5; HR I, 219–20)

And at the end of the First Meditation itself he notes:

> I know no peril or error will meanwhile follow from this [pretending that my former opinions are all false], and I cannot more favorably give myself up to distrust, in so far as it is not now a matter of action, but I apply myself only to knowing. (AT VII, 22; HR I, 148)

Commentators have frequently taken such passages to show that

Descartes's 'doubts' are, at any rate, less than full-blooded article; they lack, so to speak, cash value.[58]

Now I expect many people will impatiently declare at this point that *of course* Cartesian doubt is not real doubt—not even real theoretical doubt (whatever the theoretical-practical distinction may actually come to in this context). Neither an act of will, nor month-long reflection on the Dreaming and Deceiver Arguments, nor any combination of meditations and volitions can be expected to produce in an ordinary rational person, with ordinary experiences, actual doubt as to whether he has a body. And anyone who agrees that this is really quite obvious, may conclude that the only 'genuine doubt' that can be introduced by Cartesian arguments is doubt about how those particular arguments should be dealt with. That is, someone might genuinely doubt how the Deceiver Argument should or can be answered—or whether it should simply be ignored as epistemologically nugatory.[59] But such a person is no more in a state of genuine skepticism about *the existence of a physical world* than someone who has conceded uncertainty about the flaws in the ontological argument is in a state of religious belief. (Of course someone could, conceivably, refuse to *count himself* as knowing anything as long as he had failed to answer all arguments brought to his attention which concluded there is some margin of uncertainty in all his beliefs. But that, we might say, would be his problem.)

There is, however, another statement of Descartes's to be taken account of in this connection. He remarks emphatically to Gassendi:

> What I said, that *all testimony of the senses is to be regarded as uncertain, even as false*, is entirely serious, and is so necessary for the understanding of my Meditations, that whoever will not, or cannot, admit that, is capable of making no objection to them that is worthy of a response. (AT VII, 350; HR II, 206)

No doubt it is necessary to make allowances for the fact that while Regius had accused Descartes of being unorthodox, Gassendi had accused him of kidding (cf. AT VII, 258; HR II, 137). Nevertheless, for reasons that should already be clear, I am inclined to give much more credit to this statement than to the dismissive ones quoted previously. The reason, once again, is that the doubts generated in Meditation I are supposed to be the first important steps toward *genuine, far-reaching alterations in our former beliefs*. Even though the skeptical arguments are ultimately 'answered,' things are not left as if untouched. This is beautifully apparent from the Synopsis passage quoted above, once it is considered in fuller context:

[F]inally all the reasons from which the existence of material things can be inferred, are adduced. Not that I think they are very useful for proving that which they prove, namely, that there really is a certain world, and men have bodies, and the like, which no one of sane mind has ever seriously doubted; but because in considering these, we learn that they are neither so firm nor so perspicuous as are those by which we arrive at knowledge of our mind and of God; so that these last are the most certain and most evident which can be known by the human mind. (AT VII, 15–16; HR I, 142–3)

The upshot of the argument of the *Meditations* is that an external physical world can be proved to exist, thus *in a sense* affirming what everyone 'knew' all along; but the proof turns out to be arduous and to require immaterialist premisses: people are *wrong* in thinking that the direct evidence of the senses is sufficient. (In fact, as I will suggest below, it is not in the end quite clear that Descartes does think the existence of matter can be *proved*, if this means 'established with demonstrative certainty.') Further, it is not even the case that everything we 'knew all along' is reinstated in any sense by the end of the *Meditations*. Descartes clearly believes his conception of the mind as a distinct, immaterial substance is innovative with respect to received opinion—and a number of his contemporaries' 'objections' to the *Meditations* seem to bear him out. Further, the conclusion of the Sixth Meditation concerning external bodies is only that:

I am taught by nature that various other bodies exist around my body, some of which are to be sought after and others avoided. And certainly from the fact that I sense very diverse colors, sounds, scents, tastes, heat, hardness, and the like, I rightly conclude that there are in the bodies, from which these various perceptions of sense come, some variations corresponding to them, even if perhaps not similar to them. . . . (AT VII, 81; HR I, 192)

This is a very weak conclusion indeed. And in the next two pages Descartes will dwell at length on the various errors found in the beliefs of the unreconstructed empiricist. The theme of his reflections is that sensations (according to the results of his *Meditations*) were put in us only to guide us concerning what is beneficial or harmful to ourselves, yet we erroneously take them to reveal what objects are like in themselves.

Although in approaching the fire I feel heat, as also in approaching it too near I feel pain, there is really no reason which would persuade me that there is in the fire anything similar to this heat, any more than [there is anything similar] to this pain; but

45

only that there is something in it, whatever it may be, which causes in us these sensations of heat or of pain. (AT VII, 83; HR I, 193–4)

There is a perfectly good sense, then, in which even by the end of the *Meditations* the 'testimony of the senses' is to be regarded as 'uncertain and even as false.'[60]

I would agree that none of this strictly shows that Descartes 'ever really doubted the existence of God or the external world.' Who knows? (But why not?) I think it does at least show the error of holding, as one critic has, that 'the skepticism to which [Descartes] commits himself, is innocuously thin and undisruptive.'[61]

But what about the issue of action? We should notice, first, that in the statement quoted from the *Principles* Descartes seems to be pointing out that we sometimes have to act despite our doubts (have to act on probabilities or even arbitrarily); doubts fail to have expression in action just because practical urgencies may take precedence over the resolution of relevant doubts. But how, exactly, does this observation bear on the kind of doubts supposedly generated by the skeptical arguments in the First Meditation? And how might it be reconciled with Descartes's seemingly incompatible statement that his *Meditations* doubts involve no 'peril,' since he is concerned with knowing rather than action? (If I see that something is doubtful, but that I must act on probabilities, surely I do recognize some 'peril.')

It seems to me that Descartes was confused about the relation of his sort of 'doubts' and action, and that many of his commentators have been, too. It is evident that Descartes was at least vaguely worried that hyperbolic doubt would seem to have untoward consequences for action, and that he was anxious to dispel this impression. Commentators have thought that since Descartes explicitly severed his 'doubts' from questions of action, he thereby acknowledged that the doubts were factitious. There is a shared common assumption here: that real doubt about, say, the existence of the physical world, has a logical implication for action. I want to question this assumption.

As a starting point, let us consider what the position might be of someone who maintains that Descartes's 'doubt' is something less than genuine suspension of belief because it 'finds no expression whatever in action.'[62] Let's put the question this way.

What would be the difference between (a) entertaining the idea that there is (or might be) no physical world where this belief *does* issue in action, and (b) entertaining the idea that there is no physical world where it *does not* issue in action? This is a very curious

46

question. In the first place it is very hard to imagine what it would be to 'act as if there were (or might be) no physical world'—unless it is to act just as Descartes does in writing (more exactly in thinking) the first five Meditations. That is, one develops a philosophical argument that explicitly raises the issue of whether there is 'a world,' and proceeds for a certain distance without providing an affirmative answer to it. In the second place, someone who is entertaining the idea that there is no physical world is *ipso facto* entertaining the idea that there is no (physical) behavior. Thus he could not himself apply the criterion of action to determine whether he is experiencing genuine doubt—or rather could not do so non-circularly. Similarly, while someone who doubted the existence of a bridge over the river could manifest this doubt by approaching the river slowly, or taking a roundabout route, there is just very little someone who doubted the existence of the physical world could *do* to make this doubt, so to speak, concrete. To doubt the existence of the physical world is also to doubt the existence of the river, the roundabout route and any approach whatsoever, slow or fast.

There seem to be two natural responses to this. One is to insist that someone who doubts the existence of the physical world should either act heedlessly or do absolutely nothing—since any deliberate choice of action will unavoidably imply the conviction that there is after all something to do something to, or something to do something with. It will, in other words, imply an unskeptical commitment to common sense.[63] This is a classical response which Descartes—as we will see in a minute—both ridicules and seriously credits. Alternatively, one might deny that there can be real doubt, where nothing can in principle count as authentic expression in action.

The latter position is, obviously, one that would require considerable defense. I don't propose to go into it in any detail here. I would like to point out though, that *most* philosophical positions, including the claim about real doubt presently in question, are not tied in any obvious way to 'questions of action.' It might be difficult to make a case for the action criterion in the case of Cartesian skepticism, while avoiding the consequence that philosophical beliefs aren't 'real beliefs.'

Now it appears that Descartes himself did think that there was a 'logical' way for doubt about the world (or pretense that the world does *not* exist) to issue in action—along the lines of the first response mentioned above. The First Meditation suggests that if the 'doubt' were not explicitly restricted to matters of knowledge and meditation, it might result in 'danger.' Further, Descartes remarks to Gassendi (after explaining the 'seriousness' of the skepticism of the First Meditation):

> But it is necessary to bear in mind the distinction, emphasized [*inculcata*] by me in various places, between the actions of life and the inquiry into truth. For when it is a question of the regulation of life, it would surely be foolish not to trust the senses, and those Skeptics were completely ridiculous who neglected human affairs to the extent that, lest they throw themselves over precipices, they have to be saved by their friends; and in this connection I somewhere admonished, *no one of sane mind seriously to doubt of such things*. When, however, we inquire what can be known most certainly by the human mind, it is completely alien to reason, not to be willing to reject them as doubtful, indeed even as false, in order to discover that certain others, which cannot thus be rejected, are by this fact more certain, and actually better known by us. (AT VII, 350–1; HR II, 206)

It is perhaps not quite clear whether, in this passage, Descartes is drawing a distinction between theoretical doubt and real (i.e. practical) doubt, or merely admonishing others not to draw the classical, foolish conclusions from the supposition that the world does not exist. There is really not much suggestion that doubts about the world are any less *doubts* for not resulting in sane men jumping off precipices. The crucial point, in either case, is this. Descartes has not said, *or even implied*, that the Deceiver Hypothesis calls in question one's beliefs about the *continued constancy* of one's perceptions. And such beliefs are all that one needs to avoid directing one's will in various 'irresponsible' directions. (Of course the hypothesis *could* be used to generate a Humean, will-the-future-be-like-the-past? sort of skepticism *too*. A *really* malicious Deceiver could be expected eventually to confound my developed expectations of constancy. But the point is that this is a *separate* worry from the concerns of the First Meditation.[64])

There is, finally, a distinction between theory and 'practice' which is important to Descartes's conclusions in the Sixth Meditation, and which may in some manner have influenced his pronouncements about hyperbolic doubt. That is the claim that the senses are reliable guides to what is beneficial or hurtful, though totally unreliable guides to the intrinsic nature of things. This position requires one to say, for example, that while one's conception of the nature of fire has been changed by reading the *Meditations*, one's practice of 'remaining physically distant from it' has not. But the protagonist of the First Meditation has been given no reason to regard as unreasonable his customary volitions of 'retracting his hand from the fire.' The question of the foolishness of the ancient skeptic sectarians is, then, a separate one from the reality of their doubt. There is no clear way that Cartesian skepticism should, logically, issue in action.

II

Knowledge of Self and Bodies

1   The concerns of Meditation II

The First Meditation called into 'doubt' all the deliverances of the senses, and especially what we learn from the senses concerning the existence of nature and our physical selves. It also raised questions about the certainty of mathematics and the reality of simple natures. The aim of the Second Meditation is to establish that we can know with certainty that we ourselves exist even without knowing that bodies exist. Our knowledge of ourselves as thinking beings is, Descartes holds, primary and non-sensory. In addition, Descartes argues that we have a non-sensory awareness of the nature of body itself, which is far superior to what we take to be 'knowledge' gained by direct sensory apprehension. Another important claim of the Second Meditation is that the knowledge of ourselves as thinking things is, like the knowledge of body derived from reason, 'clear and distinct.' I will argue later that *this* claim provides an important step in Descartes's development of his argument for the independence of mind from body—an argument concluded only in the Sixth Meditation. In addition it implies what I will call the doctrine of the 'epistemological transparency' of thought or of the thinker: our awareness of our thought processes is immediate and unproblematic. Thus, thought lies outside the domain of scientific explanation. Unlike body, it is just what it seems, and there is nothing about it to explain. (As I will argue later, though, Descartes also holds some views that are in conflict—or at any rate in tension—with the doctrine of epistemological transparency of thought or mind.)

In this chapter I will be primarily concerned, first, with what is sometimes called Descartes's 'proof of his own existence,' and second with the argument through which he tries to establish some fundamental propositions about the nature of body. My treatment of the first topic is, mainly, an attempt to explore and clarify certain aspects of the so-called *cogito* reasoning, for what I regard as their great intrinsic interest. While I will argue in some detail against certain other treatments of the subject, much of this criticism is relatively independent of the over-all conception of the *Meditations* that I defend in this book. I do, however, accord fundamental importance to the role of the *cogito* reasoning in providing a basis for Descartes's later immaterialist conclusions. Thus, the interpretation of the *cogito* reasoning cannot proceed in complete independence from interpretation of the *Meditations* as a whole. However, this point will not be fully explained until a later chapter.

With respect to the treatment of body, I hold that Descartes has a rather good argument for at least *part* of the conclusion he wishes to reach in the Second Meditation—but this argument unfortunately does not appear in the *Meditations* themselves. The argument that *does* appear in the *Meditations* is, I think, terribly obscure—and gives the impression that Descartes is concerned with problems quite different from the ones that are really at issue.

2 Ego existo

The new line of thought of the Second Meditation begins with the observation that just as Archimedes had required only one fixed point to move the whole world, so Descartes will have great hopes if he can locate the 'least thing' which is certain and firm (AT VII, 24; HR I, 149). He then restates his previous supposition that he has no senses, and that 'body, figure, extension, movement, and place' are mere 'chimeras.' But perhaps, he continues, there is something 'different from all these,' of which there could not be the least occasion to doubt. Perhaps, he first suggests, there is at least some God (or whatever it should be called) who conveys these thoughts [*cogitationes*] to me? But why should he suppose so, since he might himself be their author? But then at least he is something? The ensuing crucial passage culminates in the conclusion that '*ego sum*' does escape the negations of Meditation I:

But I have already denied I have any senses, and any body. But nevertheless I hesitate; for what follows? Am I so bound to body and senses that without them I could not be? But I was persuaded there is nothing at all in the world, no sky, no earth, no minds, no bodies; [did I not persuade myself] therefore that even I am not? No indeed, certainly I was, if I persuaded myself of something [French version: or even if I thought of something]. But there is some unknown deceiver, maximally powerful and clever, who by his industry always deceives me. Without doubt [*haud dubie*] therefore I still am, if he deceives me; and deceive as much as he can, nevertheless he could never make it the case, that I am nothing as long as I think that I am something. So that, indeed, all these things having been considered enough, it is finally determined that this proposition [*pronuntiatum*], *I am, I exist*, whenever it is pronounced by me, or mentally conceived, necessarily is true. (AT VII, 24–5; HR I, 150)

This passage is widely known as an instance of the '*cogito* reasoning,' despite the fact that the famous formulation 'I think therefore I am' ('*cogito ergo sum*') appears only in cognate passages in other works—not in the *Meditations* itself. For instance, in the *Discourse* Descartes had written (at a similar stage in the argument):

Immediately I noticed that while I wished thus to think that all was false, it was necessarily required that I who thought it was something. And remarking that this truth: I think, therefore I am, was so firm and so assured, that all the most extravagant suppositions of the skeptics were not capable of shaking it, I judged that I could receive it without scruple, as the first principle of philosophy which I sought. (AT VI, 32; HR I, 101)

And the *Principles* passage is rather similar:

But having thus rejected all those things, of which we can in any way doubt, and even feigning them to be false, . . . we easily suppose there is no god, no heaven, no bodies; . . . but not in the same way [*ideo*] that we, who think such things, are nothing: for it is inconsistent to suppose that what thinks does not at the same time that it thinks, exist. And hence this cognition, I think, therefore I am, is the first and most certain, of all that occurs to one in the order of philosophizing. (AT VIII–1, 6–7; HR I, 221)

In place of the categorical assertion of 'I think therefore I am,' the *Meditations* passage concludes with a conditional proposition: '*I exist* necessarily is true, *whenever* it is pronounced or mentally conceived by me.'

Some commentators have strongly insisted on the differences between the *Meditations* formulation and that of the other works. They have been concerned to argue that what I will call the 'naïve interpretation' of the *cogito* is not acceptable for the *Meditations*, however strongly it may be suggested by the cognate passages in other writings. They also feel that the *cogito* reasoning, as naïvely interpreted, is subject to philosophical criticisms that their more sophisticated interpretations avoid. I will argue that the naïve interpretation is not in conflict with the text of the *Meditations*. It does, however, present certain philosophical problems and perplexities—not all of which are avoided by alternative sophisticated interpretations.

According to the naïve interpretation, the *cogito* reasoning is intended to present 'I exist' as a truth known by inference to be indubitable; its indubitability is inferred from the indubitability of 'I think'—or, as Descartes sometimes says, of the fact that I think, or of my thinking. The indubitability of 'I think' itself is construed as a sort of *datum*. This interpretation is suggested by the categorical assertion of 'I think,' and by the 'therefore,' in the formulation of the *Discourse* and the *Principles*. It is (one would have supposed) conclusively confirmed by Descartes's way of replying to one of Gassendi's objections to the *Meditations* argument. Gassendi had written:

> Concerning the Second [Meditation], I see that you recognize at least that you who pretend [to doubt] are; and thus establish that this proposition: —I am, I exist, is true each time that you pronounce it, or that you mentally conceive it. But I don't see that you needed all this apparatus, when you had other grounds for being certain [*aliunde certus eras*], and it was true, that you are; and could have inferred that from any other action [*actione*], since it is known by the natural light that whatever acts, is. (AT VII, 258; HR II, 137)

In replying, Descartes does not at all object to Gassendi's construal of what he was doing at the beginning of Meditation II—i.e., inferring the truth of 'I exist' from one of his 'actions.' He just denies that any action other than thought would do. He remarks:

> What reason do you have to say that there was no need of such a large apparatus to prove that I exist? . . . When you say that I could have concluded the same thing from any other of my actions, you are very mistaken, *because there isn't one of them of which I am entirely certain*—I mean with that metaphysical certainty which alone is here in question—*except thought* [emphasis added]. Thus, for example, this consequence would be no good: I walk, therefore I am, except in so far as the consciousness of walking is a thought, from which alone this conclusion [*illatio*] is certain, not from the movement of the body, which sometimes does not exist in sleep, when nevertheless it still seems to me that I am walking; so that from the fact that I think I walk I can very well infer the existence of [a] mind which thinks

this, but not that of [a] body which walks. It is the same with the others. (AT VII, 352; HR II, 207)

In replying to this objection to the *Meditations*, Descartes claims that a formulation like 'I walk therefore I am' wouldn't suit his purposes (and note that it is Descartes, not Gassendi, who here supplies the 'therefore' formulation). The reason is that I don't have metaphysical certainty of my walking—but only of my thinking. In other words, Descartes endorses Gassendi's conception of the structure of the *cogito* reasoning—while rejecting his claim that just any action would serve for the premiss.

The end of this reply suggests, further, that a particular thought or *cogitatio*, such as the 'consciousness of walking,' would serve just as well as the less specific 'I think' as the basis for concluding to the certainty of one's existence. And this accords well with passages from other writings, where Descartes endorses other propositions of the form 'I think that p (or, it seems to me that p), therefore I exist,' as able to serve the function of the *cogito* reasoning.[1] The *Meditations* passage, too, can be read as indicating that Descartes is not particular about *which cogitatio* judgment he uses:

If I *persuaded myself of something* [FV or even if I
   thought of something], I certainly was;
Without doubt I still am, if *he deceives me*;
He could never bring it about that I am nothing as
   long as I *think that I am something*.

On the other hand, there is perhaps reason for caution here. For Descartes does not assert that either 'I persuaded myself' or 'I think I am something' is certain—and would obviously not want to assert that 'he deceives me' is certain. The *Meditations*, then, does introduce, in some sense, a hypothetical approach to the problem of the certainty of one's own existence, in relation to one's thinking. What Descartes's reply to Gassendi seems to tell us is just that this hypothetical approach was not meant to supplant in any substantial way the more straightforward deployment of 'I think therefore I am' in other works.

In what follows I will consider three lines of objection to the naïve interpretation.

First, I acknowledge and try to clarify the point, made by many scholars, that the naïve interpretation requires that we read Descartes's own major presentations of his position as enthymatic. I try to show that this implication does not involve conflicts with the texts, in particular does not involve conflicts with Descartes's denial that the *cogito* is (implicitly) a syllogism.

Second, I argue against the view, developed particularly by Harry Frankfurt, that Descartes's discussion of his existence in the Second Meditation presents peculiar difficulties for the naïve interpretation from a textual point of view. (I'm inclined to think that the naïve interpretation is even *more* strongly confirmed by the *Meditations* than the other works.) However, I will agree with one implication of Frankfurt's position: that the relation of the *cogito* to the enterprise of Cartesian doubt is not fully accounted for by the naïve interpretation.

Third, I will take up the objection that the *cogito* as naïvely interpreted involves a *petitio principii*. Although this objection has been repeatedly formulated in the literature by highly perceptive critics, I do not find that its precise import has been made very clear. I will distinguish and evaluate several different lines of criticism that may be considered aspects of the *'petitio'* objection. This discussion will lead to clarification of the naïve interpretation. (It will also ultimately lead to the suggestion that certain Cartesian texts about our knowledge of substances run counter to the requirements of the *cogito* as naïvely interpreted.)

Finally, I will try to show that the so-called 'performative interpretation' does not provide a philosophically superior reading of the *cogito*.

I have characterized the naïve interpretation as the view that Descartes intends to establish the indubitability of 'I exist' by presenting it ('I exist') as entailed by 'I think'—itself indubitably and immediately known. But, evidently, we need some principle to license the inference of 'I exist' from 'I think'—otherwise it will lack formal validity. This observation is sometimes taken as equivalent to the claim that if the *cogito* is a valid inference at all, it must be construed as a syllogism, depending on a major premiss such as 'whatever thinks exists.'[2] And this is supposed to present an objection to the naïve interpretation—even apart from the oddity of a major premiss with 'exists' in the predicate place. For Descartes insists in at least two places that his *cogito* reasoning should not be construed as a syllogism, claiming that we come to know universal premisses from knowledge of particulars.[3]

Now in the first place there is probably no way to avoid all perplexity about the role of a universal principle in the *cogito* reasoning. For Descartes clearly does think that one is *somehow* involved—though different passages give different views of the nature of this involvement. Such a proposition is actually included by

Descartes in the statement of the *cogito* that we quoted from the *Principles*:

> we cannot suppose that we who think such things are nothing: *for it is inconsistent to suppose that what thinks does not at the same time that it thinks exist*. (AT VIII–1, 7; HR I, 221; emphasis added)

This suggests that knowledge of the universal is presupposed by the *cogito*—a claim that Descartes seems to have made explicitly in his conversations with Burman.[4] The relevance of a general principle seems also to be recognized in the *Discourse*. Here, however, Descartes presents the knowledge of the general principle as *posterior* to the *cogito* reasoning. For shortly after having affirmed the status of 'I think therefore I am' as his first certainty, he remarks:

> I considered in general what is required for a proposition to be true and certain; for, since I had just found one which I knew to be such, I thought that I should also know in what this certitude consists. And having remarked that there is nothing at all in this: *I think, therefore I am*, that assures me that I speak the truth, except that I see very clearly that to think it is necessary to be: I judged that I would take it as a general rule, that things we conceive very clearly and very distinctly are all true. . . . (AT VI, 33; HR I, 101–2)

Similarly, in replying to Objections to the *Meditations*, Descartes denies that the *cogito* reasoning is syllogistic, not on the grounds that a universal principle is *irrelevant*, but rather on the grounds that 'it is the nature of our minds to form general propositions from the knowledge of particulars' (AT VII, 140–1; HR II, 38).

But second, the claim that the *cogito* is an inference—even that it is a logically valid inference—is not equivalent to the claim that it is a syllogism. *Modus ponens* is a valid form of inference, and the various particular hypotheticals enunciated in the Second Meditation would provide adequate licenses for inferring from various *cogitatio* judgments to 'I exist.' I conclude, therefore, that Descartes's denials that the *cogito* is a syllogism are not directly relevant to the interpretation of the *cogito* as a valid inference of one truth from another.

But if the *cogito* is not to be construed as a syllogism, how are we to understand the role of the general principle, 'whatever thinks, exists,' which Descartes is so ready to discuss in connection with it? The best answer, I think, is that Descartes was concerned with its role in knowledge of the hypothetical 'If I think, I exist'—which is made explicit in the *Meditations* (in various versions) although left implicit in the other works. 'If I think, I exist' is presumably an *instance* of 'Whatever thinks exists.' But what does this tell us about the order of knowledge? Should we say that knowledge of principles is prior or posterior to knowledge of their instances?

Several different views on this question are suggested by the Cartesian texts. The *Principles* text, which surely comes the closest to presenting the *cogito* as an actual syllogism, suggests that an explicit knowledge of the principle is required for the certainty of the conclusion 'I exist.' The *Conversation with Burman* has Descartes holding that only an *implicit* knowledge of the principle is required. This seems to fit with the *Discourse* passage where Descartes appears to be reasoning transcendentally from the fact that he is certain of the *cogito* (in the particular version) to the conditions of the possibility of this certainty. The latter are not originally explicitly noticed: they are elicited as presuppositions. That is, Descartes seems there to hold the view that the soundness of the reasoning depends on the truth of the universal principle (so knowing the reasoning is sound requires in some sense 'knowing' the universal principle). Yet one can recognize that the inference is sound prior to achieving *express* recognition of any universal principle.

The remark quoted from the Replies is rather too terse for any confident interpretation. But it surely *could* be read as implying, in contradiction to some of Descartes's other statements, that 'universals' are not present in the mind at all until it forms them from particulars.

The question of the relation of principles and instances in the order of knowledge is, in fact, a difficult one. It became a subject of explicit and detailed treatment by two of Descartes's immediate successors, Locke and Leibniz—who defended opposite positions.[5] I think it is quite possible Descartes simply could not make up his mind. On the one hand he wanted to say that we can know the (necessary) truth of 'If I think I exist,' without having heard or thought of any abstract principle such as 'whatever thinks exists.' This does seem plausible, and it suggests that (as Locke might say) we know the instance without knowing the principle. On the other hand, he wanted to say that the (necessary) truth of 'If I think, I exist' is not strictly independent of the truth of 'whatever thinks exists' or the validity of 'if . . . a, exists a.' This seems plausible also, and tends to suggest (as Leibniz might hold) that we must in some sense, explicitly or implicitly, know the principle first.[6] It is not surprising that Descartes's treatment of the question in different contexts should reveal some vacillation.

57

One further point, in passing. In so far as Descartes tends to the view that knowledge of principles is prior to knowledge of instances, he seems inclined to the view that certain propositions may be known only *implicitly*. That is, he seems prepared to allow that we may properly be attributed knowledge of truths we have never consciously recognized or articulated. This willingness to consider and even espouse a doctrine of implicit knowledge is one of the elements of Descartes's philosophy that requires caution about ascribing to him the view that mental states are necessarily conscious.[7] I will have more to say about this issue in a later chapter.

Critics frequently remark that Descartes's presentation of the *cogito* is enthymatic. Now this statement is misleading, if one has in mind the suppression of an inference license from '*cogito*' to '*sum*' (i.e., something to fill in the 'therefore'). For in the *Principles* and the *Discourse* Descartes makes explicit a universal principle that *would* serve this purpose (although his denials of syllogistic intent make it preferable to suppose he is thinking of an *instance* of this principle as the actual constituent of the *cogito*). And in the *Meditations* he makes explicit at least five particular hypotheticals that would license the inference to 'I exist' from a particular *cogitatio* judgment (I persuade myself of something, etc.). In another respect, however, the reasoning as naïvely interpreted *is* enthymatic in all three presentations. As Harry Frankfurt writes (in criticizing the naïve interpretation):[8]

> If the peculiar value of deriving *sum* from *cogito* [as opposed, e.g. to *ambulo*] actually consisted in the certitude of *cogito*, Descartes ought to establish or at least to claim that *cogito* is in fact a statement of which he can be certain. He does not do so.

Thus, on the naïve interpretation, there would be, in Frankfurt's words, 'a serious gap in Descartes's discussion of his existence in the Second Meditations.'

And, it would seem, in the *Discourse* and *Principles* as well. For even though Descartes may be taken to affirm 'I think' in the latter works (*Cogito ergo sum; je pense donc je suis*), he does not in the *cogito* passages assert, let alone argue, that 'I think' escapes the net of systematic doubt.

It seems to me that all three presentations must indeed be regarded as enthymatic in this respect,[9] but that this is not a serious objection to the naïve interpretation. In all three works, but above all in the *Meditations*, Descartes *does go on* to indicate that propositions or judgments about his own thoughts are entirely unproblematic. Thus in the Second Meditation he writes:

What therefore am I? A thinking thing. What is this? Surely something doubting, understanding, affirming, denying, willing, opposing, imagining also, and feeling.

Surely these are not few, if they all belong to me. But why should they not belong? Am I not the same who now doubts nearly everything, who nevertheless understands something, who affirms that this one [thing] is true, who denies the others, who desires to know more, who wishes not to be deceived, who imagines many things involuntarily, who even notices many things as if coming from the senses? What is there of these, even if I always sleep, even if he who created me is in himself such as to delude me, that is not equally true as that I am? . . . For that it is I who doubt, who understand, who will, is so manifest, that nothing could occur through which it could be more evidently explained [*ut nihil occurrat per quod evidentius explicetur*]. But in fact I am even the same who imagines; for even if indeed, as I supposed, no imagined thing is at all true, nevertheless the power of imagining itself really exists, and constitutes part of my thought [*cogitationis meae*]. Finally, I am the same who senses, or who is aware of corporeal things as if through the senses: clearly I now see light, hear sound, feel heat. These are false, for I sleep. But certainly I seem to see, to hear, to feel heat. This cannot be false; this is strictly what in me is called sensing; and this precisely understood is nothing else than to think. (AT VII, 28, 29; HR I, 153; cf. AT VIII–1, 7–8; HR I, 222)

It is perhaps disappointing that Descartes does not expressly consider the question of why the Deceiver could not cause him to make false judgments about his own thoughts. It appears, though, that Descartes regards it as sufficient to insist on the distinction between the existence of a thought or experience, on the one hand, and the existence of things thought, imagined or 'sensed,' on the other. Once this distinction is recognized, observations about one's own mental states are supposed to fall within the certainty of the *cogito* itself. 'For that it is I who doubt, who understand, who will, is so manifest, that nothing could occur through which it could be more evidently explained.' These states are states of *me*, *qua* thinking thing, and *qua* thinking thing I certainly and indubitably exist. Hence the existence of these states itself is certain and indubitable. This reasoning is, no doubt, invalid; the Deceiver has not sufficiently been confronted on this level. But the point is just this: no matter how one interprets the *cogito*, one is going to have to recognize eventually that Descartes does ascribe indubitability to his *cogitatio* judgments, epistemological transparency to his thought-states—and he takes these to be impervious to the powers of the Deceiver. The naïve interpretation may indeed ascribe to Descartes an undefended premiss or assumption; but the ascription itself can be defended. Further, the interpretation does not leave a 'logical gap' in the argument in the sense of entailing that the argument is irreparably invalid.

Frankfurt advances another textual objection to the naïve interpretation. He holds that while this interpretation views Descartes as trying to establish the certain truth of 'I exist,' no such conclusion is found in the text of the *Meditations*. He writes:

> The purpose of [Descartes's] inference, however, is not to prove that *sum* is true.[10]

> Descartes' discussion [in the *Meditations*] might have been expected to end with an . . . assertion or denial of *sum* or, perhaps, with an assertion or denial that *sum* is certain. Instead, however, the final outcome of the discussion is a characterization of *sum* as 'necessarily true as often as it is uttered by me or conceived by my mind.'[11]

Frankfurt does not explain why he takes the remark he quotes as the 'end' or 'final outcome' of Descartes's discussion; in fact, Descartes affirms that he 'necessarily is' in the very next sentence after that quoted by Frankfurt—or, in the French version, that he is certain that he is (AT IX–1, 19). But perhaps the second comment quoted from Frankfurt is merely misleading. For he does not seem really to want to deny that Descartes is concerned to establish that *sum* is certain—provided we understand that a very special sense of 'certain' is at issue. According to Frankfurt, what Descartes means to show is just that 'I exist' is certain in the peculiar sense that anyone who wonders about its truth by that very fact has 'available' an adequate reason for affirming it. But this complex proposition does not, according to Frankfurt, lead Descartes to the conclusion that *sum* is *true*.

Now I have some sympathy with the positive side of Frankfurt's position on the *cogito*. That is, I think in the end it is at least rhetorically incomplete *merely* to represent Descartes as reasoning, 'I think' is indubitable and if I think, I exist; therefore, indubitably, I exist. This representation is incomplete even apart from any issue about the suppression of a general principle. For it does not bring out the peculiar relation of the *cogito* to the enterprise of Cartesian doubt. Since 'I doubt,' or 'I am deceived,' or 'I entertain the possibility I am deceived,' are themselves *examples* of *cogito* judgments, they themselves entail the truth of 'I exist,' according to the connection between *cogito* and *sum* alleged in the *cogito* reasoning. In other words, it surely is an important feature of the *cogito* reasoning that doubt and/or the supposition of deception *itself* is supposed to *lead to*, rather than undermine, the certainty of 'I exist.' This observation is not, however, at war with the naïve interpretation; the two can co-exist and complement each other.

And Frankfurt is surely wrong in supposing that Descartes is *only* interested in the relation of 'I exist' to 'I wonder whether I exist' etc. In other words, the negative side of his interpretation seems to me quite hopeless. Descartes *does* claim in the Second Meditation to be concerned with truth—'I do not now admit anything which is not necessarily true' (AT VII, 27; HR I, 152)[12]—and specifically with the truth of 'I exist':

> [Am I more than the self which I know?] I do not know, of this I do not now dispute: I can only give judgment concerning those things which are known to me. I know I exist; I ask what I am this I that I know. (AT VII, 27; HR I, 152)

> Am I not the same who now doubts nearly everything, who still nevertheless understands something; who affirms that this one thing is true. . . . (*Ibid.*)

There is I think overwhelming textual justification for attributing to Descartes the view that 'I exist'—while not of course a necessary truth in itself—may be known with certainty to be true by the thinking being.

So far I have tried to show that the naïve interpretation attributes to Descartes only premises that he could accept as premises and a conclusion that he would accept as a conclusion: 'I exist' is certainly true. I have shown that the naïve interpretation, in presenting the *cogito* as an inference, does not necessarily conflict with Descartes's intermittent denials that the *cogito* is a syllogism—even if we interpret 'inference' to mean 'logically valid inference.' I have agreed that the argument is presented enthymatically in the major passages: the *Meditations* omit altogether to affirm 'I think' in the context of the discussion of existence, and all three published works omit to affirm the *certainty* of 'I think' in the appropriate contexts. On the other hand, Descartes does stress the certainty of 'I think' and of particular '*cogitatio*' judgments elsewhere in the Second Meditation and in the Replies to Objections. It is true that he does not *defend* the claim that *cogitatio* judgments are indubitable, in the sense of being Deceiver-proof, in these or any other passages. (This is, of course, one manifestation of the view that mental states are epistemologically transparent to the mind who 'has' them.) There may well be grounds for a philosophical objection to Descartes here, but not to the naïve interpretation *per se*.

I now wish to consider whether and in what sense the naïve interpretation leaves Descartes open to the further charge of having committed a *petitio principii* in the *cogito* reasoning.

This charge is advanced, for example, by Hintikka, in his famous article, 'Cogito Ergo Sum: Inference or Performance?'[13] Hintikka indicates the objection mainly by way of an example:[14]

> One can see why some interpretation like the one we have been criticising [a version of the naïve interpretation] attracted Descartes. . . . He could always ask: How can it possibly be true of someone that he thinks unless he exists? And if you challenge the premise that he is thinking . . . , Descartes could have replied that in a sense the premise is redundant. He could have resorted to some such argument as the following: If I am right in thinking that I exist, then of course I exist. If I err in thinking that I exist or if I as much as doubt whether I exist, then I must likewise exist, for no one can err or doubt without existing. In any case I must therefore exist: *ergo sum*.
>
> This neat argument is a *petitio principii*, however, as you may perhaps see by comparing it with the following similar argument: Homer was either a Greek or a barbarian. If he was a Greek, he must have existed. . . . But if he was a barbarian, he likewise must have existed. Hence he must have existed in any case.

But Hintikka concludes, the celebrated Homeric question cannot be solved on paper. Thus the argument is fallacious.

Hintikka's presentation is not very coherent. Nothing he says really shows that the premiss 'I am thinking' is 'in a sense' redundant, and by the same token it is not clear in which way the 'Homeric' argument is supposed to be similar to the *cogito* as naïvely interpreted. It is easy to see why Hintikka's 'Homeric' argument might be called circular, or question-begging: the premiss requires the qualification, 'Homer, *if he existed*, must have been either a Greek or a barbarian.' For 'Homer is (or was) a Greek' and 'Homer is (was) a barbarian' might both be regarded as false or lacking truth value, in case Homer does not (did not) exist. But since Descartes does not, as a matter of fact, regard it as an open question whether 'I think' is true, false or lacking in truth value, he would not have *made* the move Hintikka offers him. The *cogito*, like any other demonstration, depends for soundness on the truth of its premisses. And

Descartes holds that 'I think' (on a given occasion of the *cogito*) is not only true but indubitable.

But perhaps we can reformulate the *petitio* objection in the light of these criticisms of Hintikka. The objection will now go as follows. If 'I think' is true only if 'I exist' is true, then to know that 'I think' is true and certain one must *already know* that 'I exist' is true and certain. Similarly, if 'I exist' is dubitable, 'I think' will similarly and by the same token be dubitable: one cannot know that 'I think' is *indubitable* unless one already knows that 'I exist' is indubitable. This seems to be the form in which the *petitio principii* objection is expressed by Bernard Williams (in 'The Certainty of the Cogito').[15] Some might feel that the main advantage of Frankfurt's non-naïve reading of the *cogito* is that it appears clearly to avoid this version of the 'circularity' objection. For according to Frankfurt's reading, Descartes's 'conclusion' is that 'I exist' is certain just in so far as he cannot wonder about it without its being true. This puts emphasis on the 'entailment' relation between *cogito* and *sum*, and seemingly renders the order of knowledge issue irrelevant.[16]

Yet, it seems there must be something wrong here. For this version of the *petitio* objection would cut against any valid deductive argument whatsoever, considered as a vehicle of inference.[17] Besides, as we've already seen, 'order of knowledge' issues are not necessarily so clear and straightforward. A proponent of the *cogito* might be able to argue that recognition of the indubitability of 'I think' *is* in some way more basic or immediate than recognition of the indubitability of 'I exist'—at least in so far as 'express' knowledge is at issue. He would hold, then, that in the natural order of things one notices first that 'I think' is indubitable, and *then* notices that it is a condition of the indubitability of 'I think' that 'I exist' also is indubitable. He need not be disturbed by the suggestion that the knowledge—even awareness—of my existence must in some way 'already' be implicit in the knowledge that I think. (He may further point out that the element of 'discovery' in the *cogito* reasoning is not by any means *restricted* to whatever discovery may be involved concerning the indubitability of 'I exist.' There is also the reflective discovery that knowledge of 'I think' is sufficient to know I exist: that knowledge of body is not required.)

I want now to consider another worry that arises in connection with the *cogito* reasoning as we have been interpreting it (and seems to bear also against, for instance, the *cogito* as Frankfurt interprets it). I have been interpreting the *cogito* as involving an inference from 'I think' to 'I exist,' and have suggested above that one might discover the indubitability of 'I exist' by noticing it is a condition of (the indubitable) 'I think.' But now the following question arises: what makes us think we *are justified in accepting* a principle that lets us infer from 'I think' to 'I exist'?[18] This question has been raised in one way by Hintikka, who notes that 'ϕa' entails 'Ea' (or 'a exists') only in those logical systems where we make it a condition on the truth of 'ϕa' that 'a' names an existing entity.[19] He finds here a ground for claiming arbitrariness—or, again, 'circularity'—in the *cogito* as naïvely interpreted. I take his point to be that Descartes is entitled to infer from 'I think' to 'I exist' only if he has (arbitrarily and antecedently) made it a condition of true predication in his 'system' that the subject of predication exist.

The arbitrariness, here, I take it, is supposed to come in ruling out of the realm of true predication propositions of which the subjects are (merely) possible or fictional entities. I can't after all reason without inanity: Lear loved Cordelia; therefore Lear existed. Yet there seems to be something suspicious about this criticism. For do we really want to call 'Lear loved Cordelia' a *truth*?

However, a similar worry has troubled another critic, and perhaps his approach will help to make the problem clearer. Anthony Kenny has asserted that 'the cogito and ontological argument cannot both be valid.'[20] His point is that the ontological argument will be sound only if we are permitted to treat as true, predications of non-existent entities. Thus, Descartes tries to model the ontological argument on reasoning about triangles, where statements like 'Triangles have their longest side opposite their widest angle' are necessarily true and known with certainty, whether or not triangles exist. But if we are allowed to treat as true propositions whose subjects are not actual existents, then we cannot (Kenny would claim) soundly reason from 'I think' to 'I exist.'

Now we have noticed that Descartes *does* regard the principle 'whatever thinks exists'—not to mention, 'If I persuade myself of something then I exist'—as somehow relevant to the soundness of the *cogito* reasoning. So it certainly *looks* like he wants to endorse the formula, if ϕa, then Ea. But what Kenny's observation shows, I think, is that this interpretation of Descartes just has to be wrong. The *cogito* just *can't* be taken to rest on the assumption that true predication requires an *existent* as subject. The ontological argument is only one of several important elements of Descartes's system that require that we be able to make true predications of non-existent entities.[21]

But what recourse is there, given that we are faced with Descartes's repeated endorsement of 'Whatever thinks exists'? First, I think, we should remember the exchange between Descartes and Gassendi, which concerned not bare predication, but *action*. The principle they agree on seems to be 'Whatever acts, exists.' Descartes further claims, in his answer to Gassendi, that of all his actions only thought is metaphysically certain. That is, he is metaphysically certain only of 'I think' and not, for example, of 'I walk.' While non-existent triangles may be said (perhaps) to have properties, they may hardly be said to act.

But what about Hintikka's example of Hamlet ('Hamlet did think a great many things; does it follow that he existed?').[22] And what, again, about God? (Why could Descartes not avoid the complexities of the logic of perfections by reasoning: God is (essentially) all-knowing; whatever knows, thinks; whatever thinks exists; therefore God exists?)

Perhaps Descartes *does* want to hold that a predicate expressing or implying a state of action can be truly ascribed only to existent subjects. If so, we would have to deal with predications of fictional entities in somewhat the way suggested above: i.e. we'd have to say it isn't *really true* ('a truth') that Lear quarreled with Cordelia—despite the fact that there is a right answer to the question, Did Lear quarrel with Cordelia? (and the answer is 'yes'). Triangles and other mathematical essences or natures would provide no problem. The issues about God would have to be dealt with as best one could. (Perhaps by suggesting that while actions *in time* can only be truly ascribed to an existing entity, the mysteriously timeless activities we attribute to God may intelligibly be supposed, *prima facie*, to have a non-existent essence as subject.) But there is another possibility. Consider Descartes's assertion:

> There are no affections or qualities of nothing [*nihili nullas esse affectiones sive qualitates*], so that wherever we come upon [*deprehendimus*] any, there must necessarily be found [*inveniri*] a thing or substance whose they are [*cujus illae sint*]. (AT VIII, 8; HR I, 223)

Kenny interprets Descartes as saying here that there can be true predication only of existent subjects.[23] (Hence his conclusion that the ontological argument and the *cogito* cannot both be maintained.) But it's not at all clear that Descartes's assertion should be read in this way. Descartes may rather be claiming that where we *observe* an attribute—i.e. determine it to be existent or actual—we may conclude that there is an existing subject or thing, of which it is the attribute. In other words, he may understand the principle as allowing inference not from true predication to existent subject, but from observed actual property to existent subject. Properties of fictional entities or essences, we may suppose, do not pass this test. And the *point* of reasoning from property to subject or thing in this way—rather than simply observing the existence of the subject directly—is that Descartes wants to go on from the *cogito* to conceive the self as a substance, and one *cannot* (according to Cartesian doctrine) observe substances directly.[24] They must be known through their attributes.

These considerations should draw our attention to one important point. When Descartes says that *'cogito'* is indubitable he surely is assuming some kind of direct awareness of an actual thought-process. The existence or actuality of thought should surely be construed as part of the *datum* of the *cogito*. Therefore, Descartes's principle, 'whatever thinks exists,' should perhaps be read along something like the following lines: whatever is actually thinking, has actual thoughts, must itself be an actual being, an existing thing. When it is read in this way worries about predication of possibles (or fictitious entities, or essences) do not seem to obtrude.

However, the proposition that the self must be inferred from the observation of thoughts also leads to certain problems which pose, I think, serious difficulties for Descartes's system. Descartes enunciates the principle 'There are no properties of nothing' immediately after a presentation of the *cogito* reasoning. While it is not presented as part of the *cogito* proper, this juxtaposition, together with the doctrine that we must infer the existence of substances from their perceived attributes,[25] suggests that the starting point of the *cogito* must be 'there is, presently, thought,' rather than 'I think.' The problem now is how to get to the 'I.' The principle Descartes states may allow us to infer from 'there is thought' to 'there is a thinker or subject of thought'; but this conclusion is not equivalent to *'I* think,' and does not yield 'I exist.'[26]

Further, consider the problem of continuing identity through time. It is clear we want to ascribe many thoughts to a single 'I'; and Descartes makes explicit in the Synopsis of the *Meditations* that he does regard the 'I' of the *cogito* as a continuing identical entity (AT, VII, 14; HR I, 141). Now it is not implausible, I think, to treat the subjective unity of thought, 'identity of consciousness,' as itself a *datum*. (Kant would hold that to do this involves nothing more than recognizing the tautology that all my thoughts are mine.) But if we take Descartes's talk of knowing substances through their attributes to imply that the referent of 'I' in 'I think' is an *inferred* entity, we are faced with the very intransigent problem of justifying the assumption that there is a *single* entity that is the subject of all my thoughts.[27]

It seems that if the *cogito* is to work at all, we must take 'I think' (and not merely 'there (or here) is thought') as its starting point. And perhaps if it is plausible to treat the subjective unity of thought as a datum, 'I think' may be as justifiable a starting point as 'there is thought'—contrary to the allegations of many of Descartes's critics over the centuries. But then we must ask whether this move is reconcilable (a) with Descartes's talk of knowing subjects only through their attributes, and (b) with his use of the *cogito* reasoning as the starting point for the argument that he is an immaterial substance. I would like to defer consideration of the second question till later—and only remark here that the interpretation of the *cogito* as an inference from 'I think' to 'I exist' seems to me to provide at least a good way of understanding how Descartes *thought* he could use it to argue for the distinctness of mind from body.[28] With respect to the first question, I think there may in fact be an irreconcilable conflict in Descartes's position, as to whether 'I' expresses a datum or refers to an entity known only by inference. The *cogito*, for reasons already stated, requires that it express a datum; Descartes's position that 'I' denotes a substance, together with the denial that substances are apprehended directly, requires that the referent of 'I' be (merely) inferred. However, this conflict might be avoided if some modification were allowed in Descartes's statements about the knowledge of substances through attributes. While these certainly do suggest that we *perceive* an attribute and *infer* a substance or subject, it may be that what Descartes is mainly concerned to avoid is the idea that we can perceive substances naked of attributes. But to hold we cannot perceive a subject except in so far as we recognize it to exhibit some property or activity does not seem to *require* holding that we *infer* substances from attributes.

In concluding this discussion of the *cogito*, I offer a few critical comments on some alleged alternatives to the naïve interpretation.

Sometimes the naïve interpretation of the *cogito* has been opposed on the grounds that 'I do not exist' is, in isolation, a self-stultifying or self-defeating utterance or thought, while 'I exist' is in some sense self-verifying. Thus any *premiss*, such as 'I think,' must be redundant in establishing the certainty of 'I exist.'[29] This seems to be so because 'I' merely picks out the thinker of any thought or the maker of any assertion; hence it cannot fail of reference when it occurs in an actual thought or assertion, such as 'I exist.'[30] (Note that the point here is not just that 'I do not exist' denies its own presuppositions; for this might be said of any negative existential proposition with a name or other referring term in the subject place. The point is rather that it must do so *falsely*.) Now as a matter of fact this reasoning is sound only on the assumption that there *is* an asserter of every assertion, or a thinker of every thought. And this assumption does not appear trivial.[31] This suggests, I think, that one cannot just accept as an unarguable intuition the claim that the thought or utterance of 'I do not exist' must falsely deny its own presupposition. Hence, it is not after all clear that we can do without premises in 'seeing' that 'I exist' is certain on any occasion when it is thought or uttered. Further, it is not clear how claims to the effect that 'I do not exist' is, in itself, necessarily false whenever it is thought or uttered, could provide the basis for any argument concerning the *nature* of the self. It is *essential* to Descartes's intended use of the *cogito* that it provide grounds for attributing to himself a property—specifically, the property of thought. Thus, the mere observation that 'I do not exist' is a self-stultifying thought in the sense described, even if true, cannot provide adequate basis for interpreting the Cartesian *cogito*.

This objection is also apposite to the so-called 'performative' interpretation of the *cogito*, which is, in a sense, a variation on the view that 'I do not exist' is a self-defeating utterance. Nevertheless, it is worth briefly considering the performative interpretation, in order to exhibit its contrast with the naïve interpretation. I understand it to rest on the following notion:[32]

> 'I do not exist' is self-stultifying because any use of the assertion will in fact *have the effect of persuading the audience* that I *do* exist, rather than that I do not.

Now, this statement could be viewed merely as providing a minor embellishment on one of the readings previously considered. We might suppose, for example, that the utterance of 'I do not exist' is a self-defeating performance *because* we believe that 'I' cannot fail to refer when used in an assertion. But the statement can also be interpreted as making a different and novel point. Thus, one might hold that 'I do not exist' is a self-defeating performance because there is a conflict between the 'content' of the assertion and the facts that (a) the assertion is (*ex hypothesi*) a performance of mine, and (b) any performance of mine serves to *call attention to* my existence. Thus (to restrict ourselves for the moment to verbalizations) my asserting 'I exist' may be said to create the belief that I exist, in exactly the way that my asserting 'it must be twelve o'clock' does—or, for that matter, in exactly the way that my raising a question ('Did I fall asleep while you were talking?'), by calling attention to myself, may be said to bring about the belief that I exist, or recognition of my existence. The assertion 'I do not exist,' being yet another action performed by me, serves, like the others, as one more manifestation of my existence.

Here it is instructive to compare, in the first place, vocal utterances with grosser forms of physical behavior. By performing an act such as kicking you I can under normal circumstances call attention to my existence just as effectively as by some use of language such as remarking aloud, 'Notice me' or 'I exist.' And a self-defeating element might, under suitable conditions, also attach to such non-verbal performances as a result of their ability to call attention to the performer's existence: as when someone commands, 'Believe that I do not exist or I will kick you.'

Now it is necessary to introduce a qualification concerning the proposed claim that any performance of mine serves to make manifest or cause recognition of my existence. For it is important to distinguish between the following two propositions:

(1) Any intentional action of mine is a manifestation of my existence; and
(2) Any intentional action of mine tends to call attention to or make manifest my existence.

(1) is true if it is a necessary condition of my doing something that I exist. (2) is not true even on this assumption. Playing dead or lying low are intentional actions of mine and they need not be self-defeating. It takes only a little imagination to think of cases where even *utterances* of mine (registered on a tape-recorder, conveyed over the telephone, or employed ventriloquistically) could lead others to believe that I do not exist. And, if people are independently convinced that I do not exist, an utterance of mine in my own name to the effect that I do not will be readily intelligible and metaphysically undisturbing, provided it is understood that some delayed-time mechanism is being employed. For example, I might decide to *tape* my will, in order to enhance the emotional impact of my generosity and/or punitive denial of inheritances to my survivors: 'Now that I no longer exist, and you are all greedily anticipating your share of my considerable estate. . . .' Yet it must be the second sort of 'manifestation' on which the performative interpretation rests, since it is concerned to stress the *effects* of certain activities—not their source.

The assertion 'I do not exist' is self-defeating only if it is taken to reach its intended audience at about the same time that the intention originating it occurs. And it is self-defeating not simply because it is a performance, and performances are manifestations of the existence of the performer. The crucial point seems to be that utterances are (except in very unusual circumstances) the sort of performances that tend to call attention to the existence of the performer; they are not, for instance, normally ways of lying low.

But Descartes, of course, was not concerned in the *cogito* passages with audible utterances. He is concerned rather with thought. And the *thought* that I exist (or that I do not) hardly seems to be a performance at all. Certainly it is not the sort of performance that would serve to call someone else's attention to my existence. We might, however, try to argue as follows. Just as an utterance I make in your presence (at least under uncomplicated circumstances) will make manifest to you the fact that I exist (still exist, or whatever), so a thought I entertain in your absence will at least tend to make manifest *to me* that I exist: the principal difference is in the audience.

We might then conclude that to say 'I exist' is certain is to say that its denial cannot be thought or spoken without tending to cause in any 'audience' the belief that I do exist. Hintikka, in fact, seems to hold a view something like this, at least in some passages. He seems to be arguing that to think the thought 'I do not exist' is to engage in an intrinsically absurd performance, and that the observation *that this is so* is the essential content of Descartes's 'insight' concerning the certainty of 'I exist.'[33] For someone discovering the unique certainty of 'I exist' recognizes, precisely, that to try to entertain seriously the thought, 'I do not exist,' results only in convincing oneself that one does exist: one succeeds only in convincing oneself of the opposite of the proposition one is attempting to entertain. Since this is inevitable (one perceives that) the attempt to entertain the proposition 'I do not exist' is absurd.

Now such an interpretation is far harder to justify textually than the naïve view previously discussed. (I take it that Hintikka's claims of textual support have adequately been refuted by Frankfurt, Kenny and others.[34]) But it is also no more immune to philosophical objections than the other interpretation. One problem is that the performative interpretation fails to elucidate the central point: the connection between thinking something or entertaining a thought, and becoming convinced of one's own existence. And if one attempts to remedy this problem he may find that the performative interpretation is no longer standing on its own legs; elements of the other accounts of the *cogito* reasoning tend to reappear with all *their* difficulties. Thus, as Fred Feldman has pointed out, one might try to explain Descartes's inability to think 'I do not exist' without becoming convinced of his existence, by supposing he holds the belief, If I think, I exist. But then we have reintroduced the naïve interpretation.[35]

There are certain other problems with the performative interpretation. For instance, at least as the interpretation is formulated by
Hintikka, it requires that we suppose the existence of an audience—
in the limiting case in which we are interested, oneself—whose
convictions can be observed and discussed. But this seems to point to
at least as serious a problem of presupposition as the one already
discussed, in considering the *petitio principii* objection to the naïve
interpretation. In addition, it is not clear what is supposed to prevent
a person from entertaining the hypothesis that the Deceiver causes
him to be affected in the way indicated (to become convinced of his
existence by attempting to think that he does not exist). Elsewhere
Descartes does claim that certain propositions cannot be thought of
without being believed (so, it would seem to follow, their denials
cannot be thought of and believed true).[36] Yet these propositions, he
seems to say, can be called in question by a sort of second-order
doubt: perhaps some of the propositions I cannot think of without
believing them true are nevertheless false. Hence, if anyone objects
that the *cogito*, as naïvely interpreted, should not by rights escape the
Deceiver Hypothesis, we may point out that the performative
interpretation, too, is vulnerable to this objection.

3 But what then am I?

The affirmation of his existence leads Descartes into an inquiry
concerning his nature: granted it is certain that he exists, what sort of
thing is he? He considers his former opinion that he had a body, with
face, arms, etc., and a soul that moved the body and perhaps took the
form of some very subtle gas-like stuff. However, on the hypothesis of
the Deceiver he cannot assure himself of possessing any of the
attributes he has associated with his body.

> What then of those I attributed to the soul? To nourish or walk?
> Since I now have no body, these also are nothing but figments. To
> sense? But even this requires a body, and I have seemed to sense
> many things in sleep which I later noticed [*animadverti*] that I
> did not sense. (AT VII, 27; HR I, 151)

There is, he finds, only one attribute that is not excluded on this basis

> To think? Here I find it: thought [there] is [*cogitatio est*]; this
> alone cannot be taken from me [*a me divelli nequit*]. I am, I exist;
> [this] is certain. But for how long? For as long as I think; for indeed
> it might be the case that if I ceased from all thought, at the same
> time I would entirely cease to exist. I am now admitting nothing
> except what necessarily is true; I am therefore strictly only a

71

thinking thing, that is, mind, or soul, or intellect, or reason, words of which I previously did not know the meaning. I am however a true and truly existing thing; but what sort of thing? I have answered, a thing which thinks. (AT VII, 27; HR I, 151–2)

The affirmation of thought (*'cogitatio est'*) occurs for the first time in this passage. And Descartes's editor Alquié has remarked, *à propos* of the passage, that 'not only . . . does the affirmation of thought appear as posterior to that of the self (*du moi*), but it appears to be subordinated to it.'[37] However, as we've seen, Descartes has already moved from the hypotheticals of the *cogito* passage ('If I persuade myself of something, I exist,' etc.) to the direct affirmation of the certainty of his existence. So knowledge of his own thought has already been taken for granted in some sense. Alquié himself, after indicating that the *cogito* passage presents 'une experience ontologique du moi comme existant,' comes close to admitting this point:[38]

Il convient d'ajouter cependant que le texte qui précède l'affirmation 'je suis' établit implicitement le 'je pense' à titre de condition, encore obscurement apperçue, de ce 'Je suis' (ainsi, *j'étais sans doute, si je me suis persuadé, ou seulement si j'ai pensé quelque chose*).

In any case, in the explicit affirmation *'cogitatio est'* Descartes is now including much more than the simple 'I think' as the rest of the sentence, and its further sequel, make evident. What is 'subordinated' to 'I exist' is not so much 'I think,' as the proposition that when all else has been doubted thought remains as indubitably an inseparable or essential property of mine.

Sum res cogitans ultimately includes at least five distinguishable claims (each one stronger than the one before):

(1) I think
(2) I am a thinking thing
(3) Thought is a property essential to me
(4) Thought is the only property essential to me[39]
(5) I am essentially a thinking thing, and not essentially material.

((5), but not (4) implies an affirmation of the non-identity of thought with any corporeal property.)

How many of these propositions are supposed to be established in the Second Meditation? The passage quoted almost makes it sound as if Descartes thinks he has established *all* of them. 'Thought alone cannot be separated from me; I am nothing but a mind or soul or understanding or reason.' But this is very puzzling. In the first place, it is not at all clear by what right he could claim to have established all these things at this stage of his reasoning. For instance, what could entitle him to suppose that nothing is really true of him, beyond what he is certain of at this stage? Second, Descartes will offer in the Sixth Meditation *an explicit argument* for the claim that thought is his only essential property. This argument would surely be redundant if he already considers himself entitled to affirm in the Second Meditation that 'thought alone cannot be separated from me.'

Some of this perplexity can be resolved. For in Meditation II Descartes himself goes on to point out that he is not yet entitled to the strong conclusion about the distinctness of mind or self from body that his previous words did suggest. He comments:

> But possibly it happens that these very [corporeal] things [such as the human body] which I supposed were nothing because they are unknown to me, are in the truth of the matter [*in rei veritate*] not different from this me which I know. I do not know, I do not dispute about this matter now, I can only give judgment on things that are known to me. (AT VII, 27; HR I, 152)

Descartes, then, deliberately retracts his apparent affirmation of (4) and (5). He restricts himself, for the time being, to the following, merely epistemic, versions of these propositions:

(4E) Thought is the only property I know to be essential to me (inseparable from me);

(5E) I do not know thought to be identical with any corporeal property.

However, Descartes does clearly take the *cogito* reasoning to have provided him with (2), I am an existing thing (or *res*), and not merely with what Kant would call the bare 'I think':

> I am, however, a true and truly existing thing (*res vera et vere existens*).

This fact will prove crucially important when we consider the mind–body distinctness argument of Meditation VI.

Also, it appears that Descartes does take himself to know, at this stage in his reasoning, that thought is essential to him, or pertains to his nature (proposition (3), above). This statement might be disputed, on the grounds that he also offers a qualification on the claim that 'thought . . . cannot be separated from me.' For he does not assert that he *would* cease to exist if he ceased from all thought, but only that he *might*. Also, the word 'essence' does not occur in the Second Meditation; so far as I can find, it is not used in connection with the mind or self until the Sixth. However when Descartes does come to speak of his essence he seems to treat this expression as synonymous with 'nature':

> From this very fact, that I know I exist, and that meanwhile I notice nothing else to pertain to my nature or essence, except this alone that I am a thinking thing, I rightly conclude that my essence consists in this one [thing], that I am a thinking thing. (AT VII, 78; HR I, 190)

And he does claim to make discoveries about his 'nature' in the Second Meditation, which is in fact titled, 'Of the nature of the human mind: that it is better known than body' (*De natura mentis humanae: quod ipsa sit notior quam corpus*). Since there is no further discussion of his 'nature or essence' between the Second Meditation and the statement quoted above from the Sixth, I conclude that Descartes means to hold in the Second that he does perceive, not merely that he thinks, but that thought pertains to his nature or essence. In any case, Descartes nowhere indicates that he thinks the claim that thought belongs to his nature requires any explanation or defense beyond that provided by the *cogito* reasoning and the other passages we have quoted from the Second Meditation.

It is important to notice, however, that throughout the Second Meditation Descartes tacitly observes a distinction between claims about what he knows to *belong to him*, and claims about knowledge of *his nature*. (This point is completely obscured by the French translation, which gratuitously inserts the word 'nature' at two points where Descartes's Latin has only 'me' or 'myself'—and by Haldane and Ross, who follow the French (cf. AT IX–1, 22, 23; HR I, 153, 154). Here, as elsewhere, Descartes's Latin makes more sense philosophically than the Duc de Luynes's French.) In the Sixth Meditation he will stress that he can clearly and distinctly 'conceive himself as a complete being' without the faculties of sense and imagination: in other words these faculties are not essential to him (AT VII, 78; HR I, 190). On the other hand (considered merely as faculties of thought, without commitment to any corporeal basis), they are known to *belong to* him in the Second Meditation:

> What then am I? A thinking thing. What is this? Surely [something] doubting, understanding, affirming, denying, willing, opposing, also imagining, and sensing.
>
> Certainly these are not few, if they all belong to me. But why should they not belong? (AT VII, 28; HR I, 153)

(The rest of this passage has been quoted above.) It is true that

Descartes goes on in the next lines to indicate that all these things cannot be 'distinguished from his thought,' and cannot be said to be separate[d] from him: *Quid est quod a me ipso separatum dici possit?* But there the point is, I take it, just that all these things do *belong* to him as a thinking thing, and depend on him—as he would put it elsewhere—modally. In other words, he is not claiming that all these faculties belong equally to his nature or essence. In the conclusion of this discussion Descartes stresses that imagination and sense are part of his thought. ('Even if no imagined thing is at all true, nevertheless the power of imagining itself really exists, and constitutes part of my thought. Finally, I am the same who senses. . . .')

The statement concerning sense has received special attention from Wittgensteinian critics and other recent philosophers, as exhibiting Descartes's commitment—now much disparaged—to the incorrigibility of judgments about one's own mental states. Thus, as we have seen, Descartes winds up the *sum res cogitans* discussion with the following remark:

> Finally, I am the same who senses, or who is aware of corporeal
> things as if through the senses: clearly now I see light, hear
> sound, feel heat. These are false, for I sleep. But certainly I seem to
> see, to hear, to feel heat. This cannot be false; this is strictly what
> in me is called sensing; but this is strictly speaking nothing else
> than to think. (AT VII, 29; HR I, 153)

And, as I have acknowledged above, Descartes both needs the doctrine of the certainty of *cogitatio* judgments for the certainty of the *cogito*, and fails explicitly to defend it against his own Deceiver Hypothesis. I agree, then, that Descartes's position is somewhat vulnerable here. However, the passage is not concerned solely to make the claim that *cogitatio* judgments are absolutely certain and incorrigible. It is equally concerned to establish the thesis that *sensation* can be viewed as a type of thought, and that hence our experience of sensation can be abstracted from any commitment to what are ordinarily regarded as the necessary physical aspects of sensation. There are states of seeming-to-sense that count among the *cogitationes*—that are *not* called into question by doubts about body. Whether or not my body 'really exists,' these thought-sensations *can* be attributed to me.

Descartes is concerned to establish the distinction between sensations construed as modes of thought, and sensations construed as modes of matter. It is not essential to this aspect of his argument (even though it may be essential to the *cogito*) that judgments about the former be totally or utterly or necessarily incorrigible—only that we recognize that they are not brought into question by doubts about body. Thus, critics who grant the conceptual distinction between sensations as mental states, on the one hand, and physiological states on the other hand, and then go on to consider whether there aren't esoteric ways in which judgments about even the former are 'corrigible,' really have conceded to Descartes an important part of what he is after. *To the extent that the concern with 'certainty' is in the service of establishing certain positive metaphysical conclusions, such as the mind–body distinction, they may be said to have conceded the most important part.*

At the end of the Second Meditation Descartes will hold that the perception he has gained of his own mind, in recognizing himself as a *thinking thing*, is 'clear and distinct,' and independent of the conception of body. He will also hold that he has shown the mind to be 'better known' than the body, not only in the sense that knowledge of mind is prior to knowledge of body, but also in the sense that we have fuller knowledge of the one than of the other. The former claim completes the Second Meditation's preparations for the argument for mind–body distinctness, finally presented in Meditation VI, which will be considered in due course. The latter claim, about the demonstrated superiority of our knowledge of mind, was vigorously disputed by Gassendi in the Fifth Objections. The highly interesting exchange between Descartes and Gassendi on this issue will be considered at the end of the present chapter. First, however, we must see how Descartes treats the problem of the knowledge of body.

4 This wax

The transition from the discussion of mind to the discussion of matter is effected in a way which will be important in interpreting the final conclusions of the Second Meditation. Descartes observes that it is difficult to overcome the idea that he knows bodies, which present themselves to imagination and sense, much more distinctly than the self just considered, which does not (*quam istud nescio quid mei, quod sub imaginationem non venit*). This is so despite the fact that it would be strange if,

> things which I take [*animadverto*] to be doubtful, unknown, foreign to me, were comprehended by me more distinctly than what is true, what is known, than finally myself. (AT VII, 29; HR I, 153–4)

One objective, then, of the ensuing discussion of body is to defend the claim that mind is not less 'distinctly' known. The strategy is to defeat the suggestion that knowledge of bodies gained by sense and imagination is 'more distinct' than the knowledge of mind gained without these faculties, by showing that even bodies are not known 'distinctly' by sense and imagination—but by understanding.

It follows, then, that the discussion of knowledge of the wax is meant to vindicate simultaneously the (interdependent) claims that knowledge of mind is at least as 'distinct' as knowledge of a body, and that the senses (and imagination) are not the sources of our best knowledge of things. It will also attempt to tell us something about the *content* of a distinct conception of a body—and, I think, at the same time tell us something more about the nature of mind. Finally, the passage is meant to contribute to the foundations of the Sixth Meditation demonstration of the distinctness of mind from body, by presenting a 'clear and distinct' conception of a body which is, obviously, quite different from our clear and distinct conception of the mind. On the other hand (as I will try to show) the passage is *not* meant to fill certain other roles commonly claimed for it. In particular, it is *not* meant to explain the conditions of reidentifying a given individual body over a period of time, and is *not* meant to establish any positive doctrine about sortals like 'wax' or 'stone.' What is obscure and troubling about the passage is how and to what extent it is supposed to bear on the following two fundamental tenets of Descartes's philosophy of matter: (a) the essence of matter is just extension; (b) the only properties *a body really possesses* at a given time are its size, figure, location, motion, number, etc.; its color, odor, hardness, warmth, etc. are mere subjective appearances. I will argue that neither of these conclusions is actually reached in the wax passage, though some *related* points are made. In this case it will be illuminating to compare with the *Meditations* certain passages on matter from the *Principles* and the *Replies to Objections*.

Descartes introduces his discussion of knowledge of body in a way that makes clear his intention of opposing commonsense assumptions, thus continuing the assault on commonsense empiricism begun in the First Meditation:

> Let us consider those things which *commonly are thought to be* the most distinctly comprehended of all [*quae vulgo putantur omnium distinctissime comprehendi*; emphasis added]: namely bodies, which we touch, which we see; not indeed body in common, for these general perceptions are usually a little more confused, but one in particular. Let us take, as an example, this wax. . . . (AT VII, 30; HR I, 154)

77

yellow? It's coloration

Descartes goes on to describe the sensible properties of the wax: recently taken from the hive, it is hard, white, cool, easy to touch, of certain shape and size, emits a sound when struck, and still retains the sweetness of honey and the scent of flowers. In short, 'all those things are present which seem to be required that any body can be known most distinctly' [*possit quam distinctissime cognosci*] (*ibid.*). We are then asked to imagine what happens when the wax is brought very near a fire. It loses its sweet taste and its odor, 'the color is changed, the shape is destroyed, the size increases, it becomes liquid, it becomes hot, it can scarcely be touched, and now, if you hit it, it does not emit a sound.' Nevertheless, he continues, the same wax remains ('no one would deny it, no one would think otherwise'), despite the comprehensive alterations of its sensible properties. What are we to conclude from this? According to Descartes, that whatever we had 'distinctly comprehended' in the wax is not included in the things attained by the senses.

> What therefore was there in [the wax] which was comprehended so distinctly? Certainly none of those things which I attained by the senses; for everything that came under taste, or odor, or sight, or touch or hearing, now is changed: the wax remains. (*Ibid.*)

It is evident that at least up to *this* point in the argument Descartes is not trying to draw a distinction between 'primary' and 'secondary' qualities. *All* the features the senses originally perceived in the wax —size and figure as well as color and coolness—are gone: this seems to be the one crucial point. It is worth observing though, that Descartes's conclusion that the senses provided (after all) no distinct knowledge of the wax apparently requires the assumption that the senses attain only to *particular* or determinate size, color, shape, etc. That is, he must be supposing that the senses bring to his attention *this* shape, *this* color, *this* size—not the fact that the wax has some shape, some color and some size. For in these latter respects the wax has *not* changed in the course of the experiment, despite the fact that it may have lost *one or two* sensory modalities—such as odor— altogether.

But what is really going on here? What does Descartes *mean* in denying that what came under the senses was what was known 'so distinctly' in the wax? He has already been using the term 'distinct' for several paragraphs—but always without explaining it:

> I must recall the mind from [imagination] . . . in order that it may be able to perceive its own nature with maximum distinctness.

> I cannot help thinking, that corporeal things . . . are much more

distinctly known than that I know-not-what of me [*istud nescio quid mei*] which does not come under the imagination. (AT VII, 28; HR I, 153)[40]

Shortly this term will be coupled with the equally unexplained term 'clear,' as in 'clear and distinct mental inspection [of the wax],' where this sort of perception is contrasted with the imperfect and confused (AT VII, 31; HR I, 155).

In both the *Principles of Philosophy* and (in a way) later in the end of the wax discussion Descartes offers some kind of abstract account of what a distinct perception is.[41] However, these passages are themselves too obscure, problematic and in need of interpretation to provide any direct and immediate illumination of the question we have raised. It is better, I think, to try to follow out the details of the piece of wax passage, and then try to relate these to the general indications of what is involved in having a *distinct* perception of x.

One theory that may occur to the reader is the following. Since the conclusion that the sensible properties were *not* distinctly comprehended in the wax is supposed to follow from the observation that the sensible properties change without the wax ceasing to exist or to be 'the same,' distinct comprehension must at least have something to do with grasping the unchanging or permanent properties of a thing. A *prima facie* objection to this theory is that Descartes, in his previous discussion of knowledge of *himself*, did not in any way suggest that the knowledge he had of himself as characterized by *changing modes* (I feel heat, etc.) lacked distinctness (in comparison, say, to knowledge of his 'faculties' in general—or of those intellectual faculties that will later be found essential). Nevertheless the theory should be kept in mind, as it seems the best we have to go on at the moment.

Descartes's positive conclusion about distinct knowledge of the wax is drawn in his next remarks, which I break into three sections for purposes of commentary.

(1) Perhaps it was that which I now think: that this wax was not indeed that sweetness of honey, nor fragrance of flowers, nor that whiteness, nor [that] figure, nor [that] sound, but a body which a little while ago appeared to me perceptible by modes of a certain kind, now by others [*ante modis istis conspicuum, nunc diversis*]. (2) But what is this exactly that I thus imagine? Let us consider and, removing those [things] that do not belong to [*pertinent*] the wax, let us see what is left. (3) Surely nothing other than something extended, flexible, mutable. (AT VII, 30–31; HR I, 154)

79

(1) The particular sweetness, fragrance, color, figure, etc. 'were not' the wax, but only modes by which at a given time it could be perceived. (Note that there is still no distinction introduced between primary and secondary qualities.) (2) What do I then have in mind in talking of a 'body that appears perceptible by different modes at different times'? We will see by separating out those things that do *not* belong to the wax (here conceived, surely, as a body distinct from the modes 'under' which it is perceived). (3) Answer: nothing other than something extended, flexible, mutable. This phrase does for the first time single out certain *favored* properties;[42] as far as the preceding argument goes, it comes out of the blue. The conclusion Descartes so abruptly arrives at is that all that 'belongs to' the wax is to be extended, flexible (capable of changing figure) and mutable. It does not 'belong to it' to have a particular figure or color—nor to *be colored* in general.

What does Descartes mean here by 'belong to'? Now we know that Descartes does accept some version of the primary–secondary qualities distinction. He is going to go on to hold, later in the *Meditations* (as well as in other works) that perceived color, odor and so forth, (a) are not 'distinctly perceived in' bodies and (b) should not be ascribed to bodies *at all*. (The first point is made in Meditations III and V, and the second in Meditation VI; they will be discussed in later chapters.) E. A. Burtt has assumed that the purpose of the wax passage itself is to introduce a distinction between properties that 'inhere in objects as they really are' and those that do not. He then maintains (understandably) that the passage is irrelevant to its purpose. Burtt writes:[43]

> Why, now, are we sure that the primary, geometrical qualities inhere in objects as they really are, while the secondary qualities do not? . . . Descartes' own justification for this claim is that these [primary] qualities are *more permanent* than the others. In the case of the piece of wax, which he used for illustrative purposes in the second *Meditations*, no qualities remained *constant* but those of extension, flexibility, and mobility. . . . But, we might ask, are not colour and resistance equally constant properties of bodies? Objects change in colour, to be sure, and there are varying degrees of resistance, but does one meet bodies totally without colour or resistance? The fact is, and this is of central importance for our whole study, *Descartes' real criterion is not permanence but the possibility of mathematical handling.* . . .

Burtt seems to conclude that Descartes's claim to have philosophical foundations for his science is, at least in this respect, a sham. For he continues:

the whole course of Descartes' thought from his adolescent studies on had inured him to the notion that we know objects only in mathematical terms.

Burtt's objection is that color, for example, is just as 'permanent' a property as extension. But if his interpretation of the passage is correct, an even more fundamental question must be raised, namely: how can changes of the sort Descartes observes in the wax tell us anything about 'inherence' at all? For example, how could the fact that a thing can *change* from being white to being, say, yellow, serve to show that whiteness was *never* 'truly to be recognized as in the object'?

But I believe Burtt's interpretation is mistaken. The conclusion that only properties 'capable of mathematical handling' are really in bodies is reserved for later Meditations; the wax passage has a different concern. A passage from the Sixth Replies shows that Descartes regards the conclusion about the real modes of body as the second, not the first, issue to be raised about body. The first is the problem dealt with in Meditation II: the problem, namely, of what belongs *to the concept of a body*, or what is involved in the nature of the body. He writes:

Afterwards, however, I proceeded further, and resting on this foundation [the determination that mind is really distinct from, and better known than the body], I passed over to consideration of matters of Physics, and attended first to the ideas, or notions, which I found in myself of some one thing [*de unâquâque re*], and carefully distinguishing each [idea] from the others, so that all my judgments would agree with [the ideas], I remarked that nothing at all belonged to the concept of a body [*ad rationem corporis pertinere*], except only that it is a thing with length, breadth, and depth [*res longa, lata, et profunda*], capable of various figures and various motions. . . . (AT VII, 440; HR II, 253–4)

After making this point—which goes beyond the explicit conclusion of the Second Meditation only in specifying that bodies can change motions as well as shapes—Descartes continues:

and of which the figures and motions are only modes, which by no power could exist without [the body]; but colors, odors, tastes and [other] such things, are merely certain sensations existing in my thought, and not less different from bodies than pain is different from the shape and motion of the instrument that inflicts it. (AT VII, 440; HR II, 254)

(Descartes goes on to assert that the various powers and qualities of bodies 'consist only in' motion or the privation of motion, and the configuration and location [*situ*] of the parts.)

The 'theory' introduced above seems to be confirmed. In determining what is 'distinctly perceived' in the wax, Descartes intends to be making clear the necessary elements of the concept of a body. As noted, this leaves us with a certain asymmetry between the treatment of body and the treatment of mind. However, perhaps this asymmetry can be explained as follows. In obtaining a distinct knowledge of himself, Descartes can rely on the direct and immediate observation of what is in him, his individual thoughts. In the case of bodies, however, only the concept is initially given. Since sensory data are not to be relied on, there is no direct or immediate knowledge of the existence of bodies or their properties. What we find distinctly given in ourselves, with respect to ourselves, are both our essential faculties, and non-essential faculties and states. What we find distinctly given in ourself, with respect to bodies, is only their abstract concept.

Now it may be objected that we have once again attributed to the Second Meditation a concern that really belongs to a later stage of Descartes's argument. For isn't the *Fifth* Meditation concerned to establish the 'essence of matter'? The answer to this is straightforward. The Fifth Meditation introduces the concept of *res extensa*—the material continuum of Cartesian physics. According to my reading, the concern of the piece of wax passage is the somewhat less esoteric notion of the essence or nature of a single body. (I will deal with this distinction at somewhat more length below.)

However there is a more important objection to be considered. For it seems that even on the present reading the conclusion of the wax passage is not really supported by argument, and a version of Burtt's criticism is still apposite. Given that the wax retains *some* color (and Descartes does not state the contrary) why should we conclude, on the basis of this passage, that color is any less essential to a body than extension or figure?

In fact Descartes does go a considerable way to answering this challenge in another work—though not in the *Meditations* themselves. The answer is sufficiently close in form to the 'wax' argument to suggest that Descartes simply failed to make explicit the crucial point in his earlier work. (His argument was foreshadowed by Galileo in *The Assayer*, published almost twenty years before the *Meditations*.)[44]

In two passages of Part II of the *Principles* Descartes offers arguments directly relevant to 'constancy' of color and resistance.

82

Superficially the logic of these two passages is rather different, but it is likely that the underlying intent is the same.

In *Principles* II, xi, Descartes maintains that we have experienced bodies that are altogether lacking in color, bodies that lack weight, bodies that lack hardness. He claims that we will easily recognize that extension constitutes the nature of body just as it constitutes the nature of space, if we perform an easy thought experiment. Thus,

> [A]ttending to the idea that we have of any body, such as stone, we reject from it all that we recognize [*cognoscere*] not to be requisite to the nature of body. First, then, we reject hardness, because if the stone were liquified or reduced to powder . . . it would lose that and yet would not cease to be body; we also reject color, because we have often seen stones so pellucid that there is no color in them; we reject weight, because although fire is very light it is not less thought to be body; and finally we may reject cold, heat, and all other qualities, because either they are not considered in the stone or because if they change, the stone is not on that account thought to have lost the nature of body. (AT VIII–1, 46; HR I, 259)

He concludes:

> Thus we discover [*advertemus*] that nothing at all remains in the idea of body, except [*praeterquam quod sit quid extensum*] a certain extension in length, breadth, and depth: which is the same contained in the idea of space. . . . (*Ibid.*)

At first sight, this passage strikes one as surprisingly empiricistic. Descartes seems to be resting his claim concerning the nature of body on observations concerning which properties are such that we do sensibly perceive bodies without them. Further, the properties he considers as candidates in this passage are exclusively those that would occur to a commonsense empiricist, and are 'rejected' according to the naïve reasoning that would occur to such a person (as opposed to more recondite properties such as mass that might occur to a physicist). However, it seems that Descartes's underlying purpose is really to get us to consider what belongs to our *concept* of body; he merely uses the concrete examples as rhetorical means of showing we wouldn't 'refuse to call something a body' if it lacked color, hardness, etc. Although the examples are handled in a rather crude way, the idea is not unsophisticated. Descartes is really asking what properties are analytically contained in the concept of body in general. What is really important is not what 'we have often seen,' but rather what we can conceive. (Note that in fact it is not *really* the case that we *could* see bodies 'so pellucid that there is no color in them.') The other relevant passage in the *Principles* makes fully apparent Descartes's concern with what is contained in the *concept* of body:

> II 3–4 Thus we shall easily set aside the prejudices of the senses and here make use of our understanding alone, attending carefully to the ideas placed in it by nature.
>
> Doing this we perceive that the nature of matter or of body regarded in the universal [*in universum spectati*], does not consist in its being a thing.[that is] hard, or heavy, or colored, or one that affects our senses in some other way, but only in the fact that it is a thing extended in length, breadth, and depth. (AT VIII–1, 42; HR I, 255–6)

What shows the inessentiality of hardness and so forth is that we *can conceive of* bodies lacking such properties:

> For as to hardness, the senses indicate nothing else to us of that, except that the parts of hard bodies resist the motions of our hands when they strike against them; but if, whenever our hands moved toward some area, all the bodies existing there receded with the same speed as [our hands] approached them, we would never feel hardness. But in no way can it be understood that bodies which recede in this way would on this account lose the nature of body; which hence itself does not consist in hardness. (*Ibid.*)

According to Descartes, this case can be generalized:

> And by the same reasoning it can be shown that weight, and color, and all the other qualities of this kind, which are perceived in corporeal matter, may be taken from it, itself remaining complete [*integra*]: whence follows that the nature [of body] depends on none of these. (*Ibid.*)

In the *Principles*, then, Descartes does argue that a body need not be colored, hard or otherwise sensible: we can completely subtract these qualities mentally without subtracting 'what makes it body.' On the other hand, Descartes thinks we cannot subtract extension without subtracting 'what makes it body': as Kant remarks in the *Critique of Pure Reason*, 'All bodies are extended' is an analytic truth, whereas 'all bodies have weight' is at best a synthetic truth. This reasoning suggests that there is nothing inconsistent in the notion of an absolutely insensible body. For, it seems, we can perceive the extension of a body only if it manifests itself to sight by color, or to touch and kinesthesis by resistance.[45]

Before returning to the *Meditations*, I would like to consider one line of criticism of this rather interesting argument in the *Principles*. This criticism will lead us to examine a further feature of Descartes's treatment of body in the *Principles*, which also helps to illuminate the piece of wax argument.

Anthony Quinton has maintained that Descartes is entitled only to the position that a body may lack either color *or* resistance to touch; not that it may lack both. According to Quinton,

> A material thing is not just extension, it is a piece of observable extension, a visibly or tangibly characterized region of space. There is more to the occupancy of space than mere voluminousness, the occupancy must be perceptible and that means that it must be either visible or tangible.

Quinton endorses the Berkeleyan claim that 'a thing could not be thought to have shape and size unless its shape and size were either visible or tangible or both, unless the thing had some colour or texture.'[46]

Quinton offers little or no argument in support of his contention, and I find it unconvincing. In the first place, there is a confusion in Quinton's statements about tangibility. A body would be tangibly detectable if it merely offered *resistance* to touch—and this is not the same thing as 'having texture.' But further, it seems to me that Descartes's reasoning is successful in showing that there is no contradiction or repugnancy in the notion of a body that is perfectly transparent and *also* (because of its tendency to recede from touch) tangibly indetectable. We need to be shown why, if there is no difficulty in conceiving a body that satisfies one or the other of these descriptions, there *is* difficulty in conceiving a body that satisfies both. I think the burden of proof here is on Descartes's opponent. To this extent it seems to me that Descartes's argument in the *Principles* is successful.[47]

In the passage I have quoted, Quinton seems to treat as equivalent the claims that 'a material thing is not just extension,' and that 'it is a piece of *observable* extension.' Elsewhere in his article, however, Quinton rightly notes that a distinction should be recognized between mere extension or geometrical voluminousness on the one hand and impenetrability on the other hand.[48] A material thing could be held to differ from mere spatial extension, in that mere spatial extension can have material things in it, whereas a material thing precludes the presence of another material thing within its boundaries. And it seems that a body could be impenetrable in the sense just defined without being detectable to touch, at least in any obvious or ordinary way. And this brings us to a final important point about Descartes's treatment of body.

Descartes does maintain that matter in general or as a whole is 'just extension'—or more exactly, a subject with extension as its only essential attribute. This is why he mentions only extension as essential to body in the *Principles* passages we have been considering. On the other hand, with respect to *particular* bodies and spaces he recognizes a sort of distinction between body and space. This distinction, which is explained in terms of movement, may account for the appearance of mutability and flexibility in the piece of wax passage, together with the 'extension' of *Principles* II, iv and xii (and of Meditation V). It even appears that Descartes recognizes *impenetrability*, in the sense sketched in the last paragraph, as somehow bound up with this notion of an individual body. Let us examine this neglected aspect of his position a little more closely.

Descartes's account in the *Principles* of the distinction between body and space is intriguing, but difficult. Space, he says, is to body as genus or species is to individual; however, this distinction itself is only a conceptual one. Thus,[49]

> Space, or internal place, and (a) corporeal substance contained in it, do not differ in reality [*non etiam in re differunt*], but only in the way in which we are accustomed to conceive them. For truly the extension in length, breadth, and depth, which constitutes (a) space, is entirely the same as that which constitutes (a) body. But the difference is in this, that in (a) body we consider the same [extension] as singular, and we think that it always moves whenever (the) body moves: while in (a) space we attribute to it only a generic unity, so that, when the body moves that fills (the) space, nevertheless the extension of (the) space is not supposed to move, but to remain one and the same, as long as it remains of the same magnitude and figure, and keeps the same position [*situm*] among certain external bodies, through which we determine that space. (AT VIII-1, 45; HR I, 259)

So far as I can make out, this says that *we consider* what is *really* the same extension *as* moving (in so far as we think of it as in, or as constituting, a body and hence as particularized), and as not moving (in so far as we think of it as constituting [a] space, and hence not individualized, but having only the unity proper to a genus or universal). The point is made a little clearer in Principle xii, where Descartes explains that we say a stone and a piece of wood can have, successively, *the same extension* in the generic sense, when the second comes to occupy the place (defined in terms of shape, size and relative position) previously held by the first. On the other hand, in so far as we think of the extension of the stone as particular to it, it can never be 'had' by any other body (AT VIII-1, 46–7; HR I, 260).

The distinction here, is, I take it, exactly the same as the one we draw on when we say the blue of my shirt, which exactly matches a particular flower, is and is not the same as the blue of the flower.

In this analysis it is a tautology that two bodies cannot have the same extension, when we are conceiving the extension as particular. For the body individuates the extension. What is not so far clear, though, is what individuates *the body*. Further (I am not sure this is ultimately a different problem) it is not clear why two bodies can have the same extension in the generic sense only *successively*—which is precisely the issue of impenetrability. Descartes does seem to assume this, though,[50] and to relate it (in both *Principles* II, x and II, xii) to the question of relative location. But relative location is location relative to certain bodies—which takes us back to the question of what individuates bodies.

Descartes thinks that 'all variety of matter, or all diversity of its forms' 'depends on motion'; moreover a given clump of extension constitutes one body if 'it' moves as a whole (*Principles* II, xxiii, xxv; AT VIII-1, 52-4; HR I, 265-6). (Matter, being essentially extended, is essentially divisible, which is to say 'movable according to its parts'; and

> All the properties which we clearly perceive in [matter] are reduced
> [*reducuntur*] to this one, that it is divisible, and movable
> according to its parts, and hence capable of all those affections,
> which we perceive can follow from the motion of its parts. (II,
> xxiii; AT VIII-1, 52; HR I, 265; cf. *Principles* II, xx)

But motion, again, is relative motion—i.e., motion relative to other bodies, individuated in the same way. The upshot, then, is that a given bit of extension is particularized by being conceived as movable relative to other bits of extension, similarly conceived. But since the difference between particularized and movable, and unparticularized and unmovable extension rests on a merely conceptual distinction, there may be a genuine question in what sense particular bodies are *real*, for Descartes. In any case, we should not lightly assume a direct relation between sensible bodies and sensible motion, and the concepts of individuation and motion that Descartes expounds in the *Principles*. Thus, to mention only one consequence, we should not assume that ordinary assumptions about the individuation and 'impenetrability' of sensible objects should have any easy connection with the conceptual system of the *Principles*. This suggestion might be judged incoherent if 'insensible body' were a contradictory notion. But I have already argued that Descartes gives good reasons for denying that it is.

Returning now to the piece of wax passage, we may notice that there are certain clear affinities between the argument presented there, and parts of the analysis of the concept of body that we have been considering from the *Principles*. When Descartes says at the end of the discussion of the wax that we have quoted:

> [R]emoving those [things] that do not belong to the wax, let us see what is left,

he concludes without further ado,

> surely nothing other than something extended, flexible, and mutable. (AT VII, 31; HR I, 154)

There is, I am suggesting, a gap here that can more or less be filled in by the reasoning concerning the nature of body in *Principles* II, 3–4, 12, together with that concerning individuation and movability of parts in the other passages discussed. The *Principles* tell us, first, that we can find by thought experiment that extension alone belongs to the nature of *body* as we *really* conceive it (as opposed to how we may think we conceive it); and second, that 'all the properties we clearly perceive in [matter] are reduced [*reducuntur*] to this one, that it is divisible and movable according to its parts.' That the wax is *extended* is a conceptual truth deriving from its nature as matter. That it is mutable at least in respect of being subject to different *motions* is a conceptual truth deriving from its nature as a *particular* body. But to understand why the wax, *qua* body, must be 'flexible' requires a careful interpretation of that term. I take it that 'flexibility' must here be taken to mean 'capable of assuming different figures,' rather than 'malleable,' as one might at first assume. (This seems confirmed by the passage quoted above from the Sixth Replies (AT VII, 400).) Once the term is so interpreted, it is possible to argue that (on Descartes's principles) flexibility must be involved in the concept of an individual body, just as extension and movability are. For, any given body, being extended, is itself divisible into parts. This is to say that it has, necessarily, parts capable of *movement relative to each other*. But the possibility of change in the relative position of parts (e.g., the parts of the wax) will entail flexibility in the sense defined—or will do so unless change in the mutual relations of the *surface* parts is somehow arbitrarily ruled out.

5 Intellectual inspection

In the remaining part of the wax discussion, Descartes tries to derive the further significant conclusions that the nature of the wax has been understood all along 'by the mind alone' (F. *entendement*), rather than by imagination or sense. This conclusion in turn is related to the question of what constitutes a 'distinct' perception of the wax—and also, implicitly, to the issue of the nature of the mind itself. Thus, he goes on to argue that the wax, considered now only as something extended, flexible and mutable, is understood as having a capacity for *innumerable* changes: it is conceived as admitting of more variations than have ever been encompassed [*complexus*] by the imagination.

> What truly is this [being] flexible, mutable? [*Quid verò est hoc flexibile, mutabile?*] Perhaps what I imagine, this wax can change from a round figure to a square, or from this to a triangular? Not at all; for I understand [*comprehendo*] that it is capable of innumerable changes of this sort, and nevertheless I cannot run through innumerable [changes] by the imagination: and therefore this comprehension is not accomplished by the faculty of imagination. What is [its being] extended? [*Quid extensum?*] Is not even its extension unknown? For it was greater in the melted wax, greater in the boiling, and once more greater if the heat is increased [*augeatur*]; and I would not rightly judge what [the] wax is, if I did not think it admitted even more variations in extension, than were ever encompassed by the imagination. (AT VII, 31; HR I, 154–5)

Since I recognized from the beginning that the wax when melted and otherwise transformed was 'the same,' it follows that all along my real, underlying conception of the wax depended on the understanding, rather than sense or imagination alone:

> It remains therefore that I concede that I do *not* imagine what this wax is, but only perceive it by the mind; I say this in particular, for it is clearer for wax in common. What, really, is this wax, which is only perceived by the mind? Surely the same that I see, that I touch, that I imagine, the same finally that from the beginning I judged to be. But—what must be noted—the perception of it is not by vision, not by touch, not by imagination, and never was, although it previously seemed so, but only an inspection of the mind, which can be either imperfect and confused, as it was before, or clear and distinct, as it is now, according as I attend less or more to those [things] of which it is composed [*ad illa ex quibus constat attendo*]. (AT VII, 31; HR I, 155)

Thus, to understand body, or a body, a human mind is required. For it is only mind, not sense or imagination, that is capable of conceiving the possibility of innumerable variations; sense and imagination are restricted to the determinate, or to a limited series of determinates. (In more recent lingo, our physical object concepts are not reducible to any finite set of propositions concerning sense data or images.)

The end of this passage tells us that our perception of the wax goes from being imperfect and confused, to being clear and distinct, according as we 'attend less or more to those [things] of which it is composed.' With this statement should be compared a sort of definition of 'distinct perception' from the *Principles*:

> In order for a perception to be able to support a certain and indubitable judgment, it not only is required that it be clear, but also that it be distinct. I call that [perception] clear, which is present and open to an attending mind: just as we say that we clearly see whatever, being present to the attentively regarding (*intuenti*) eye, sufficiently strongly and openly affects it (*illum movent*). However [I call] that [perception] distinct, which, while it is clear, is so precise and so separate from all else, that it contains in itself nothing at all but what is clear. (AT VIII-1, 22; HR I, 237)

From this, one might at first suppose that the problem with the original perception of the wax was that not everything in the *conglomerate of sense perceptions* affected the mind 'strongly and openly.' This would suggest that a sense perception is transformed into a clear and distinct perception, in so far as we become more explicitly.aware of its elements.[51] But in the wax passage Descartes seems to be saying something else. He seems to be more or less setting aside the original sense perceptions as not relevant to the real perception 'of wax' or 'of what the wax is'—even though he does not wish to deny that we *do* see, touch, and so forth, the wax. What was indistinct at first was our intellectual 'perception' of the wax, or of 'what the wax is.' We could make a sort of implicit use of this perception, in recognizing that the 'same wax' could appear under various sensory forms, but we were not explicitly aware of what was contained in the perception until Descartes's analysis had concluded.[52] In addition, the *Principles* passage tells us that a distinct perception must be 'precise and separate from all else.' Perhaps we could say that the 'mental' or intellectual perception of the wax is distinct in this sense, whereas the sense perception, or compound of sense perceptions, is not. For in the former, but not the latter, the wax is conceived precisely in itself and separately from all admixture of sensible appearances.

Now sometimes Descartes's discussion of the wax is taken to be concerned with problems I have not so far even mentioned in the analysis—notably problems about reidentification of individuals and/or the determination of what is required to be of one sort rather than another (e.g., wax, rather than stone). Descartes does after all remark with seeming emphasis that the *same wax remains*, after the various changes in its sensible properties. And I imagine that most people would under the circumstances agree to the proposition that this piece of wax, which was hard, has become soft, and so forth. Readers of the French translation, or of Haldane and Ross, will also point out that in concluding the wax discussion Descartes considers the 'ordinary language' objection that,

> we say that we see the same wax, if it is present, and not that we simply judge that it is the same from its having the same colour and figure. From this [it seems] I should conclude that I knew the wax by means of vision and not simply by intuition of the mind. . . . (HR I, 155; cf. AT IX–1, 25)

Doesn't this show clearly that Descartes is concerned with some form of the question, how do we know the wax is the same individual, or that it remains the same specific sort of thing (i.e. wax), through various alterations? However, consultation of the original Latin text yields a startlingly different reading of the first sentence of the above quotation, namely,

> [W]e say we see the wax itself, if it is present, not that we judge it to be present by the color or figure. *Dicimus enim nos videre ceram ipsammet, si adsit, non ex colore vel figura eam adesse judicare*. (Possibly the original translation confused *eam* (it) with *eandem* (the same)). (AT VII, 32)

Descartes's position is that the sensible 'modes' (as he calls them in this context) are merely the starting point for the mind's direct perception of the nature of a body. The objection he wishes to deal with is that to perceive the sensible modes is the same thing as to perceive the body, in its true nature or in its very self (*ipsammet*). This is even clearer from his way of *answering* the objection: he is accustomed to say he 'sees men' when he only sees clothes that 'could cover automata' (AT VII, 32; HR I, 155). The point is not that he reidentifies the *same* men, from the clothes or otherwise. The point is that ordinary talk of 'seeing x' can be loose and misleading.[53]

Besides, the answer Descartes gives to 'what belongs to the wax?'—to be something extended, flexible, mutable—obviously provides no sort of answer at all to the question, 'what makes wax

wax?' or to 'what makes this thing the same individual?' In fact Descartes has already asserted in the Synopsis that a body that changes 'its' shape *is in reality no longer* the same individual! (Cf. AT VII, 13–14; HR I, 141.)[54] The point that Descartes is beginning to try to get across in the wax discussion is the conclusion required (as he sees it) for his physics: that it is the nature of *any body at all* (just) to be something extended, flexible and movable. And he thinks in recognizing this we must necessarily recognize at the same time that it is 'the mind' rather than sense that perceives the nature of body. He characteristically tries to reach these conclusions from a commonsense starting point by proceeding from the fact that we don't commonly require constancy of sensible appearances in order to make judgments about body.

6 Mind 'better known' than body

The idea that I just *saw* the wax, that 'I knew it by the external sense itself, or at least by the common sense, as they say, that is by the imaginative faculty,' is, Descartes goes on to insist, an error I make about my own cognition. It occurs when that cognition is not rendered sufficiently distinct to make its unique nature manifest (AT VII, 32; HR I, 155–6). My original empiricist conception of knowledge of body would make that knowledge 'capable of being had by some animal,'

> but surely when I distinguish the wax from external forms, and consider it as if naked with its clothes taken away, even though it is possible that there is an error in my judgment, nevertheless I cannot truly perceive it this way without a human mind. (*Ibid.*)

In this subtle remark Descartes intends, probably, to insinuate a point of basic importance to his conception of the mind–body distinction. Examination of our knowledge of body has told us something new about our knowing minds: that they have powers incompatible with the material mechanisms adequate, in his view, to account for animal 'perceptions.' The piece of wax passage not only provides the basis for a concept of body that will contrast with the conception of mind through the extension–thought distinction. It also provides the basis for a conception of thought—or more specifically of understanding—that is, I believe, intended to make more evident how different it is from mechanical processes. Physical mechanisms, which include the sense and imagination of animals—i.e. these functions divorced from rational intelligence—

are determinate, structured, finitary. Our minds, on the other hand, are capable of encompassing 'innumerable variations.'[55]

But Descartes takes his discussion of the wax to provide the basis for a more curious and, in a sense, even more fundamental and controversial claim: namely, that 'nothing can be more easily or more evidently perceived by me than my mind'; that I know the nature of my mind 'more distinctly' than any body (AT VII, 33; HR I, 156-7). Gassendi objected vehemently and not uncogently to Descartes's claim to have proved any such conclusion (AT VII, 275-7; HR II, 149-51). Their exchange on this issue is quite relevant to Descartes's intended use of the *Meditations* to provide a 'foundation' for his science, and to his conception of the mind–body distinction. But before turning to this issue specifically, let us briefly take note of a less perplexing aspect of Descartes's final claims, in the Second Meditation, concerning the superiority of our knowledge of mind.

Having observed that the clear and distinct perception he has achieved of the wax requires a human mind, and could obviously not be attributed to an animal, Descartes continues:

> But what shall I say of this mind itself, or of my self? For I now admit nothing else to be in me except mind. What, I ask, [of] I who seem to perceive this wax so distinctly? Do I not know myself not only much more truly, more certainly, but even much more distinctly and evidently? For, if I judge the wax exists, from the fact that I see it, certainly it follows much more evidently that I myself exist, from the very fact that I see it. For it can be that this which I see is not truly wax; it can be that I do not even have eyes, by which anything is seen; but it obviously cannot be, that when I see, or (what I now am not distinguishing) when I think that I see, that I, thinking this, am not something. By similar reasoning, if I judge the wax is, by the fact that I touch it, the same thing again follows, namely that I am. If from the fact that I imagine, or any other cause, the same is obvious. But this same thing that I observe [*animadverto*] about the wax, may be applied to everything else that is posited outside me. (AT VII, 33; HR I, 156)

The conclusion here seems to be that of any particular body that appears to the senses I know myself more clearly than I know it. For if I judge that it exists it follows that I exist (and, after the early part of the Meditation, I am in a position to recognize that this is certainly true). However, my judgment the wax exists, whether based on 'the evidence of the senses' or something else, is compatible with there being no piece of wax—at least until the specter of the Deceiver is dispelled.

Later philosophers, from Kant to Strawson, have denied that knowledge of one's own existence is possible independently of belief in the existence of an enduring world in space. However, what Descartes explicitly argues in the latter half of Meditation II is not directly threatened by such a position. He is there explicitly concerned with particular bodies that appear to the senses. That I make the judgment, 'I see a piece of wax before me,' may (setting aside the difficulties discussed in the last chapter) entail that I exist; it certainly does not entail that there is a piece of wax before me.

But would Descartes not also want to hold on the same grounds that he knows himself more clearly than corporeal nature in general? Very likely he would. But even if he became convinced, by say the argument of *The Bounds of Sense*, that such a position is untenable, he would not have to give up the claim that he knows himself more clearly than any particular body. Still, the significance of this claim appears on inspection to be very slight: that I 'know myself clearly' seems to come to little more than that I am certain that I exist. That I 'know myself more clearly' than a particular body so far comes to no more than the claim that the existence of the body is subject to (at least) hyperbolic doubt, while the existence of myself is not. Even Gassendi does not seem particularly concerned to dispute *this*. But there is more to come:

> Further though, if the perception of the wax is more distinctly perceived [*magis distincta visa*], after it has become known to me, not by sight or touch alone, but from many causes, *how much more distinctly must I now be said to know myself, inasmuch as no reasons can aid the perception either of wax or of any other body, without all the same better proving the nature of my mind*! But also so many others are in the mind itself besides, from which its notion [*notitia*] can be rendered more distinct, that those, which emanate to it from the body, hardly seem to count.
>
> But there at last I have without effort [*sponte*] returned where I wished; for since I now know that body itself, is perceived not properly by the senses, nor by the faculty of imagining, but by intellect alone, and that it is not perceived in that it is touched or seen, but only in that it is understood, I clearly know [*aperte cognosco*] nothing can be more easily or evidently perceived by me than my mind. (AT VII, 33–4; HR I, 156–7; emphasis added)

While the first half of this quotation is the more germane, it may be helpful first to see what can be done about the thumping non-sequitur that appears in the second half. *How* can the observation that 'body itself is perceived . . . by the intellect alone,'

94

lead to the conclusion that 'nothing can be more easily or evidently perceived by me than my mind'? Actually, the way Descartes introduced his discussion of the wax makes it fairly easy to see how this question should be answered. Having claimed that he began to know himself more distinctly in so far as he detached himself from sense and imagination, he found it necessary to consider the objection that corporeal things, explored by sense and presented to imagination, seemed in a way most distinctly known. The implication was, we may assume, that corporeal things seemed more distinctly known just *because* they come under sense and imagination.[56] However, Descartes has now argued that corporeal things, too, are properly known only in so far as we withdraw from sense. Hence, he claims, the fact that they fall under sense and imagination no longer provides grounds for the worry that objects that fall under the senses are more distinctly known than the mind.

But how is Descartes's reasoning intended to show that the *nature* of mind is *better known* than body? Gassendi protested: 'your conclusions about wax prove only the perception of the existence of mind, and fail to reveal its nature' (AT VII, 275; HR II, 149). Gassendi's objection is very clear and explicit: we cannot claim to understand the nature of a thing if all we can do is list its obvious or superficial properties; this holds for the mind or thinking substance as much as for any ordinary physical thing. Yet in the case of mind all Descartes has provided us with is a catalogue of what was already obvious. In Gassendi's words:

> Surely, if a conception of Wine superior to the vulgar is asked of you, it will not be enough to say; Wine is a liquid thing, pressed from grapes, white or red, sweet, inebriating, etc.; but you will undertake to investigate and declare in what manner its internal substance, insofar as it is observed to be compounded, [is constituted] of spirit, phlegm, tartara, and other parts, mixed together in some quantity and proportion or other. In the same way, when a conception of yourself superior to the vulgar, that is, possessed up till now, is asked for, you doubtless see that it is not enough if you announce to us that you are a thing thinking, doubting, understanding, etc.; but it is incumbent on you, to examine yourself by a certain chemicallike labor, so that you can determine and demonstrate to us your internal substance. (AT VII, 276–7; HR II, 150)

Gassendi goes on to insinuate that since a good deal is known about body by the various established sciences (chemistry, anatomy, etc.), a great deal would have to be determined 'beyond the vulgar' about mind, if Descartes's claim that his mind is better known than the body is to have any plausibility at all.

Gassendi's point then, is that Descartes claims a superior knowledge of his mind on the basis of a catalogue of its most superficial properties—the sort of catalogue that no one, least of all Descartes, would regard as establishing a distinct knowledge of body. If Gassendi's point seems well-taken, it is apt to seem even more so after one has considered Descartes's reply:

> I have never thought anything else was required for the manifestation of substance, except its various attributes, so that, in so far as we know many attributes of a substance, we thereby understand its nature more perfectly. But, just as we can distinguish many different attributes in the wax, one that it is white, another that it is hard, another that from being hard it becomes liquid, etc.; so also there are just as many in the mind, one that it has the power of knowing the whiteness of the wax, another that it has the power of knowing its hardness, another that [it has the power of knowing] the change of hardness, or liquefaction etc.; . . . Whence it is clearly inferred that there is nothing of which so many attributes are known, as our mind, because, as many as are known in any other thing, just as many can be enumerated in the mind, from the fact that it knows them, and thus its nature is the most known of all. (AT VII, 360; HR II, 213)

A very similar passage is found in the *Principles* (I, xi):

> [I]t is most evident to the natural light . . . that we know a thing or substance the more clearly, the more [qualities or affections] we observe [*deprehendimus*] in it. And that we observe many more in our mind than in any other thing, is surely manifest from the fact that nothing causes us to know anything else, which does not even much more certainly lead us to knowledge of our mind. (AT VIII-1, 8; HR I, 223)

In these passages Descartes is clearly saying mind is 'better known' than body, in so far as any judgment I make about the nature of a body provides grounds for recognizing one or more facts about me (my mind)—e.g., that I make that judgment, and consequently have the 'power' to make it, or to recognize the facts contained in the judgment. (Whereas the converse does not hold: judgments I make about myself, my thought, need not entail propositions about the nature of body.) Yet it is highly surprising to find Descartes espousing such a simplistically quantitative conception of 'perfect comprehension.' For the predominant epistemological theme in his

96

writings on knowledge of nature is that perfect comprehension of material substance is obtained not by lengthening the list of observed properties (as Bacon's program, for instance, demanded), but by providing an account of the extension, figure, and motion of body's internal parts. As we have seen from the wax discussion, one's knowledge of material substance is said to be distinct, not in proportion to the number of one's sensory judgments, but only in so far as one has overcome the prejudices of childhood to the extent of achieving an intellectual perception of the essence of body behind the fluctuating modes presented to the senses. The series of sensory judgments about wax that Descartes enumerates in the passage just quoted from the Replies are precisely of the sort that he usually represents as providing only a 'confused knowledge.' In fact, this is the very point he has just finished making in discussing the piece of wax!

Gassendi had suggested in his criticism that examination of the piece of wax did not provide any knowledge whatsoever of the nature of the mind, since it revealed nothing about the mind's 'internal substance.' Descartes ridicules this idea in his reply:

> I am surprised that you here grant that all those things that I consider in the wax, *indeed demonstrate that I distinctly know that I exist, but not who or what I am*, since the one thing cannot be demonstrated without the other. Nor do I see what more you expect about this matter, unless that it be said what is the color, odor, and taste of the human mind, or of what salt, sulphur, and mercury it is composed; for you wish us to examine it, as though it were a wine, *by a sort of chemical labor*. That is really worthy of you, O flesh, and of all those who, since they conceive nothing except what is wholly confused, are ignorant of what should be asked about a given thing. (AT VII, 359–60; HR II, 212)

There follows the passage I have already quoted, concerning perfect comprehension. However, since Descartes does not, in fact, generally subscribe to the 'quantitative' view about the nature of substance that he there ascribes to himself, he is not really entitled to this line of defense. Perhaps if all one's knowledge of A is confused, and all one's knowledge of B is just as confused, then one might be said to know A better than B if one knows (confusedly) *more* about A. But from what Descartes has already said, a qualitative assessment must be highly relevant, and this the argument has not so far provided.

It might be suggested on Descartes's behalf that at least we know everything we are aware of in our minds—e.g., the thought that the wax is white—really is in our minds, while it will turn out that we err in supposing there is in the wax, the whiteness that we think we see in it. The reason the unqualified quantitative view won't do for bodies is just that bodies aren't really what they seem.

However, this is surely not (even on Cartesian terms) the only reason the quantitative 'list' view of superior knowledge won't do for bodies. In the case of bodies what is required is—just as Gassendi has indicated—*explanations* of their observed properties and behavior in terms of general laws and the unobserved constitution of things. Gassendi is right to demand of Descartes why mental phenomena should be regarded differently in this respect—as not requiring any non-vulgar explanation.

We have come, here, to a point of crucial importance in the Cartesian system. Mind is said to be better known than body—but this cannot *really* be because our knowledge of mind fulfills to a higher degree the same standards by which we evaluate knowledge of body. There seem to be two points Descartes *could* draw on to defend the position—insinuated at the end of his reply to Gassendi—that the standards appropriate to the one are not appropriate to the other.

First, our previous account should make clear that Descartes *does* think he has provided, in the Second Meditation, a knowledge of mind 'superior to the vulgar'—without resorting to 'chemical labor.' He has distinguished the true idea of the mind from the ideas of sensible things, with which it had been 'confused' (cf. AT VII, 130–1; HR II, 31–2). And he has gone on to show that the operations of our mind have a unique range and variability which distinguishes them from the 'perceptual' apparatuses of animals. Moreover, in making a similar point in the *Discourse*, he has there argued that this aspect of our mentality shows that a mechanistic account of the mind's operations is 'morally impossible' (AT VI, 57–9; HR I, 116–17). It would follow that Gassendi's 'chemical labor' is ruled out.

Second, Descartes could appeal to his repeatedly stated position that the mind is in some sense transparent to itself: 'there can be nothing in me, that is in my mind, of which I am not conscious' (AT III, 273; PL 90; cf. AT VII, 107). Such a view—in so far as Descartes seriously accepts it—would imply that there is no point or possibility in attempting to apply a 'chemical labor' to the mind, since the mind *has* no 'hidden constitution.'[57] The questions of how consistently Descartes held this view, and to what extent he may have been justified in holding it, will be considered in more detail in a later chapter.

Both the notion that mind is not machine-like in its operations, and the notion that it is epistemically transparent to itself, provide grounds for Descartes's rejection of Gassendi's claim that the same model of explanation should be held relevant to mind as to body. Both notions could contribute to the philosophical foundations of Descartes's science by showing what does and what does not appropriately fall within the explanatory range of that science. Lacking a 'chemical' explanation of mind, and of the more mind-governed aspects of human behavior, Descartes can still lay claim to explaining 'all the phenomena of nature,' providing that mind is deemed to lie outside of nature, by virtue of being fundamentally different from matter in its essence and operations. Further, there is no embarrassment in lacking an explanation of thought, if one holds that thought, being epistemically transparent, needs no explanation.

It seems likely that Descartes's conception of mind as outside the appropriate realm of scientific explanation includes both the view that the operations of mind are mysteriously non-mechanical, and the view that mind is somehow transparent to itself. Unfortunately, it also appears that these two views are in tension with each other. The human mind, on Descartes's view, can do things that cannot be modelled mechanically. But our explanations, and hence in an important sense our understanding, are limited to what can be explained on mechanical models. How are we then to avoid the conclusion that there is an important sense in which the mind is not at all transparent to itself? Its mode of operation must elude our understanding, according to the Cartesian account, regardless of what kind of 'certainty' we may achieve about the occurrence of various thoughts, or the possession of mental 'powers.'[58]

III

Some Perspectives on the Third Meditation

1 Introduction

In the previous chapters I have followed quite closely Descartes's development of his argument in the first two Meditations. However, my purpose is not to provide a continuous commentary on the whole argument of the *Meditations*, but rather to analyze closely certain parts of that argument, within the framework of a general conception of the nature and purpose of the work. In the present chapter, and in later ones, I will depart from systematic exegesis. I will consider in detail only certain prominent features of Descartes's development of his argument in Meditations III, IV, V, and VI. I will be concerned, particularly, with further aspects of his theory of our knowledge of mind and body, and also, in the present chapter, with the notion of a deceiving creator and the doctrine of the creation of the eternal truths. This will result in a rather foreshortened picture of the central part of the *Meditations*. For I will have very little to say about the arguments for the existence of God that occupy most of the Third and Fifth Meditations. While these arguments are interesting enough, I don't think Descartes is in a position to defend their soundness very forcefully. (I give one or two reasons for this view in passing, though I don't think it is a very problematic one.) In any case, I'm mainly interested in the place of the arguments in the over-all strategy of the *Meditations*, rather than in their logical details. I see them as, in part, vehicles for certain concepts and commitments whose importance is not limited to their roles in specific arguments: for instance, the distinction between finitude and dependence on the one hand, and infinitude and independence on the other, the theory of 'true and immutable natures,' and the perplexing concept of material falsity.

2 *Material falsity and objective reality*

In the Second Meditation Descartes has held that the wax is clearly and distinctly perceived as just something extended, flexible and mutable. The Third Meditation develops further the themes of the contrast between the clear and distinct perception of body, and bodies as sensibly perceived. In doing so, it begins the transition from general conclusions about the nature of a body, to conclusions about which of the sensibly 'perceived' properties of bodies have correspondents in physical reality. Thus, Descartes argues that only a subset of the properties that a body seems to sense to have are clearly and distinctly 'perceived in' it. This leaves him only a step from the Sixth Meditation conclusion that only geometrical properties *can be ascribed* to the physical world. Also in the Third Meditation, as I will try to show, Descartes gives us a sort of explanation of why we so often fall into the error of confusing our subjective states or sensations (color, odor, heat) with real properties of physical things.

Descartes opens the Third Meditation with a reaffirmation that

> even if the things which I sense or imagine are perhaps nothing
> outside me, nevertheless I am certain that those modes of
> thinking, which I call sensings [*sensus*] and imaginings, in so far as
> they are only certain modes of thinking, are in me. (AT VII, 34–5;
> HR I, 157)

While he had formerly admitted as certain 'earth, sky, stars, and all other things which I perceived by the senses,' which he has now come to doubt, it is questionable what of these he had perceived clearly. True, 'the ideas themselves, or the thoughts, of such things' he had observed in his mind,

> But even now I do not deny these ideas to be in me. (AT VII, 35;
> HR I, 158)

There was, however, something else that he had thought he perceived clearly which he did not, namely that,

> There were certain things [*res quasdam*] outside me, from which
> these ideas proceeded, and to which they were entirely similar.
> (*Ibid.*)

Having reminded us of the difference, with respect to certainty, of the existence of *ideas* of things and the existence of *things*, Descartes again brings up the issue of the apparently superior certainty of simple mathematical propositions. He remarks again that the latter cannot be doubted, except through the hypothesis of a deceiving Creator. Thus, he must inquire 'as soon as possible' whether there is a

God and if so whether he might be a deceiver. He initiates this quest—which I will consider more systematically in the next section—by a return to those mental states, of which he has no doubts.

'Order requires,' Descartes says, that he divide his thoughts into certain types, and find out in which of these 'truth or falsity properly consists' (AT VII, 36–7; HR I, 159). There follows a passage which will be of key importance in analyzing the treatment of *cogitationes*, and specifically the sensing of bodies, in Meditation III:

> Of my thoughts some are like images of things [*tanquam rerum imagines*], to which alone the term 'idea' is strictly appropriate: as when I think of man, or Chimaera, or Heaven, or Angel, or God. Others, though, have certain forms besides: as when I will, when I fear, when I affirm, when I deny, I always indeed apprehend some thing [*aliquam rem*] as the subject of my thought, but I also comprehend by thought something more than the similitude of this thing; and of these some are called volitions, or affects, but others judgments. (AT VII, 37; HR I, 159)

This passage strongly implies that *all* thoughts have an element that is 'like the image of a thing'; those that are not ideas in the strict sense, 'have other forms besides.' (Thus, when I fear a lion, I have a mental state composed out of the passion of fear and something that is like an image of a lion.) In other words, as Norman Malcolm has remarked, this passage seems to indicate that 'in every instance of thinking there is a representation.'[1] But what, exactly, does the term 'representation' mean here? With respect to the Cartesian position there are, I think, two important points to note. First, when Descartes says that ideas are *'tanquam rerum imagines'* I think he is saying more than that thoughts have 'objects,' according to which they are classified (as ideas *of God, of heat* or *cold*, etc.). He means also that ideas are received by the mind *as if exhibiting to it* various things—or as if making things *cognitively accessible*. (Descartes seems to use the terms 'represent' and 'exhibit' as interchangeable.)[2] To say this seems to be to say *more* than that ideas are, necessarily, 'ideas of'—though it might not be easy to determine exactly how *much* more. Second, when Descartes speaks of ideas being *'tanquam rerum imagines,'* he does *not* mean that every idea involves a mental picture with *visual* properties: an idea, in other words, can purport to bring something into cognitive ken without purporting to represent it visually. (In fact, as Descartes stresses in the *Replies*, it need not purport to represent the thing via *any* sensory modality.[3]) I will use the expression 'representational character' to designate that feature of ideas by which they are *'tanquam rerum imagines.'*

In a general way, the representational character of ideas is related to erroneous judgment. Ideas considered just as 'certain modes of thought,' Descartes says, 'cannot properly be false.' But,[4]

> the principal and most frequent error which can be found in them, consists in this, that I judge the ideas which are in me to be similar or conformable to certain things posited outside me. (AT VII, 37; HR I, 160)

We suppose that objects are as our ideas 'exhibit' them—and we may be wrong. Of particular interest in this connection are those ideas which seem to 'come from without' (as opposed to the other two categories Descartes discerns: ideas that seem to be innate, and those that seem to be constructed by himself).

> But here the principal issue is to ask of those, that I consider taken up as if from things existing outside me, what reason moves me to suppose that they are similar to those things. (AT VII, 38; HR I, 160)

Descartes concludes in effect that he has no good reason. While he has a 'spontaneous impulse' to believe this, such impulses can by no means be regarded as uniformly reliable. The fact that such ideas come to him against his will proves nothing conclusively, since he might have within himself some unknown power to cause them. In any case, even if such ideas do come from external objects, he has no good reason to suppose that they resemble them. In fact his knowledge of astronomy leads him to believe that the idea of the sun that (he is inclined to think) comes directly from the sun itself via the senses 'resembles the sun' less than the idea derived from astro-nomical reasonings (ultimately based, he hints, on innate cog-nitions). All this 'sufficiently demonstrates' that

> it was not by certain judgment, but only by a certain blind impulse, that I have up to now believed that there exist certain things [*res quasdam*] different from me, that impart [*immittant*] to me their ideas or images through the sense organs, or some other path. (AT VII, 39–40; HR I, 161)

The parts of Meditation III that we have been considering, and related passages to be considered below, are sometimes treated as little more than 'lead-up' to the argument that concludes to the existence of God from the need to postulate an appropriate cause for the idea of God. I think, however, it is at least equally valid to view matters the other way round. The Third Meditation argument for

God's existence can be viewed as a way of bringing home the distinction between ideas and their 'objects' that Descartes requires for the presentation of his ontology of nature.

At this point of the argument of the *Meditations* one can begin to see clearly the change from (mere) 'hyperbolic doubt' to outright criticism of the world-views of commonsense empiricism, and of the Aristotelian-Scholastic tradition. With respect to the requirements of hyperbolic doubt, Descartes needed to say here only the following: *however* good my reasons are for believing in a physical world such as the senses portray to me, it is still after all possible that I might, in trusting these reasons, be deceived by a powerful god. What he says instead—indeed stresses—is that he has nothing *like* a good reason; it is only by a 'blind impulse' that he believes what he sees.

Descartes's strategy is rather subtle. He has, it is true, relied essentially on hyperbolic doubt to get us to acknowledge *some sort* of distinction between perceptions (as states of the self) and the 'external' objects that we take ourselves to perceive. But the representationalism itself, in virtue of which the mind is supposed to apprehend things by means of thoughts or ideas distinct from the things, is in the service of a further objective. As I have already repeatedly indicated, Descartes is concerned to establish not just that things *need not be* just the way they appear, that the 'inferences' from ideas to things is somehow *shaky*. He wants us to accept a view of the world according to which things *are not* the way they appear; according to which (what he must regard as) our habitual inferences from sensations to things are *wrong*. As a result of passing through the various stages of 'withdrawal from sense' we are supposed to find ourselves able to accept the strange world-view of geometrical physics—strange to the senses though natural, Descartes thinks, to unimpeded mind.

In the end, ordinary sense perception will be pitted fairly sharply against the alleged deliverances of imagination and understanding. (Descartes thinks of imagination not just as the faculty of production or reproduction of sense-derived images in general, but also as a faculty of mathematical illustration, one that can be used to reproduce or construct *geometrical* images.)[5] We are expected to conclude with Descartes that the ideas of sense are by far the inferior source of information about the world: they are less reliable, less certain and (repeated again and again) less clear, less distinct, less evident than what is directly revealed to us by the natural light. At the same time, the ideas of sense, like all ideas, have representational character. That is, they purport to represent *res quasdam*. In this section I want to examine particularly Descartes's discussion of the representational character of ideas of sense in the Third Meditation. I will suggest that at the time of writing the *Meditations* he takes this feature of our sensations as providing a sort of explanation of our persistent error in embracing the world-view of commonsense empiricism. I will also show how, under criticism from Arnauld, Descartes retreats from the *Meditations* position—which had in fact led him into incoherence. In the *Principles*, I will argue, Descartes moves away from the doctrine that all ideas, and specifically the ideas of sense, are *tanquam rerum imagines*. We can see him there casting about for an alternative account of our life-long tendency to conflate mere sensations with ideas that clearly and distinctly represent the (real) properties of things. In passing, I hope to bring out one or two curious aspects of Descartes's treatment of the concept of 'objective reality' in the Third Meditation.

In the next stage of Descartes's argument, the notion of the representational character of ideas is used to introduce the concept of 'objective reality.' An idea has more or less 'objective reality,' Descartes seems to indicate, depending on the metaphysical category of its object—that is, of what it 'exhibits to us':

> Insofar as these ideas are just certain modes of thought, I do not
> recognize any inequality among them, and all seem to proceed
> from me in the same way; but, insofar as one represents one thing,
> and another another, it is evident that some are very different from
> others. For surely those which exhibit substances to me are
> something more and, so to speak, contain more objective reality in
> themselves, than those which only represent modes, or accidents;
> and in the same way the idea by which I understand a certain
> supreme God, eternal, infinite, omniscient, omnipotent, and the
> creator of all things besides himself, has certainly more objective
> reality in itself than those ideas by which finite substances are
> exhibited. (AT VII, 40; HR I, 161–2)

Descartes will go on to argue that it is evident 'to the light of nature' that for every idea there must exist a cause with at least as much 'formal reality' (in effect, reality *simpliciter*) as the idea has 'objective reality.' One conclusion will be, of course, that since the idea of God has infinite objective reality, it must be caused by a being with infinite formal reality—i.e., by God.

Between the introduction of the concept of objective reality, and the conclusion of the proof of God's existence, Descartes interposes an account of the 'material falsity' of the ideas of sense—a 'falsity' deriving from their representative character. This account forces us to recognize a distinction between the representative character of an idea and its objective reality—a distinction which appears more an impediment than a help to the proof of God's existence. But, I have suggested, Descartes had other motives for explaining material falsity to us.

Pursuing the question of whether he can infer beyond his ideas to the existence of some being other than himself as (perhaps) their cause, Descartes considers first the ideas of bodies. He here asserts, without argument or clarification, the position I have already referred to—that only a subset of the properties that objects seem to the senses to possess are 'clearly and distinctly' perceived in them.

> If I very thoroughly inspect [the ideas of corporeal objects], and examine them one by one in the way that I have yesterday examined the idea of the wax, I notice that there is very little that I clearly and distinctly perceive in them: namely magnitude, or extension in length, breadth, and depth; figure, which arises from the termination of this extension; position, which different figures hold among themselves; and motion, or change in this position; to which can be added substance, duration, and number: the others however, such as light and colors, sounds, odors, tastes, heat and cold, and the other tactile qualities, are not known by me except very confusedly and obscurely, so that I am even ignorant whether they are true, or false, that is, whether the ideas, which I have of them, are the ideas of some sort of things [rerum quarundam], or not of things. (AT VII, 43; HR I, 164)

Clearly, the assertions in this passage go beyond those in the wax passage (of which we are, however, carefully reminded). What we are now said to perceive clearly and distinctly in bodies are magnitude, figure, position (situm), motion, substance, duration, number. (The last three qualities are mentioned as 'added' to the others, without doubt for the reason that they pertain to incorporeal as well as corporeal beings.) To say that we clearly and distinctly perceive figure and motion in bodies, is obviously different from saying we clearly perceive them as flexible and mutable—even if 'mutable' is taken implicitly to connote 'capable of changing position as a whole,' together with 'capable of changing shape.' Also, the list is longer. However, it is important to notice that Descartes does not really make clear in precisely what sense we distinctly perceive, say 'figure in body.' Does he mean to imply that we distinctly perceive the particular figure of a particular body (at a given time)? Even in the Sixth Meditation (as I will argue in a later chapter)

106

Descartes's statements on this issue remain rather vague and ambiguous.

Apart from the lack of specificity in Descartes's claim, there is a difficulty—a crucial one for the *Meditations'* argument—in seeing why we should accept it at all. Or (to put the matter in a perhaps less anachronistic way) it is hard to see how to *make sense* of this distinction, apart from the strictly psychological and historical considerations adduced by Burtt: 'the whole course of Descartes's thought from his adolescent studies on had inured him to the notion that we know objects only in mathematical terms. . . .'⁶ We have seen that in the *Principles* he does try to show that extension (and hence divisibility and movability according to its parts) differs from color and so forth in being conceptually involved in the idea of body. But even this does not seem sufficient to show that we clearly and distinctly perceive figure, motion and position *in bodies*—or even to explain what exactly this proposition comes to. I will defer further consideration of this problem till a later section. Meanwhile, it is important to bear in mind that clear and distinct perception is not supposed to be just an especially vivid and reliable sort of sense perception. A clear and distinct perception is an act of the understanding.

For present purposes, what we must specially note is Descartes's claim that

> light and colors, sounds, odors, tastes, heat and cold, and the other tactile qualities, are not known by me except very confusedly and obscurely, so that I am even ignorant whether they are true, or false, that is, whether the ideas, which I have of them, are the ideas of certain things or not of things [*sint rerum quarundam ideae, an non rerum*]. (AT VII, 43; HR I, 164)

Now, what is the issue here? It is natural at first sight to suppose that Descartes is saying he can't tell whether or not these sense-ideas represent *existent* entities. For what else *could* he be talking about? And he is after all engaged in an inquiry to determine whether there are other things that exist besides himself. Yet by the same token, one might object that his criticism of the ideas of color, cold, and so forth is out of place. For isn't he supposed to be in ignorance whether *any* of his ideas (other than those pertaining to himself) represent existing entities or not?

In fact, when Descartes asks whether or not his ideas are of 'certain things' he is *not* raising the question whether they represent to him entities that actually exist. For he indicates very explicitly, in both the *Meditations* and the *Principles*, that what represents *res* and what does not, depends on a concept of reality that is not equivalent to existence. For instance, he says a little later in the Third Meditation that 'although perhaps it is possible to imagine that such a being [as God] does not exist, it is nevertheless not possible to imagine that his idea exhibits nothing real to me' (AT VII, 46; HR I, 166). Several texts strongly suggest that when Descartes asks whether an idea represents something real, or *rem*, he is asking whether or not in some way it gives him cognizance of a *possible* existent. With a clear and distinct idea there can be no question: 'In the concept or idea of everything that is clearly and distinctly conceived, possible existence is contained. . . .' (AT VII, 116; HR II, 20). From obscure and confused ideas, however, we 'cannot tell' whether or not they represent a possible object. But we are assuming all ideas are 'of things' in the sense that they have representational character.

Consequently, the claim that an idea or thought is 'of a thing (*res*)' must be distinguished *both* from the claim that it represents something that in fact exists, *and* from the claim that it has representational character. An idea may have representational character, yet fail, in the relevant sense, to represent *any thing*.

Descartes, then, is not claiming at this point of his argument that he can know from considering his ideas 'very thoroughly' whether some definitely do represent actual external existents. He does claim, however, to be able to know whether some definitely represent *some thing*.[7] With respect to entities other than himself, the issue of real possibility is treated as prior to the problem of existence. As the Fifth Meditation will make clear, the issue of physical-mathematical truth is first to be resolved on the level of possible things ('true and immutable natures'), *then* on the level of actuality or existence.

But how can Descartes consistently speak of ideas as 'true' and 'false'? He has only recently remarked that ideas considered simply as modes of thought 'cannot properly be false' and—later in the same paragraph—that 'they can scarcely give me any material for error.' He has held that truth or falsity is to be found only in judgments, especially those that relate ideas to something beyond themselves. He goes on to explain, however, that ideas can be 'materially' false:

> For although I noted a little before that falsity properly so-called, or formal falsity, can only be found in judgments, there is nevertheless a certain other material falsity in ideas, when they represent what is not a thing as if a thing (*non rem tanquam rem repraesentant*). Thus, for example, the ideas that I have of heat and cold, are so little clear and distinct, that from them I cannot

108

tell whether cold is only the privation of heat, or heat the privation of cold, or each is a real quality, or neither. *And because there can be no ideas that are not as if of things [nisi tanquam rerum]*, if indeed it is true that cold is nothing else than the privation of heat, the idea which represents it to me as something real and positive, will not improperly be called false, and so of the others. (AT VII, 43–4; HR I, 164; emphasis added)

At first sight Descartes seems to be contradicting himself in this and the previously quoted passage. For he seems to be saying *both* that his ideas of light, color and so forth are of such a nature that he cannot tell whether they represent what is real or not, *and* that the ideas represent light, color and so forth *as real*. But, in view of the preceding discussion, we can see that what he is saying is not really self-contradictory. The point is just that while these ideas do not have the marks of clarity and distinctness that would allow us to conclude with philosophical assurance to the 'reality' of light, color and so forth, they nevertheless, like all ideas, present themselves 'like images of things.' In this respect they can possibly *mis*lead anyone who does not exercise the proper philosophical caution with respect to his affirmations. As Descartes later explains to Arnauld, to say an idea is materially false is to say that it provides 'material' for falsity in the strict sense, or formal falsity: i.e., it tends to lead its unwary possessor into making false judgments (AT VII, 233–5; HR II, 106–7). If 'in fact' light, color, heat, cold and so forth are 'nothing real' or 'non things' [*nullas res*], the ideas that represent these 'qualities' as if they were real [*tanquam res*] are to this extent materially false. In other words, the fact that an idea has representational character—that it presents itself *as if* exhibiting some thing to the mind, or making it cognitively accessible—leads us falsely to suppose that it does make something real cognitively accessible to us.

One point that needs to be made about this passage is that the notion of a *privation* is perhaps not as essential to the argument as it may at first appear. If cold is 'merely a privation of heat' then *it* is not 'something positive'—but heat is. However, Descartes is really saying here that *none* of the qualities mentioned need be 'real.' As already noted, this is the real objective of the distinction between properties that are clearly and distinctly perceived in bodies and those which are not. The distinction between privative and positive qualities would be familiar to Descartes's scholastic audience, and that presumably is why he employs it in explaining the notion of material falsity, for these purposes running together the ideas of the 'real' and the 'non-privative.'[8]

109

This passage led Arnauld to inquire how a non-entity, or a privation, could *be* represented by a 'positive idea,' since the idea of something is just that thing itself, 'as it exists objectively in the understanding' (AT VII, 206; HR II, 86–7). And in fact, Descartes has provided us with no direct answer to the question: 'What is it, exactly, for an idea to *represent 0?*' Therefore, it is not easy to know exactly how Arnauld's question should be answered. (Descartes's own answer, in the *Replies*, is a model of confusion confounded (AT VII, 233; HR II, 106).) However, we do know roughly what Descartes ultimately wants to say. He ultimately wants to say that in response to a certain sort of occurrence, describable in terms of extension and motion, and involving, at least typically, interaction between the human body and other bodies, a certain sensation is experienced. This sensation, for most people, constitutes the idea of cold. Because the sensation, like all 'thoughts' comes to us *tanquam rei imago* we refer it to the realm of things, take it to tell us something about things. In fact, however, all that there is in the realm of things to 'correspond to' this sensation is just the chain of (geometrically describable) events that precede and give rise to the occurrence of the sensation in the human mind. (This is all there *can* be: all that is distinctly conceivable.) The real nature of cold—what cold really is—must be located somewhere in this chain of physical events. Thus 'it' might even turn out to be a privation of the physical activity constituting heat. This, I assume, is what Descartes means when he replies to Arnauld that the idea of cold is not cold itself existing in the mind, but something else 'we wrongly take for that privation' (AT VII, 283; HR II, 106). We mistakenly take the sensation to be the privation just in the following sense: (1) We in some manner take the sensation to be what is out there when we experience cold; (2) What is out there when we experience cold is a privation.

In the continuation of this account of ideas of sense, however, Descartes gives a peculiar twist to the story of how they are caused. There is no reason, he remarks, to suppose at this stage of his inquiry that these 'obscure' ideas have causes outside himself:

> For if they are false, that is, if they do not represent things [*hoc est nullas res repraesentent*], the light of nature makes known to me that they proceed from nothing, that is, they are not in me on account of any other cause except because there is something lacking in my nature, and it is not completely perfect. If however they are true, nevertheless because they exhibit so little reality to me, that I cannot even distinguish it from non-entity [*ne quidem illud a non re possim distinguere*], I do not see why they cannot have being from myself. (AT VII, 44; HR I, 165)

Descartes claims, then, that the idea of cold, for instance, if materially false, must issue from nothing, or from 'some defect in [his] nature.' This is puzzling since it seems to rule out the possibility that sensations arise in the mind as a result of changes in the body, effected by external physical circumstances. But surely Descartes does *not* want to rule this out?

Perhaps the answer is this. Considered as modes of thought, sensations have positive formal reality, and like any other real occurrence must have an equally real cause. Considered though from the cognitive point of view—from the point of view of content, or 'objective reality,' sensations are mere nothings. They do not require a positive cause, and may be said to arise from 'some defect in my nature' for the rather interesting reason that a perfect or unlimited being would not have such confused or cognitively empty ideas. It is because I am limited and embodied that I experience the confused ideas of sensation, rather than only contemplating the clear and distinct ideas of the scientific image. (Descartes will explain the bodily use of sensations later.)

But notice that the view that sensations, from the objective point of view, are 'caused by nothing' has an interesting and surprising implication: sensations must *lack objective reality, despite having representative character*! That they have representative character has been an assumption of the whole discussion. That they lack objective reality follows directly from the premiss that they are 'caused by nothing,' together with the principle, soon introduced in this Meditation, that there can be no more objective reality in an idea than there is formal reality in its cause.[9] This divorce between the representative character of an idea and its objective reality is, I want to hold, an embarrassment, not an asset from the point of view of the Third Meditation's ultimate goal of proving God's existence from the idea of God. I will first try to show that this is so, and then go on to consider in more detail why Descartes should have allowed this awkwardness to arise in his argument.

First, we should observe that the notion of material falsity is not *needed* for setting up the argument for God's existence, and in particular is not needed to establish the point that knowledge of God is prior to knowledge of physical things. Ostensibly, of course, Descartes introduces the notion that ideas of sense may be materially false, in order to argue that *they* do not provide the basis for concluding to a cause outside himself. (He would be a sufficient cause; indeed his 'defects' are.) But actually from this point of view the notion of material falsity is a red herring. For in the next paragraph Descartes will conclude that his *clear and distinct* ideas of

111

bodies—which he contrasts with those tarred with the brush of material falsity—could *also* have been produced by himself (AT VII, 44-5; HR I, 165).

And second, the notion of material falsity provides the basis for an *objection* to Descartes's proof of God's existence, because it entails that the objective reality of an idea is *not* something the idea wears on its face. Descartes would have it otherwise: in his initial exposition of the concept of objective reality he seems to indicate that an idea's objective reality is transparent, deriving directly from its representative character:

> There cannot be in me an idea of heat, or of stone, unless it is placed in me by some cause, in which there is at least as much reality as I conceive to be in heat or stone. (AT VII, 41; HR I, 162)

This suggests that my idea of x has n degrees of objective reality just in so far as I conceive of x *as having n* degrees of (formal) reality. Yet this cannot be correct, or else there could be no such thing as material falsity.[10] For I do (or may well) think falsely that my materially false ideas represent something real—that they have objective reality. They are said to be materially false just because, representing *nullas res tanquam res*, they *tend* to mislead me into thinking they represent something real.

With respect to the demonstration of God's existence, this complexity in determining objective reality leads to the following problem. If our ideas can provide 'material for error' concerning that which they represent, and can to this extent be misjudged with respect to whether they represent *res* or *nullas res*, what justifies our assurance that the idea of God in fact does possess infinite objective reality (and therefore must have an 'infinitely real' cause)? Descartes does consider this question explicitly:

> And it cannot be said that perhaps this idea of God is materially false, and thus could have existence from nothing, as a little before I noticed concerning the ideas of heat and cold, and similar ones; for on the contrary, since it is clear and distinct to the highest degree [*maxime*], and contains more objective reality than any other, there is none that is in itself more true, nor any in which less suspicion of falsity is to be found. The idea, I say, of a being of greatest perfection and infinity is true to the highest degree, for though perhaps I can imagine that such a being does not exist, I cannot nevertheless imagine that the idea of him *exhibits nothing real to me*, as I said before about the idea of cold. It is also clear

and distinct to the highest degree, for whatever I clearly and distinctly perceive that is real and true, and that implies any perfection, is entirely contained in it. (AT VII, 46; HR I, 166; emphasis added)

Here Descartes seems to say that he can know the idea of God is *not* materially false, both because it is very clear and distinct, and because it 'contains more objective reality than any other.' The trouble with the second part of this statement is that it seems simply to ignore the question: how can we be certain that our idea of God actually does contain or exhibit infinite reality, given that we may make mistakes about the amount of reality exhibited by other ideas, such as that of cold (because they may represent *nullam rem tanquam rem*)? The problem with the first part of the statement—the appeal to clear and distinct perception as the criterion of material truth—is that we have been told the proof of God's existence is required to vindicate the clarity and distinctness of ideas as the criterion of truth.[11]

Nevertheless, we may now recall, the original introduction of the notion of material falsity does indicate that the clarity and distinctness of an idea are supposed to be the crucial features that allow us to conclude that the idea *represents some thing*:

The ideas that I have of heat and cold are *so little clear and distinct*, that from them I cannot tell whether cold is only the privation of heat, or heat the privation of cold, or each is a real quality, or neither. (AT VII, 43–4; HR I, 164)

And perhaps the appearance of the problem of circularity at this point should not disturb us unduly: we knew we would have to contend with *that* problem eventually anyway. Still, from the point of view of Descartes's strictly theological objectives, the notion of material falsity is a problem and a distraction. To understand its introduction in the Third Meditation, we must acknowledge that this Meditation is concerned not merely with the proof of God, but also with developing the theme of knowledge of body.[12] Thus, an important part of Descartes's purpose in Meditation III is to establish the distinction between obscure or confused and distinct ideas of bodies, and to make us aware that causal inferences from our ideas to external reality are not always justified—even *apart from* the esoteric notion of 'justification' introduced by the hyperbolic doubt. But then Descartes also needs some sort of explanation of the fact that we so regularly do make the inferences that produce our ordinary commonsensical world-view. (To say these inferences rest on 'blind impulse' says *something*—namely, that they aren't rationally

113

warranted—but the picture needs to be filled out, made more comprehensible.) In the *Meditations*, I am suggesting, this explanation is provided in part through the notion of material falsity—the notion that, since all ideas are *tanquam imagines rerum*, even those that are really of non-things, *nullas res*, present themselves as if images of things, thereby leading the unwary percipient into deceit.[13]

Now we may still wonder why Descartes should subscribe fully to the view that the idea of cold (for example), if materially false, must issue from nothing, or from some 'defect in his nature.' We may wonder, in other words, why Descartes should commit himself to the view that materially false ideas *lack* objective reality. Why doesn't he just say that the *confusion* of these ideas results from some defect in his nature, and that *because* they are confused these ideas do not provide sound basis for inference to the nature of the world? This would allow them to *have* objective reality, in the way that fictional ideas, such as that of a hippogryph, do. And their 'representative character' could still be the cause of their misleading us.

One reason Descartes may have had for rejecting the latter alternative is the following: he was determined at all costs to maintain that the ideas of sense, even if they are *tanquam rerum*, nevertheless fail to exhibit to us any possibly existent quality in an intelligible manner. He may have felt that openly to allow these ideas 'objective reality' would be to undermine his position that in an important ('*de re*') sense they are *not* 'of things.'

In any case, Descartes's implication in the Third Meditation that most ideas of sense may lack objective reality (excluding extension, figure, motion and situation, which are supposed to be ideas of intellect as well) was evidently not a mere slip. For under questioning from Arnauld he alters other features of his position, rather than abandoning this one. Arnauld maintains that Descartes's proof of God's existence requires assuming (what Arnauld regards as true) that 'positive' ideas have objective reality. And Arnauld continues:

> While it can be imagined that cold, which I judge to be
> represented by a positive idea, is not positive, it nevertheless
> cannot be imagined that a positive idea exhibits to me nothing real
> and positive; since a positive idea is not said to be positive
> according to the being it has as a mode of thinking (in that sense
> all ideas would be positive), but from the objective being which it
> contains and displays to our intellect. Hence, that idea is possibly
> not the idea of cold, but it cannot be false. (AT VII, 207; HR II,
> 87)

114

Arnauld is insisting that we can't say a given idea both represents x 'as something positive' or 'as if a thing,' *and* completely lacks objective reality. A little later he concludes his objections to Descartes's notion of material falsity with the following remark:

> What is the cause of that positive objective entity, that brings it about that the idea is materially false? Myself, you say, in so far as I come from nothing [*a nihilo sum*]. Therefore the positive objective being of some idea can come from nothing, which overthrows [M. Descartes's] own fundamental principles. (*Ibid.*)

The point, again, is that the representative character essential to material falsity necessarily involves a positive content, and must by Descartes's 'principles' have a positive cause. In other words, Descartes contradicts himself in saying that materially false ideas come from nothing, from the 'objective' point of view.

This shrewd line of questioning gave Descartes a ripe opportunity to separate himself, if he had wished to, from the view that a materially false idea lacks objective reality. It also gives him the opportunity to correct the implication—if he wishes to correct it—that an idea in so far as it is materially false 'comes from nothing.' But he does neither of these things. Instead he seems simply to abandon the view that the representative character of ideas of sense (which is surely 'something positive') is a source of our mistaken beliefs about the real qualities of objects. Now, in the Fourth Replies, ideas are said to be materially false *merely* because they are *obscure*—not because they represent *nullas res tanquam res.*

> I only call that materially false because, since it is obscure and confused, it is not possible to determine whether what it exhibits to me is something positive outside my sensation or not; and this is why I have occasion to judge it as something positive, even though perhaps it is only a privation. And hence one should not ask, what is the cause of that positive objective being, from which I say it results that the idea is materially false; for I do not say it is made materially false by any positive entity, but only by the obscurity, which nevertheless has a positive entity as subject, namely the sensation itself. (AT VII, 234; HR II, 106–7)

This must, I think, be viewed as a significant departure from the doctrine of the *Meditations*. And while it may get Descartes out of one difficulty, it does get him into another. For now the *same feature* of ideas, their 'obscurity,' is being assigned the tasks of explaining *both* why I 'cannot tell' whether or not the idea exhibits something real, and why I judge that it does. Further, even if we were able somehow to resolve the appearance of inconsistency on this point, we are left with a very weak 'explanation' of our false judgments concerning the qualities of objects. For, while the representational character of ideas was said in the *Meditations* actually to mislead us on the matter of objective reality, the 'obscurity' of ideas can be said only to provide an 'occasion' or opportunity for error.

Did Descartes become aware of these difficulties in his response to Arnáuld? Was he conscious of changing his position on the issue of material falsity? Did this change of position have any effect on his readiness to affirm the 'representational' character of all ideas? I believe there is some basis for affirmative answers to these questions in Descartes's treatment of ideas of sense in the *Principles*. At least, his treatment there does suggest a continuing development of his views. He seems to give up or at least to downplay the *Meditations*' position that all ideas of sense have representative character, and to cast about for some other account of our taking them to be 'of things.'

In *Principles* I, 66–7, Descartes notes that all of us, from youth on, have had the habit of judging that what we sense are 'sorts of things [*res quasdam*] existing outside the mind, and entirely similar to' our sensations. Even in the case of pleasure and pain we make the same mistake:

> For although these are not thought to be outside of us,
> nevertheless they are not customarily viewed as in the mind only or
> in our perceptions, but as in the hand or in the foot, or some other
> part of our body. (AT VIII–1, 32–3; HR I, 247)

The views that pains exist in our foot, and that 'light exists outside of us in the sun' are equally 'prejudices of our youth'; but, 'as a result of the habit of judging in this way it seems to us that we see so clearly and distinctly that we take it for certain and indubitable.'

But what accounts for the original formation of this unfortunate habit? The closest Descartes comes to introducing the *Meditations* notion of material falsity is in the following passage from Principle 68:

> When [pain, color and the rest] are judged to be some kind of
> things [*res quaedam*] existing outside our minds, in no way at all
> can it be understood what things [*quaenam res*] they are, but when
> someone says he sees a color in some body, or feels a pain in some
> limb, it is just the same as if he said he there sees or feels that the
> nature of which he is completely ignorant. . . . For even if,
> attending less, he should easily persuade himself that he . . .
> has some notion of it, from which he supposes it to be some-

116

thing similar to that sensation of color or pain, which is experienced in himself: if nevertheless he examines what it is that this sensation of color or pain represents, as if existing in the colored body or in the painful part, he will realize that he is totally ignorant of it. (AT VIII–1, 33; HR I, 248)

However, the emphasis has changed. Descartes neither asserts nor denies that all ideas are *'tanquam rerum'*; the point he is rather stressing is that we have no coherent answer to the question: what in external reality is represented by 'sensations' of color, pain and so forth? It is different, he goes on to claim (in Principle 69), with extension, figure and motion, which are 'known in a very different way,' and 'clearly perceived in bodies.'

What then accounts for our failure to observe this difference? In Principle 70 Descartes remarks that we 'do not notice' that colors and so forth are *not* clearly perceived in bodies, while we do recognize that extension and so forth are perceived as they are in bodies; *therefore* we judge that there is something 'in' the body similar to the 'sensation of color':

When . . . we think we perceive colors in objects, even though we do not know what it is which we then call by the name of color, and we cannot understand any similarity between the color which we suppose to be in objects, and that which we experience as being in the sensation: because nevertheless we do not notice this fact, and because there are many others, such as magnitude, figure, number, etc., *that we clearly perceive are not otherwise sensed or understood by us than they are, or at least can be, in objects*: we easily fall into this error, that we judge that, which we call color in the objects, to be something entirely similar to the color that we sense, and thus think that what we do not perceive in any way is clearly perceived by us. (AT VIII–1, 34–5; HR I, 249)

In other words, for no good reason we assimilate our mere sensations to qualities clearly perceived in bodies. Descartes, however, does not leave the matter here. He expatiates on it in the following Principle, with a long and rather elaborate account of how the empiricistic 'prejudices of our youth' came into being. And while the account does not become a great deal more precise, it does seem clearly different from those we have previously encountered. And the detail lavished on this problem shows, I think, the seriousness of Descartes's interest in it.

Descartes explains that at the beginning of our lives, when the mind was 'very tightly bound to the body' it felt various sensations when the body was affected. Originally none of these were referred outside the body, but

> When something occurred disadvantageous to the body, it felt pain, and when something advantageous, it felt pleasure; and when the body was affected without much advantage or disadvantage, for the diversity of parts in which, and the ways in which it was affected, it had different sorts of sensations, those that is which we call the sensations of taste, odor, sound, heat, cold, light, color and the like, which *represent nothing posited outside thought*. At the same time the mind also perceived magnitudes, figures, motions, and the like, *which were exhibited not as sensation, but as certain things (res quaedam), or modes of things, existing outside the mind, or at least capable of existing, even though it did not yet recognize this difference among them*. (AT VIII-1, 35; HR I, 249-50)

This seems to indicate that whether or not an idea 'represents something capable of existing outside thought' can be determined by inspecting the idea. And, most important, this feature *is not said to be a function of an idea's clarity and distinctness*. Perhaps, then, our error in taking colors to be real qualities is supposed to arise from our simply failing to heed the difference between mere sensations and the perceptions of things. And in fact the rest of Descartes's account in the *Principles* does suggest that it is by a sort of *carelessness* that the mind assimilates sensations like color and pain to real properties like extension and figure, after it has formed the concept of an external physical world:

> Since afterwards when the mechanism of the body, which is so fabricated by nature that by its own force it can move in various ways, turning itself fortuitously here and there, in order to approach the advantageous or flee the disadvantageous, the mind attached to it began to notice that what it thus approached or fled were outside itself, and *not only attributed to them magnitudes, figures, motion and the like, which it perceived as things or modes of things, but also tastes, odors, and the rest, the sensation of which it noticed to be caused in it by the same things*. (AT VII, 35-6; HR I, 250; emphasis added)

Descartes is vague on whether at this second stage of development the mind does or does not have some realization of the difference between mere sensations and the perceptions of extension, figure and motion. However, the general drift of the *Principles* discussion seems to me to go against the line taken in the *Meditations*—against, that is, the view that sensations and other perceptions are superficially alike in that both seem to represent things. Here Descartes stresses that the two are *different*: colors, tastes, sounds and so forth not only 'represent nothing outside thought,' but also 'are exhibited as sensations'; while extension, figure and motion are exhibited or perceived as 'certain things or modes of things, existing outside the mind.' At the same time, Descartes still sees a need to give some kind of account of our tendency to attribute color, tastes and the like to physical objects. And he accordingly still allows (which is in any case undeniable) that we *think* our ideas of color and so forth 'represent something existing outside thought.' But this tendency is no longer said to result from an intrinsic feature of sensations: that they are *tanquam rerum*, as if of things. Rather, it is supposed to result from their confusing *association* with the really representative perceptions of extension, figure and motion.

From the point of view of the *Meditations*, our ability to grasp the crucial difference between the true scientific image and the false commonsense image of the world rests on our acceptance of the proposition that the perceptions of the former are clear and distinct, while those of the latter are obscure and confused. It is, I have suggested, a major failing of Descartes's argument there, that he gives us so little reason, or compelling basis, for accepting this proposition. One is just supposed, somehow, to 'see' it. But the situation seems to be still worse with respect to Descartes's hints in the *Principles* that there is a further difference between sensations and real perceptions, having to do with their representational character. As I have interpreted him, Descartes is suggesting there that ideas of colors, tastes and so forth are presented as mere sensations, while those of extension, figure and motion are given to us as exhibiting certain things or modes of things. And *this* proposition seems to be not obscure or ill-defended, but *false*. At the very least it is difficult to overcome the prejudices of one's youth to the extent necessary to perceive a relevant phenomenological difference between the 'ideas' of color and extension—or between the perceived color and the shape 'of' a particular object.[14]

A phenomenological distinction of the sort in question really does exist, I think, between pleasures and pains on the one hand, and the remaining 'sense perceptions' Descartes discusses, on the other hand. Descartes wants us to draw the subjective–objective distinction in another way, grouping colors, odors, tastes and so forth with pleasure and pain. He would like to believe that a phenomenological distinction can, in the end, be made to support this regrouping. I believe he is wrong.[15]

3 A God who can do anything

At the beginning of Meditation III Descartes reaffirms the certainty that he is a thinking thing, and raises the question whether he cannot derive from this single certainty a general conclusion about truth:[16]

> I am certain that I am a thinking thing. But do I not then also know what is required for me to be certain of anything? For in this first cognition there is nothing else, except a certain clear and distinct perception of what I affirm; which surely would not be sufficient to render me certain of the truth of the thing, if it could ever happen that anything which I perceived so clearly and distinctly were false; and hence I now seem to be able to establish as a general rule, all that is true which I perceive very clearly and distinctly. (AT VII, 35; HR I, 158)

He goes on to acknowledge that he had previously accepted as 'certain and manifest' many things which he now regards as doubtful: 'the earth, heaven, stars and all other things which I perceived by the senses.' But nothing of these had been clearly perceived, except 'the ideas or thoughts of such things,' which he still does not deny are in his mind. On the other hand, he only *thought* he clearly perceived that there were 'certain things outside of me, from which these ideas proceeded, and to which they were entirely similar.' In this he either erred, or, 'if I judged truly, this did not happen from the force of my perception' (*ibid.*). In other words, the certainty of the senses, which is now rejected, was not clear and distinct perception in the first place. Nevertheless, the 'general rule' he has proposed cannot be accepted without further question. The hypothesis of the Deceiving God returns in full force. According to his 'preconceived opinion of the pre-eminent power of God' [*summa Dei potentia*], it would be easy for God to bring it about that he errs 'even in those things that I intuit as evidently as possible by the mind's eye,' including the simplest propositions of arithmetic and geometry (AT VII, 36; HR I, 158). Since he has no reason to believe there is such a God, the reason for doubt that depends on this idea is 'very tenuous and so to speak Metaphysical.' Nevertheless to remove it he must investigate whether there is a God, and if there is, whether it is possible that he is a deceiver; 'for as long as this is unknown, I do not seem capable of ever being completely certain of anything else' (AT VII, 36; HR I, 159).

This suggestion that 'the mind's eye' might fail to perceive the truth under, so to speak, the best possible circumstances of 'vision' is, surely, the most striking and extraordinary part of the argument of the *Meditations*. It is the more remarkable when we remember that

Descartes is, with some justice, regarded as the founder of classical modern rationalism.

Now one might be tempted to suppose that the very feature of Descartes's thought that underpins his 'rationalism'—namely the thorough-going critique of the 'certainties of sense'—also generates or leads to the employment of the Deceiving God Hypothesis in its fullest force. Perhaps, to put it rather crudely, he felt bound to deal in some direct way with the question: If, as you say, the senses mislead us about the world, why should we trust our 'understanding' any more? However, it has sometimes been suggested that a different, still more extraordinary tenet of Descartes's philosophy lies at the root of his extraordinary questioning of mathematical certainty, and the deliverances of the 'eye of the mind' generally.[17] According to this suggestion, the Deceiver Hypothesis is connected in some fundamental way with Descartes's doctrine that the eternal truths are dependent on God's will and power no less than is the existence of creatures. I believe this suggestion is correct, and that it is of very considerable importance for understanding the argument of the *Meditations*. In what follows I will first expound the doctrine in more detail (with considerable reliance on Descartes's own statements), and consider some issues of interpretation and criticism. I will then try to show how the doctrine appears in the Third Meditation, in connection with the Deceiving God Hypothesis. Afterwards I will re-examine the problem of Cartesian circularity, with reference to this connection. Finally, I briefly take up the question of why Descartes should insist so strongly on (what I will call for the sake of brevity) the 'creation' doctrine.

Descartes expresses insistently his view that the eternal truths depend on God's will and power, beginning with a series of letters to Mersenne in 1630,[18] then in letters to other correspondents,[19] in *Replies to Objections*,[20] and in the *Conversation with Burman*.[21] One point that emerges as fundamental in most of these contexts is that it is inconsistent to deny that the eternal truths depend on God's will, while acknowledging the infinitude and incomprehensibility of God's power. (And it is blasphemous and 'unworthy' to think of God as lacking infinite and incomprehensible power; cf. for example letter to Mersenne, 6 May 1630: AT I, 149; PL 13–14; also to Mesland, 2 May 1644: AT IV, 119; PL 150–1). In the same contexts, Descartes repeatedly affirms that will and understanding are 'one' or indistinguishable in God (e.g. AT I, 149; PL 13–14), and some commentators have construed this notion of God's simplicity as the most fundamental basis for the doctrine.[22] However, it can also be viewed as a sort of corollary of the dependence of all truth on God's will—and I think the texts suggest that the latter doctrine is indeed more basic. Everything that is (and 'these truths are something') depends on God's creative will; *hence* there is no distinct realm of ideas or *pays des possibles* that is prior to his will. This view seems to lead to the conclusion that God could have made true what we cannot comprehend as possible: 'could have made contradictories true together.' But once we have granted God's incomprehensibility, it is perfectly in order (Descartes thinks) that this notion cannot be ruled out. Thus, to say we cannot comprehend how 'an aggregate of one and two' could be other than three is not to put a *limit* on His power; it is only another way of saying we can't comprehend His power. The following passages are representative.

[I]n general we can indeed affirm that God can do everything that we can understand, but not that He cannot do what we cannot understand; for it would be presumption [*temerité*] to think that our imagination has as great an extent as His power. (to Mersenne, 15 April 1630: AT I, 146; PL 12)

[S]ince God is a cause the power of which surpasses the bounds of human understanding, and since the necessity of these [mathematical] truths does not at all exceed our knowledge, they must be something less than, and subject to, this incomprehensible power [of God]. (to Mersenne, 6 May 1630: AT I, 150; PL 14)

You ask me by what kind of causality God established the eternal truths. I answer you that it is by the same kind of causality as He created all things, that is, as their efficient and total cause. For it is certain that He is as much the author of the essence as of the existence of creatures: but this essence is nothing other than these eternal truths, which I do not at all conceive as emanating from God like rays from the sun; but I know that God is the author of all things and that these truths are something, and consequently that He is their author. I say that I know it, and not that I conceive it or that I understand it; for one can know that God is infinite and all-powerful although our soul, being finite, cannot understand or conceive Him. . . . (to Mersenne, 27 May 1630: AT I, 151–2; PL 14–15)

As to the difficulty of conceiving how it was free and indifferent for God to make it not be true that the three angles of a triangle were equal to two right angles, or in general that contradictories could not be [true] together, one can easily remove it, by considering that the power of God cannot have any limits; then also, in considering that our mind is finite, and created of such a nature, that it can conceive as possible things which God has willed to be in fact possible, but not of such [a nature], that it can also conceive as possible those things which God could have made possible, but which He has still willed to make impossible. For the first consideration shows us that God cannot have been determined to bring it about that it was true [à faire qu'il fust vray] that contradictories cannot be [true] together, and that, consequently, He could have done the opposite; and the second [consideration] assures us that even though this is true, we should not try to understand it since our nature is not capable of doing so. (to Mesland, 2 May 1644: AT IV, 118; PL 150-1)

This doctrine seems to have provoked mainly bewilderment in Descartes's correspondents; from Leibniz to the present it has occasioned shock reactions as well.[23] Just how radical the doctrine is depends, however, on the answers to two interpretive questions, on which commentators have disagreed. The first question of interpretation is whether or not Descartes means the doctrine to extend to absolutely *all* truths, including truths about God's own nature and the most elementary logical principles. The second is whether or not he really means to affirm that any truth dependent on God's will is such that God *could have* made it false. It is evident that if the answer to both these questions is affirmative, Descartes is indeed committed to some weird results. He is committed, for example, to holding that God could have made it the case that nothing depends on His power, or that He never existed, or even that it's both true and false that everything depends on His power, and both true and false that He exists. Faced with these mind-bogglers, commentators have understandably turned to the texts for evidence in support of a negative answer to at least one of the questions.[24]

With respect to the first, it is in fact notable that Descartes, in presenting his doctrine, very often speaks specifically just of mathematical and physical truths, and the essences of *creatures*, as dependent on God's will—not of truths about God Himself. Also, he singles out the existence of God as the 'first' of the eternal truths—the one on which 'all others' depend; and he denies that the eternal truths are 'attached to God's essence' (AT I, 150, 152; PL 14, 15). (Could he deny that God's essence is attached to His essence?) Further, he twice indicates that God can't change the eternal truths He has once willed, which at least tells us that God can't make the same truths eternal and not eternal! (AT VII, 380, IX, 233; HR II,

226, B, 22) Finally, he seems to hold back from affirming that God is, strictly, his *own* efficient cause, though He *is* said to be the efficient cause of the eternal truths that depend on Him.[25] There is then some case for the view that Descartes primarily intended his doctrine to cover the truths of mathematics and physics.

On the other hand, Descartes does seem to countenance 'all creatures depend on God' as falling within the scope of his doctrine (AT IV, 119; PL 151). It is not easy—if it is possible at all—to avoid the conclusion that he must accordingly accept 'God is omnipotent' as falling within the scope of his doctrine.[26] But this is surely a theological proposition, and indeed an 'essential' one, if anything is; what's more, it is the very theological proposition on which Descartes's creation doctrine most squarely rests. Further, he does more than once say that 'all truth' depends on God (AT VII, 432-6; cf. V, 224; HR II, 248-51; cf. PL 236). Finally, even if Descartes did want to limit his doctrine to the eternal truths of mathematics and physics, it is not at all clear how the limitation could be other than arbitrary and *ad hoc*. If what we cannot conceive in the realm of mathematics is no guide to strict or absolute impossibility and necessity in that realm, why should our mental constraints be any surer guide in the realm of theology? It is by no means clear then, that we are entitled to 'save' Descartes from the more flagrant paradoxes by treating his doctrine as limited in scope.

The second question was whether Descartes means his doctrine to imply that God could have made the eternal truths different from what they are. This question is prompted by two considerations. First, Descartes does after all hold that will and understanding are *one* in God. But the idea that God could have made the eternal truths different seems to give primacy to will *over* understanding. Second, Descartes holds that God's 'indifference' is incomprehensible to us—and this *could* be a way of saying we don't really know *what* it implies.[27] If so, we are not justified in supposing it implies that He 'could have' created the eternal truths—or anything else—differently.[28] But whatever the merit of these observations, the last passage quoted above seems conclusive on the other side: 'God cannot have been determined to make it true that contradictions cannot be true together, *and therefore* He could have done the opposite.' Another letter, to Arnauld, has a somewhat similar implication, although it is more cautiously expressed:

It does not seem to me . . . that one should ever say of anything that it cannot be brought about by God; for since all concept of truth and goodness [*omnis ratio veri & boni*] depends on His

124

omnipotence, I would not dare to say that God cannot bring it about that there is a mountain without a valley, or that one and two should not be three; but I only say that He has endowed me with such a mind that it is not possible for me to conceive a mountain without a valley, or an aggregate of one and two which is not three, etc., and that such things involve a contradiction in my conception [*in meo conceptu*]. (to Arnauld, 29 July 1648: AT V, 223–4; PL 236–7)

It is clear enough from this that Descartes holds at least the following: there is no proposition of which we may say that God could not have made it true.[29] For we all know, in other words, it is within God's power to make true some proposition we regard as inconceivable. And the letter to Mesland that was previously quoted gives good grounds for attributing to him the stronger claim: we know that (at least) most of the propositions that seem to us necessarily true could have been false.

Should we then conclude that Descartes really is committed to the weird consequences mentioned above? Perhaps we should rather conclude, more cautiously, that he has not built into his position a way of avoiding these consequences. On the other hand, there is hardly any evidence that he ever confronted or recognized them—or, in other words, 'intended' them. Since some of his writings on the subject, such as the letter to Arnauld quoted above, do reveal a certain streak of agnosticism, one may speculate that Descartes might hold we simply cannot know what the implications of the creation doctrine are in such 'limiting cases' as truths about God himself. And this position is probably at least as defensible as would be an attempt dogmatically to restrict the implications of the doctrine to creatures' essences alone.

It is clear enough, in any case, that Descartes did regard the 'necessity' we perceive in mathematical propositions as in some sense and degree a function of the constitution of our minds—themselves finite 'creatures.' And even this relatively limited claim has been found extreme by some philosophers (such as Leibniz).[30] It would appear, however, that the history of epistemology and philosophy of mathematics since Descartes has tended very clearly to demonstrate that his position was far from wild, or excessively idiosyncratic. From Hume and Kant onward it has been widely held that alleged perceptions of 'necessity' cannot be taken for granted, and that we must in some sense or other have recourse to the structure and workings of our own minds to give an account of these 'perceptions.' In addition, there have been increasingly extensive doubts about the alleged ineluctable necessity or eternity of the traditional necessary (or eternal) truths. There is even a lively controversy among some leading philosophers of the present century whether logical necessity might not go the same way as the traditional 'necessity' of Euclidean geometry.[31] From this point of view what is really extraordinary is not Descartes's creation doctrine itself, but the fact that he has not been given more credit for arriving at it. Perhaps the theological basis of his position has stood in the way of a fair historical assessment of the original and important insight it embodies.

This brings us, however, to what may seem a crucial objection to Descartes's position. For doesn't his argument for the creation of the eternal truths rest on the premiss that *something* is inconceivable and *therefore* impossible: namely, that God's power be limited by independent necessities? And doesn't it conclude that inconceivability is not, absolutely speaking, a guarantee of impossibility? Doesn't it seem then, that Descartes's premiss requires an inference from the inconceivable (in his thought) to the impossible (*in res*), whereas the conclusion affirms that no such transcendent inference is possible? The problem could be avoided if theological and logical truths were exempted from the doctrine, but as we have just seen, there is not much to support such a proposed exemption.

I think Descartes can avoid this difficulty, without placing arbitrary restrictions on the scope of his doctrine. For he can express his position in the following manner, which does not require any inference from what is inconceivable to us, to what is really impossible.

> We must recognize that our *concept* of God has certain implications incompatible with the idea that the truths of mathematics, for example, absolutely could not have been otherwise than they are. We are then able to reconcile our *concept of* God's omnipotence with our conception of mathematical necessity, only by supposing that God, in creating us, has placed certain restrictions on what we can conceive—restrictions that make the scope of what we can (directly) conceive narrower than the scope of what He can actually do.

From this point of view the goal would be to render *harmonious* certain theological and mathematical intuitions or concepts. It is not a question of 'getting outside' certain of our conceptions (those of God), in order to determine that we are imprisoned behind the 'veil' of certain others.

There is a parallel to be drawn here with the problem of the illusoriness of the manifest image, as that problem arises for Descartes. The manifest (sensory) image of the world and the scientific (rational) image are in conflict—with the former seeming, initially, more vivid, compelling, obvious, even more 'distinctly known'[32] than the latter. The conflict is resolved by the thorough-going critique of the senses that is not concluded till Meditation VI, where Descartes establishes the limits of the usefulness and reliability of sensations. From the cognitive point of view, this critique involves placing the data of sense on a sort of *scale*, on which they can be judged inferior to the intellectual apprehensions of Cartesian science. The second major generative conflict of Descartes's philosophy arises (I now suggest) from the seeming incompatibility of the *theological* intuition that God's power must be absolutely infinite, and mathematico-scientific intuitions of necessity. The conflict is resolved in the position—so explicitly stated by Descartes in his letters—that God has created our minds in such a way that we cannot directly conceive the opposite of things he has willed to be necessary or eternal. Here too, then, the conflict is resolved 'upward.' For the intuition of God's infinite power is accorded priority over our seeming intuitions of ineluctable mathematical necessity. The latter are, like the data of the senses, ultimately 'put in their place': they are admitted as guides to our mind and the world, but not to the nature of God. And here again there is some question of a *scale* of intuitions: the idea of God is said to be 'the most clear and distinct' of any we find in our minds.[33]

I think, then, that Descartes's position can be defended against the charge of denying in its conclusion what it assumes in its premises—namely, the legitimacy of taking the inconceivable as a guide to what is really impossible. On the other hand, there is still a *sense* in which the doctrine does require us to get outside our own thoughts. It requires us to think of our minds as limited—limited in a way that will not be internally evident in a given perception. Thus, as a result of our own conceptions, we are forced to say that what is (specifically speaking) inconceivable to us may be possible in itself.[34] We are forced, then, to step back and recognize a sort of bifurcation between the deliverances of our intuition and what may be really the case. Our clearest thinking cannot be regarded as directly mirroring truth and reality; for God is introduced as a mediator, manipulating the workings of our mind at least in certain crucial respects. And this is where the doctrine of the creation of the eternal truths impinges on the Deceiving God Hypothesis—and returns us to the causal perplexities of Meditation I.

To put the matter succinctly, Descartes's creation doctrine in itself requires him to think of the human understanding as limited and constrained by God in certain respects. And this naturally if not

127

logically leads to the consideration that God, if perhaps malevolent, could in general be manipulating our thought to deprive us of access to the truth. The obvious solution, then, is to try to establish that the conception or intuition that originated the problem—that of God's omnipotence—is closely tied to another that will remove it—that of his 'perfection' and consequent benevolence.

Before considering the Third Meditation in this light, however, a note of caution is in order. I am suggesting that the creation doctrine *generates* (or helps to generate) the Deceiving God Hypothesis. But there is a very important logical distinction between the two. The creation doctrine tells us that the eternal truths 'could have been different' in a metaphysical sense of 'could have.' Except for rendering problematic certain of our modal intuitions in connection with these truths, however, it does not directly impugn our knowledge of what the truths *are*. The Deceiver Hypothesis, on the other hand, suggests that *for all we know* the eternal truths (and other 'distinctly perceived' propositions) *could be* different from what we take them to be. The Deceiver Hypothesis directly impugns (all our) knowledge; the creation doctrine does not.[35]

Returning now to the Third Meditation, I want to suggest that the connection between the doctrine of the dependence of the eternal truths on God's will, and the supposition that God is a deceiver, emerges rather clearly at just the point where clear and distinct perceptions are brought into question. To show this, it will be necessary to quote at length from a passage summarized above.

> When I considered anything very simple and easy concerning Arithmetical or Geometrical matters, as that two and three joined together are five, or similar [things], did I not at least intuit these things perspicuously enough that I might affirm them to be true? Indeed I have afterwards judged them to be doubtful, from no other cause than because there by chance came into my mind that some God could have endowed me with such a nature, that I was deceived about even those things that seemed most manifest. But whenever this preconceived opinion of the pre-eminent power [*summa potentia*] of God occurs to me, it is not possible for me not to allow that if he wishes, it is easy for him to bring it about that I err, even about those things which I think I intuit as evidently as possible by the eye of the mind. (AT VII, 35–6; HR I, 158)

It is, explicitly, the 'preconceived opinion of God's pre-eminent power' which causes one to doubt his simplest mathematical intuitions. Now of course it would be *consistent* with this passage to suppose that *all* that is at issue is God's power over our minds, and not his power over the eternal truths themselves. That is, the following hypothesis seems both logically consistent and consistent with this text: ' "2 + 3 = 5" is either true or false quite independently of God's power, but God does have the power to mislead the human mind into "perspicuously intuiting" that the proposition is true when it is in fact false.' Further, the passage does not so far directly raise any issue of necessity, impossibility or 'contradictoriness.' However, the remainder of the passage does provide a quite direct confirmation that the doctrine of the creation of the eternal truths is indeed connected with the Deceiving God Hypothesis, in the manner I have suggested above. Descartes continues:

> Truly whenever I turn towards those things which I believe I perceive very clearly, I am so completely persuaded by them, that I spontaneously break out in these words: let whoever can deceive me, nevertheless he may never bring it about that I am nothing, as long as I think I am something; or that it ever be true that I never was, when it is now true that I am; or even by any chance [*forte*] that two and three joined together be more or less than five, or similar things, in which I certainly recognize a manifest contradiction [*in quibus scilicet repugnantiam agnosco manifestam*]. (AT VII, 36; HR I, 158–9)

The affinities of this passage with Descartes's statements about the eternal truths should, I think, be apparent. His mind is unable directly to conceive the possibility that certain truths be other than they appear to him to be: to his mind their negations involve a 'manifest contradiction.' It is only consideration of the omnipotence of God that causes him to think that what seems to him impossible might be, or become true. And here the suggestion that the truths *themselves* depend on God is much clearer: the hypothesis of God's '*summa potentia*' is in conflict with Descartes's spontaneous conviction that no one can 'bring about' that he is nothing when he thinks he is something, that 2 + 3 = 5, and so forth.

Thus, the preconceived opinion of God's omnipotence calls into question Descartes's intuitions of necessity and impossibility, and with these even the *truth* of propositions he takes to be necessary. In fact, in this passage Descartes clearly *links* 'perspicuous intuition' of a proposition with perception of the contradictoriness of the opposite. Now we would not want to say that Descartes supposes we can only perspicuously intuit truths of which the opposite seems contradictory. (If he did, he could not make the claims about distinct perception of our own mental states, that appear in the Second Meditation.) On the other hand, consideration of the piece of wax passage has already shown some *tendency* in Descartes's thinking to assimilate the two. To the extent that he does make this assimilation, the creation doctrine may be even more closely linked with the Deceiver Hypothesis than I have previously suggested. For to this extent clear and distinct perceptions of truth are more or less equivalent to apprehensions of the contradictoriness of the opposite—i.e., apprehensions of necessity. But the latter are just what the creation doctrine serves to render problematic.

At this stage of the Meditation's argument, of course, the preconceived opinion of God's omnipotence is so far only an *opinion*: Descartes indeed goes on to remark that the reason for doubt that it generates is 'very tenuous and as I would thus say Metaphysical' (AT VII, 36; HR I, 159). This is just the sort of talk that has led later philosophers and critics to emphasize the 'undisruptive' and 'unreal' character of Cartesian doubt. And of course Descartes intends to *repudiate* the Deceiver Hypothesis, just as he eventually repudiates the supposition that for all he knows there might be no physical world at all. On the other hand, we must once again clearly recognize that the reason for doubt is not at all *fanciful* from Descartes's point of view, and is tied in with a fundamental positive doctrine. For he does want to hold that there really is an omnipotent God—and that the eternal truths really are dependent on His power. And this position does have implications for at least the *limitations* of our understanding.

In theory, it would be possible for Descartes to defeat the reason for doubt offered by the hypothesis of Divine deception, by going on to argue that it *is not after all tenable to suppose* that any being could 'bring it about that' propositions contradictory to my understanding are true. But of course he does not do this. Instead, he argues first that he *is* the creature of an infinitely powerful being, but that this being must be ascribed infinite perfection, and that it is inconsistent to suppose that an infinitely perfect being *would* create a creature so intrinsically defective as to be wrong even in his clearest perceptions:

> The whole force of the argument is in this, that I recognize it could not be the case that I exist of such a nature as I am, having the idea of God in me, if God did not also exist in truth, the same God, I say, of which the idea is in me, that is, having all those perfections, which I cannot comprehend, but can in some manner attain by thought, and which is liable to no defect. From which it

sufficiently appears that He cannot be deceitful; for it is manifest
to the light of nature that all fraud and deception depends on
some defect. (AT VII, 51–2, cf. 53; HR I, 170–1, cf. 172)

The idea of God that leads us to assert his omnipotence also reveals
his non-deceiving nature: a deceptive being would be an imperfect
being; but God as I conceive Him has 'all perfections.' Descartes thus
banishes the supposition of systematic error in a way consistent with
the doctrine that God *does* have the *power* to bring about things in
which he sees a manifest contradiction. (At the same time he answers
the other sort of worry that arose in connection with his sense of
dependence and creatureliness: that his cause might be too *imperfect*
to yield any perfection to his understanding.[36])

4 Circularity

The classical objection that Descartes's argument is 'circular' may be
formulated as follows. Consider just the final part of the argument of
Meditation III—the part quoted just above. Descartes claims to see by
the light of nature that deceptiveness is incompatible with perfection.
Now what can this mean except that he sees—perspicuously or clearly
and distinctly—a manifest contradiction in conjoining the ideas of
(complete) perfection and deceptiveness? But if he can trust such
perceptions, the proof is not needed. And if he cannot trust them,
the proof is not possible. In other words, the argument can proceed
only by presupposing what it is ostensibly trying to prove: that
perceptions of a very high degree of evidence or perspicuousness can
be relied on.

Now one might try to reply as follows, on Descartes's behalf.
Descartes's procedure is not circular, but dialectical. Descartes
expressly says that the only consideration that can cause him to doubt
of his most evident perceptions is the idea of God's pre-eminent
power. By subsequent reasoning he is able to disarm this
consideration, by recognizing that God must, by virtue of being
all-perfect, be non-deceptive as well as omnipotent. Descartes's
argument therefore consists in showing that his original notion of
God as a cause for doubt depended on an incomplete understanding
of his idea of God and its implications. Where is the circularity?

I do not think this reply succeeds. It does not avoid the original
difficulty: that to remove the Deceiver Hypothesis we must rely on
something the Hypothesis says we cannot rely on. Thus, if the idea of
God's omnipotence provides us with a reason for doubting our
mathematical intuitions, it seems to provide us with exactly the same

reason for doubting any other intuition, including further intuitions about God Himself.

In Chapter I I argued that when the hypothesis that our understanding is radically defective or deceptive is given its fullest scope, it not only undercuts any attempt to answer it, but also undercuts itself. If this is correct, Descartes can avoid circularity, or worse, only if the scope of his hypothesis can be non-arbitrarily limited. Now if the doctrine of the creation of the eternal truths *could* reasonably be limited to truths other than elementary theological and logical ones, and if it is true that the Deceiver Hypothesis arises more or less directly from the creation doctrine, we might have some hope of obtaining the necessary limitation on the scope of the former. For as we've seen, God's power *over* mathematical truths is implicated in the Third Meditation statement of the possibility of error in what seems most manifest. However, I have argued that there is really little textual basis for limiting the creation doctrine, and that from the philosophical point of view such a limitation would seem arbitrary anyway. (The doctrine does not leave us in a position to say that after all *some* 'necessities' are just as ineluctable as they seem.)

An alternative way of limiting the scope of the Hypothesis is suggested by Descartes's observation that the idea of God is the most clear and distinct of all. For suppose we designate the degree of distinctness possessed by the idea of God (as the all-perfect being) Dm, where 'm' stands for 'maximum.' Then we could ascribe to Descartes the claim that 'doubts' of distinct perceptions of lesser distinctness $Dm-n$ are removed by the *absolutely* distinct perception of God's perfection. What we rely on in the argument are perceptions of distinctness Dm; what the argument establishes is that other distinct perceptions of distinctness $Dm-n$ (variable n) are reliable also.

There are, I think, two things wrong with this suggested alternative. First, it too is vulnerable to charges of arbitrariness. If I am going to suppose that my understanding may be systematically deceptive/defective, there is simply no reason to feel reassured as the degree of 'distinctness' increases—even if it reaches something I detect as a maximum. Second, the assertion that the idea of God *is* the most clear and distinct is just not especially convincing. As in the case of perceptions of the physical world, one finds Descartes designating one idea as more clear and distinct than another, without providing his reader with sufficient illumination about the relevant difference between them.

Despite the difficulties, I think this might still be the best alternative for a supporter of Descartes to take. He could then combine the creation doctrine with the Deceiver Hypothesis—and its refutation—in something like the following manner.

> I have a perception of maximal distinctness (Dm) of an omnipotence so great that I am forced to recognize that it has power over even those truths that I perceive, distinctly but not to degree Dm, to be necessary and ineluctable. (In fact I perceive this power as being so great that I can't say that any truth—even those I perceive with *maximal* distinctness—is independent of it.) This perception of omnipotence, being still more distinct than my perceptions of mathematical necessity, and showing that the latter are even in some way misleading, gives me general reason to distrust all my intuitions, except those with distinctness of Dm. However, the reason for distrust can be removed if it turns out that perceptions proving God's non-deceptiveness (and existence) are equally distinct (Dm) as the original perception of His omnipotence. And in fact. . . .

The position Descartes actually takes in response to the circularity objection is a different one, however. He maintains in the *Replies* that the Deceiver Hypothesis renders doubtful only those conclusions that can recur in memory without our fully attending to their proofs (AT VII, 140-6, 246; HR II, 38-43, 115). That is, he tries to exempt from the scope of the Hypothesis not some sub-set of *maximally* distinct perceptions, but every distinct perception that does not rely on memory, *at the time we are having it*. This might mean that our *inability to doubt* while in the grips of a distinct perception somehow makes the Hypothesis irrelevant to what we're perceiving then. (And we can 'attend' to the premises needed to prove God till we reach the desired anti-skeptical conclusion.) But this line is unpromising. The crucial issue is whether we can *know* certain propositions prior to proving God; the observation that there are certain moments when we cannot for the moment doubt is epistemically irrelevant.[37]

Descartes may eventually have seen this. Thus Burman reports him as making, in a remarkable statement, the crucial epistemic move:[38]

> [The author] does use . . . axioms in the proof [of God], but he knows [*scit*] he is not deceived about these as long as he is attending to them, but while he does that he is certain he is not deceived. (AT V, 148; B xix, 6)

If Burman is to be trusted then, Descartes came to hold that he in fact could *know* the axioms of his proof (or anything else distinctly perceived) at the time of perceiving them; at that moment he knows no one is deceiving him. However after the moment passes he can no longer know that he knew—until the possibility of a Deceiver has been disproved.

This position may be internally inconsistent. If I *know* at t_1 that I'm not being deceived, I have *thereby* refuted the Deceiver Hypothesis with respect to t_1. How can I go on to claim at t_2 that an additional proof is needed to refute the Deceiver Hypothesis for t_1? Conversely, the claim Descartes is making at t_2 (that he might be of such a nature to be deceived in what seems most manifest), seems inconsistent with his *being able to know* at t_1 that he was not deceived. Descartes would have to reply that for all he knows at t_2 there is no time when he is not deceived, even though at t_1 he did know there is a time (namely, *now* = t_1) when he is not deceived. But then his position seems set up for the objection: if your knowledge at t_1 was useless at t_2, how can your knowledge of God at t_3 be useful at t_4?[39]

In any case, a philosophically serious (and somewhat less intricate) problem of consistency emerges when we compare the 'Burman position' with the text of Meditation III. As we've seen, Descartes there relates the Deceiver Hypothesis to his conception of God's omnipotence:

> Whenever this pre-conceived opinion of the pre-eminent power of God occurs to me, it is not possible for me not to allow that if He wishes, it is easy for Him to bring it about that I err, even about those things which I think I intuit as evidently as possible by the eyes of the mind (AT VII, 36; HR I, 158)

But Descartes cannot consistently maintain both this proposition about God and his later position on the circularity issue. If it is a *feature* of p's being 'most manifest' to him that he *knows* he's not being deceived, then it is not 'easy' for God to bring it about that he's deceived 'even in his most distinct intuitions.' But this proposition is not one that Descartes can nonchalantly abandon as a temporary misconception. To deny it would surely be to acknowledge a striking limitation on God's power.[40]

One other suggestion should be considered in conclusion of this discussion. According to an interpretation that has had considerable influence, there is no need to limit the *scope* of the Deceiver Hypothesis to avoid circularity. Rather, we must accept a more limited conception of its strategic role. According to this view, the objective of refuting this Hypothesis is not to establish that Descartes (or anyone) is not deceived in his clearest and most distinct perceptions. The issue at stake in Meditation III is rather the following: could it turn out that our understanding is in conflict with itself, in the sense that it provides a distinct perception that its most distinct perceptions might be wrong?[41] The task then, is to show that understanding is after all consistent, in that the possibility of a Deceiver is banished rather than confirmed by distinct perceptions.

The degree to which this interpretation can find support in Descartes's texts is a controversial matter.[42] But once again the more interesting question is how well it can stand up philosophically. It seems to me that this interpretation, while certainly ingenious, still does not avoid ascribing to Descartes a position that is ultimately arbitrary. After all, the Deceiver Hypothesis *does seem* to provide a reason for *doubting* that *distinct perceptions are true*—not just that they are consistent. *This* doubt cannot be removed by showing that distinct perceptions lead to a denial of the Deceiver Hypothesis. If one could show that in fact the Hypothesis does *not* provide a reason for doubting the truth of distinct perceptions, the restriction of concern to questions of internal consistency (including 'meta-consistency') might make sense. But the interpretation in question does not show this.

Nor do I quite see the *point* of Descartes's project on the interpretation we have been considering. Suppose it turned out that, sure enough, our understandings *are* inconsistent in the sense supposedly at issue. That is, we cannot rule out the possibility of constant deception, and we even 'clearly and distinctly perceive' that such constant deception is possible. So what? This discovery would have significance only if it tended to show that *our distinct perceptions might be false*. But according to the interpretation the Deceiver Hypothesis is not supposed to raise any such issue.[43]

Descartes's best hope of establishing a position that is significant, relatively non-arbitrary, consistent and non-circular seems to lie, then, in the notion of a scale of distinctness, as already indicated above. The perception of God's power is even more clear and distinct than perceptions of mathematical necessity; thus we are entitled to hold that the latter perceptions are subordinated to God's power. Similarly, the perception of God's perfection is more clear and distinct than our best intuitions of mathematical and scientific truth. We are entitled to rely on the latter just because they receive 'confirmation' from the most evident perception of all. However, it must again be remarked (and conceded) that this is not the line of defense that Descartes himself adheres to in his replies to the 'circularity' objection.

5 Physics and the eternal truth: a speculation

Why did Descartes attach such importance to the doctrine of the creation of the eternal truths? I have been assuming that the unlimited creative power of God, the dependence of all being on his will, was a genuine primitive intuition or basic premiss of Descartes's—just as he seems to present it.[44] But it is also natural to suppose that this doctrine must have seemed in some way *convenient* to Descartes—more congenial to other aspects of his system than the entrenched alternative position that necessity and possibility depend only on God's *understanding*.[45] It is certain, I think, that Descartes intends to mark off the *comprehensibility* of the world to us, from the incomprehensibility of God. That the eternal truths are God's creatures, his effects, means that we do not have to understand His nature in order to understand them. This point has been made in different ways by different commentators.[46] I would like to offer just one additional speculation. It is apparent from Descartes's very first statement of his doctrine (to Mersenne), that he regards it as connected with the view that the 'laws of nature' are knowable to us and imprinted in our minds. Now it is a conspicuous feature of Descartes's thinking about physical science that in this respect, as in others, the laws of nature share the traditional status of mathematical axioms. Descartes, however, does not want to deny that the laws of nature are dependent on God's will or power: indeed he relies on the conception of their dependence on God in expounding them.[47] To acknowledge the independence of mathematical truths of God's will or power would, then, have meant acknowledging a distinction between the status of mathematics and physics that seems repugnant to Descartes's whole conception of science.[48] Once again, Descartes's perspective, for all its archaism, has almost uncanny affinities with some 'advanced' present-day trends of thought.[49] It seems only fair to recognize that Descartes's philosophy of science, while crude in comparison to the well-developed theories of Leibniz and Kant, was not altogether lacking in inspiration and genius.

6 The proof of an all-perfect God

The 'circularity' objection is, of course, only one of many significant objections to Descartes's reasoning in Meditation III. Descartes's proof of the existence of an all-perfect God, from the idea he finds in himself of such a being, seems to be subject to even more difficulties than most purported theological proofs. I do not propose to discuss this argument in detail. I will merely briefly sketch the argument (or the core of the argument), and offer one specific objection to it.

136

Descartes claims to find in himself, among his other ideas, the idea of an infinitely perfect being. As a mode of a finite mind, this idea can have only finite 'formal' reality, or reality as what it *is*. However, as the idea *of* an infinitely perfect being, it has infinite objective reality: that is, its object is infinitely real.[50] (Here again reality must not be confused with existence: otherwise the existence of God would be overtly assumed in the premisses of the argument.) But, Descartes holds, it is self-evident that, just as everything must have a cause equal (at least) to itself, so any idea must have a cause with (at least) as much formal reality as the idea has objective reality. That is, there must exist a cause of my idea of God that has no less formal reality than the idea has objective reality. Hence, an infinitely perfect being must exist.

This proof relies on assumptions about causality that have been regarded as highly problematic at least since Hume. However, the argument can also be criticized without going very far beyond Descartes's own framework. For Descartes seems to have no plausible way of defending the crucial principle that the cause of an idea must have as much formal reality as the idea has objective reality. In the first place, there is the problem already mentioned of what exactly determines the degree of objective reality an idea possesses. But suppose we allow, for the sake of discussion, that an absolutely clear and distinct idea of an infinitely perfect being has infinite objective reality. Are we obliged to suppose that this idea has an infinitely real cause?

Well, 'where can an effect derive its reality, if not from its cause?' (AT VII, 40; HR I, 162). Yes, but why should we suppose that objective reality to degree n is as much reality *überhaupt* as formal reality to degree n? Isn't objective existence something less than formal existence? Descartes himself seems to reply affirmatively to this question:

> For if we suppose that any reality appears in the idea that was not in its cause, it therefore has this from nothing; but however imperfect is this mode of being, by which a thing is objectively in the intellect by an idea, nevertheless it is certainly not completely nothing [*non tamen profecto plane nihil est*], and hence it cannot come from nothing. (AT VII, 41; HR I, 163)

Descartes has simply made an arbitrary stipulation here. Why should the imperfection of objective being relative to real existence not mean that a cause with n degrees of formal reality—since it possesses this reality in the comparatively perfect mode of actual existence—bring about an idea with $n + m$ degrees of objective reality? If this objection has merit, Descartes has not successfully refuted the hypothesis that his creator is much less than all-perfect—and therefore perhaps a Deceiver.

IV

Judgment, Ideas and Thought

1 Regulating assent

The Third Meditation removed the 'doubt' of clear and distinct perceptions that derived from consideration of our mind's creatureliness and finitude, in comparison with our apprehension of the *summa potentia Dei*. In the Fourth Meditation, Descartes expands on this result.

> I experience that there is in me a certain faculty of judging, which certainly, together with all the other things that are in me, I received from God; and since he does not want to deceive me, he surely [*profecto*] did not give me such [a faculty] that, when I use it rightly, I can ever err. (AT VII, 53–4; HR I, 172)

But, of course, he does in fact err, and must admit this. The problem then is to explain the possibility of error, without supposing intrinsic defects in his 'faculty of judging.'

Descartes resolves this problem in a way that follows—at least from a superficial point of view—the traditional Christian solution to the problem of evil.[1] He maintains that judging involves, together with 'perception of the understanding,' a voluntary act of affirmation or denial, an assent or dissent towards what is 'perceived.' It is only by the concurrence of these two causes that error can arise,

> For by the understanding alone I perceive only the ideas of which I can make a judgment, and no error strictly speaking appears in it thus precisely regarded. . . . (AT VII, 56; HR I, 174)

While not itself directly the source or subject of error, the understanding is finite, lacking ideas—or clear and distinct perceptions—of a great many things. This is not a charge against

139

God: there is no reason why God should 'place in a single one of his creatures all the perfections which he can place in others.'[2] The will, on the other hand, is not even limited, and in particular is not limited by the perceptions of the understanding. The will is in fact the most perfect of our faculties: it alone is experienced as not circumscribed by any limits.[3] Descartes goes on to explain that will, or free will ('*voluntas, sive arbitrii libertas*')

> consists only in this, that we can do or not do a given thing (that is affirm or deny, pursue or flee), or rather only in this, that to that which is proposed to us by the intellect for affirming or denying, or pursuing or fleeing, we are so impelled [*ita feramur*], that we feel ourselves to be determined to it by no external force. (AT VII, 57; HR I, 175)

The more clearly the understanding perceives something, the more the will is impelled to affirm it; but since the impulsion is not experienced as external this in no way derogates from our freedom of choice. Rather, on the contrary,

> the more I am inclined in one direction, whether because I evidently understand in it the reason of truth and goodness, or because God so disposes the inmost part of my thought, the more freely I choose it. (AT VII, 57–8; HR I, 175)

On the other hand, the indifference I experience when no reason 'impels me in one direction rather than another' is 'the lowest grade of liberty.' This is the point at which error arises:

> since the will extends more widely than the understanding, I do not contain it in those limits, but extend it even to those things which I do not understand; to which since it is indifferent, it easily deviates from truth and goodness, and thus I err and sin. (AT VII, 58; HR I, 175–6)

Seemingly, then, Decartes thinks of the will as rashly attaching an act of assent to something that the understanding does not perceive or understand with sufficient clarity and distinctness.[4] In these cases the will is misused—and God is hardly to blame for any resultant error. The prudent and virtuous course in these cases is to 'abstain from judging' (AT VII, 62, HR I, 178).

The motivation of this account of judgment seems clear enough. Together with the theodicidic aspects, Descartes is concerned to ground the policy also put forward in the *Rules* and in the *Discourse*: do not try to exceed the limits of the understanding, only affirm what you clearly and distinctly perceive.[5] But the account itself is fraught with difficulties and confusions. I want to consider first certain problems in the account of understanding, and the notion of clear and distinct perception, in relation to the theory of *right* use of the will. I will argue that these are *partially* resolvable. I will then focus on the account of error—of the *wrong* use of the will in judging. I will suggest that we distinguish two lines of thought in Descartes's approach to the issue of erroneous judgment. One is neither plausible nor intelligible nor consistent with other aspects of his system; the other is more coherent and more credible.

One of the central difficulties in Descartes's treatment of the role of 'the understanding' in judgment has to do with the 'objects' of the understanding, ideas. Descartes tells us that ideas are what the understanding 'perceives,' and what it affirms and denies. Now previously he has said that ideas are like images of things, and as such neither true nor false. But clearly, what we affirm or deny are not 'images of things,' but propositions or propositional contents—and these *are* true or false independently of our affirmations or denials. (After all, what could error be but the affirmation of *what is false*, or the denial of *what is true*?) Descartes does not distinguish carefully enough the various *sorts* of mental representation (for example concepts and propositions), and he also tends to run together the notions of *falsity* and *error*. A mental image may fail to be true or false because it is a 'mere image,' not the sort of thing that has truth value. A proposition cannot fail to be true or false (except in special cases of vagueness or indeterminacy or failure of reference, etc.), but one may have a false proposition 'in the understanding' without being in *error*, if he merely considers it, without taking it to be true. Descartes should say that the ideas 'perceived by the understanding' may be (true or) false, but error arises not in the 'perception,' but in the affirmation.

But now we are confronted anew with the problem of what it can be to perceive an idea clearly and distinctly. And the problem arises here in a very untractable form. It cannot be sufficient, surely, to understand fully the *sense* of a proposition—for in that case clear and distinct perception would be no more closely allied with truth than with falsehood. We would not want to say that everything we fully understand in this sense is true, or compels the will. In the same way, it cannot be sufficient that the 'ideas' contained in a proposition are rendered distinct in the sense that the idea of the wax was rendered distinct (whatever exactly that was). For it seems that an idea *of* anything, however distinct it may be, could be combined with other ideas in such a way as to generate a false proposition. On the other hand, Descartes's doctrine of judgment effectively rules out the

141

possibility that to 'clearly and distinctly perceive p' (where p is a proposition) involves perceiving in some overwhelmingly lucid and evident way that p is true. For in that case there would be no logical gap between clearly and distinctly perceiving p and assenting to p. Assent would be inevitable not because of an irresistible impulsion of the will, but because of logical entailment. Thus, clearly and distinctly perceiving p must be more than merely *understanding* p, but less than apprehending p *as true*.

There seems to be one middle course. In discussing the Third Meditation, and also the piece of wax argument, I have called attention to the fact that Descartes to some extent associates the notion of clear and distinct perception with the notion of perceiving the contradictoriness of the opposite. Now, as the Third Meditation made clear, perceiving that the denial of p is contradictory is not the very same thing as perceiving that p is true. It is even in a sense conceivable that the negation of p be inconceivable, and yet that p is false. Yet we cannot help assenting to something when we perceive that the denial is contradictory (or inconceivable).

This provides us with a way of seeing how 'clear and distinct perception' of p might be more than mere understanding, without amounting to perceiving that p is true. According to the Third Meditation we don't strictly perceive that any proposition is true, since the best perception we can have is that of the contradictoriness of the opposite—and even this is not tantamount to truth.

From this point of view, Descartes's theory of judgment may seem not only consistent with other aspects of his position but positively required. That is, assent to p (taking p as true) cannot be reduced to an act of perception: 'something more' is required to bridge the gap between recognizing a proposition as intrinsically evident and affirming it as *true*. (The 'something more' might be supplied by postulating an irresistible attraction of the will.)

There are certain limitations on this suggestion, for, as we've already seen from his discussion of mind in Meditation II, Descartes does not want to say that we distinctly perceive only (what one might loosely call) necessary truths. I can also distinctly perceive that I am at a given moment thinking about God, seeming to see light, or doubting the existence of my dressing gown. In these cases, then, distinct perception cannot be understood in terms of perception of the contradictoriness of the opposite. The above suggestion about how it can be more than mere understanding but less than perception of truth is therefore not helpful here.

Now one could perhaps argue that perceptions of one's own mental states form a special class, and are not even meant to come within the scope of the theory of judgment. For it really appears that Descartes consistently thinks of these as somehow impervious to the Deceiver Hypothesis. Hence, he might be implicitly assuming that in the special case of *cogitatio* judgments there is no gap between perception and truth—between my perceiving that I seem to see light, or that I'm thinking of God, and its being true that I seem to see light, or am thinking of God. However, even if we accept this line of argument for *cogitatio* judgments, there are presumably still other distinct perceptions that also do not involve perception of the contradictoriness of the opposite: e.g. that 'the sun is of such and such a size,' etc. So I should limit my proposal to the following: very evident perception of the contradictoriness of the opposite of a proposition provides us with an *instance* of clear and distinct perception—one that allows us to see how such perception could be more than mere understanding, and less than apprehension of truth.

I don't mean to imply, in any case, that Descartes has a very clear and consistent grasp of the problem—had we but eyes to discern it. He does speak of clearly and distinctly perceiving *that* something is the case,[6] and it's hard to avoid supposing that he just didn't notice (or somehow didn't think) that this entails *taking* as true, and hence 'assenting.' Also, he seems to be rather carried away with the 'mind's eye' analogy—as many critics, of course, have pointed out. Thus, the fact that one needs to be able to view objects clearly in order to make reliable judgments about them (rather than say, perceiving them from afar) gives some sense to the admonition: 'Don't commit yourself ('internally') to views about objects that you don't perceive clearly.' But it's not easy to distinguish 'perceiving something clearly by the understanding' from simply understanding it. And while to understand a proposition is simply to know its sense, to understand an object or state of affairs is already to have views about it, to have made judgments. In order to form a reliable view about what's wrong with your car's engine I may have to view the engine in good light. But we can't say that in order to *understand* your car's engine, or the internal combustion engine generally, it's important that I fix an image or idea of the engine with a steadfast mental gaze without making any judgments. This picture is plausible, at most, in the special cases when intrinsic features of the proposition are the basis for affirming its truth—i.e. when the proposition is a 'necessary truth.' It's not at all clear that Descartes took account of this limitation of his analogy.

I believe Descartes's account of judgment is mixed up with another misleading analogy as well: the assimilation of truth with goodness. Descartes has indicated that a distinct perception of truth compels the will to assent to 'the true thing,' just as a distinct perception of goodness compels the will to pursue or seek the good thing. As 'all goodness and truth' depends on God's will, so our creaturely wills are determined by our perceptions of truth and goodness.[7] In the case of God, the attempted assimilation may be tied up with some of the paradoxical implications noted previously in Descartes's creation doctrine—and with his failure to take account of them. Thus, there is no evident paradox in supposing that it's good that God exists, because he wills to or wants to; what is paradoxical is to suppose that it's *true* that God exists, just because he wills to or wants to. In the case of man, such an assimilation also leads to confusion. Thus, there is no difficulty in distinguishing 'perceiving that x is good' and 'pursuing x': the first is a cognition and the second is not. But it is deluded to suppose that the same distinction can be made between 'perceiving that p is true' and 'assenting to p.' It's not clear that Descartes did not succumb to this delusion. However, as I've tried to show above, we can provide a partial interpretation of his theory that doesn't require this non-existent—or at least extremely problematic—distinction. According to this interpretation, that I 'clearly and distinctly perceive' p doesn't logically entail that I 'assent to' p, or accept p as true—even though such perception may be somehow *causally* sufficient for assent.

I turn now to certain problems that emerge for Descartes's theory when we consider cases of judgment where clear and distinct perceptions are supposed to be *absent*—in other words, those cases where we 'use our free will wrongly' and hence are liable to 'going astray.' (It is only here that we confront his theory of error *per se*.) Descartes's account suggests that in these cases the will arbitrarily and, so to speak, wantonly affirms propositions that are only 'obscurely perceived,' not 'known by the understanding.' There is even some suggestion that a special effort is involved in doing this: in the absence of distinct perceptions the will is in a state of 'indifference,' is not impelled. Here it is clear there *has* to be something wrong.

First there is the question of *motivation*: why, one may ask, would the will do a thing like this? Descartes's account is sometimes assimilated to believing something on inadequate evidence because one *wants it to be true*, but I think this is a mistake. There is no basis for this construal in the text, and it would not fit easily with Descartes's stress on the will's 'indifference' between affirmation and denial in these cases. A perhaps more warranted view is that Descartes supposes a sort of lust for knowledge leads us to affirm or deny things we are not justified in believing or disbelieving. This suggestion

144

would fit in with a good deal of what is said in the *Discourse* and, especially, the *Rules* about the sources of human error and confusion.[8] Or it is possible that, at least some of the time, Descartes thinks of the will as wandering among confused perceptions like a lost soul with no fixed purpose in life: embracing this or that one for no definite reason.

This account of the will's role in our cognitive life still seems on the slightest reflection most implausible; it may in fact postulate as a *general* occurrence something that is psychologically impossible under even the most recondite conditions. Thus E. M. Curley has argued that Descartes's account of erroneous judgment must be wrong just because it falsely implies the *possibility* of coming to accept something or believe it to be true by a bare act of will.[9] In particular, the assimilation of judging to 'pursuing or fleeing' suggests that accepting or rejecting a proposition is something we do on the basis of a *decision*. The more evidence we have the easier the decision is, but, it seems, we might just make a decision when we have no evidence at all, and know we don't—in an arbitrary manner, so to speak. But of course we can't just decide to believe or assent to something, and forthwith believe or assent to it.[10] Curley argues plausibly that we can discover phenomenologically that this is impossible.

In any case, according to the story of the Fourth Meditation, affirming obscure ideas is a lot like picking and eating apples in the dark. If in our greed for apples, or simple insouciance, we consume them all under palpably bad conditions of discrimination, we can't fairly blame God for our subsequent bellyaches. In other words, I get myself into error just in so far as the following conditions hold: (a) I perceive my evidence for p is inadequate;[11] (b) I decide to affirm p; (c) I forthwith, inwardly, commence to believe p. To the extent that Descartes's account implies this picture—and it surely does, to a considerable extent—it is a very poor account. I will argue, shortly, that it is also inconsistent with much of what Descartes says elsewhere in the *Meditations*, and set forth an alternative line of reasoning that Descartes might (more consistently and coherently) have offered. First, though, I want to show that *one* seemingly cogent objection to Descartes's account is not really effective against it.

We noted above that if 'clearly and distinctly perceiving p' is taken to mean or imply, 'perceiving that p is true,' all the work of assent is already ascribed to the understanding—there is no room, logically, for an act of will. And it may seem that a similar objection can be raised with respect to Descartes's account of what does or should happen when we do *not* 'clearly and distinctly perceive that p.' Thus,

145

Spinoza has claimed, against the Cartesian view, that 'when we say that someone suspends judgment, we are saying only that he sees that he does not perceive the thing adequately.[12] Curley restates, and endorses, Spinoza's position in the following terms:[13]

> Suspending judgment—insofar as it is something mental, not the abstention from a public pronouncement—is not an action I take as a consequence of finding the arguments pro and con are pretty evenly balanced. It is simply the state itself of finding them to be so.

Curley goes on to comment that the claim is 'a sample of' conceptual analysis, rather than introspective psychology or armchair linguistics. So, according to the Curley-Spinoza position, there is no room logically for an act of will, or an abstention, in cases where one does *not* distinctly perceive that p is true—as long as one is aware that this is so. To say that one is aware of one's perception not being sufficiently evident, or one's arguments not being conclusive on either side, *is to say* that one suspends judgment.

In this case, however, the objection is not so convincing. That one perceives that p is true does seem to entail that one assents to p. But it is not at all clear that one's 'seeing one perceives p inadequately' or seeing that the arguments for and against p are inconclusive (or 'evenly balanced') entails that one suspends judgment on p. May one not believe or judge *in the face of* the evidence, the arguments, or the awareness of 'inadequate perception'? If so (and it does seem that this is possible) there is so far no *logical* absurdity in the Cartesian view that something *more* than 'perception' is involved in judgment—or in the Cartesian injunction to avoid assenting under conditions of less than distinct perception, or less than conclusive evidence. (Curley himself, on the page before the statement quoted above, remarks: 'We can withhold our judgment, all the while allowing that the weight of evidence favors p.' I am unable to see how this statement, which I regard as quite correct, is consistent with the further, Spinozistic, claim that suspending judgment 'is simply' the state of finding the arguments pro and con pretty evenly balanced.) Descartes's theory of error is not, then, objectionable just because it implies the logical compatibility of recognizing one's evidence is less than adequate, and *not* suspending judgment. Nevertheless, we have seen that there are other conclusive grounds for rejecting his account.

I want now to see how much can be salvaged of the essential philosophical purposes of the Fourth Meditation, with respect to the problem of avoiding error, if we set aside the notion of random acts of will directed at palpably obscure 'perceptions,' and concentrate on some other features of what Descartes is holding or implying. A fundamental point, surely, is that while we 'can' and very frequently do assent to propositions that are not distinctly perceived, so we 'can,' at least in principle, avoid doing so. It is this second theme that I now want to explore.

First we should observe that Descartes's use of the concept of 'obscurity' has certain weasel-like features which figure prominently in the difficulties of Meditation IV—as they did in the treatment of material falsity. If we can't see the apples we're picking we generally know that; their obscurity is manifest. But what about the obscurity of our ideas? It seems that in the Fourth Meditation Descartes lets us suppose that obscure ideas are palpably obscure, in order to put us in a position of very extreme culpability for our errors. Hence the problems we have noticed with respect to motivation (why would the will do that?) and possibility (and *can* it do that?). But we already know very well from the First and Second Meditations that obscure ideas—at least of the senses—may very well have the specious quality of *seeming distinct*. According to the Third Meditation, they may have the even more specious quality of material falsity. The ideas of sense, then, do not strictly *seem obscure*—certainly not to routine commonsense, and much of the time not even to the critical philosopher. Far from wantonly embracing them by an act of will, Descartes has need of a constant effort of will to avoid constantly succumbing to them! The seeming clarity of the senses tempts us to believe—even apart from any immoderate desire to feel we 'know.' Affirmation of an obscure idea, then, must be more *like* following a natural bent than like making arbitrary decisions when all paths seem equal. From a rational point of view the act is not compelled; it may still have another sort of determination.

Here, then, we meet again the ambivalence about 'obscurity' that was manifest in Descartes's reply to Arnauld's criticism of his treatment of material falsity. There Descartes wanted to say that the obscurity of the ideas of sense were responsible both for 'our not being able to tell' whether they represented something rather than nothing, *and* for our being inclined to take them as objectively real. What Descartes *should* hold, I think, is that we don't customarily notice that our ideas of sense, for instance, are obscure, but this feature (or rather the absence of distinctness) can be discerned by someone with a steady resolve to seek the truth. (The argument of the *Meditations* would admittedly be much strengthened if only he could tell us how this feature of obscurity can become evident.)

147

This view would avoid some of the salient difficulties in the 'random acts of will' account while still, I think, allowing Descartes to argue that error is in principle avoidable. Since the absence of distinctness is discern*ible*—though not always and indeed seldom discerned—and since distinctness is a sufficient guarantee of truth, in principle one *can* avoid falling into error.

Let me spell out more formally my reconstruction of this theme in Descartes's treatment of judgment.

(1) One risks error if and only if one assents on less than completely adequate evidence. (This is to be read as a tautology: 'adequate' here means 'truth guaranteeing' rather than, say, 'sufficient to warrant publication.')

(2) One has completely adequate evidence for p (on a given occasion) if and only if one then clearly and distinctly perceives p.

(3) One can know whether one's perception on a given occasion is clear and distinct.

(4) One can know 1 and 2.

(5) On any occasion when one knows one risks error by assenting or dissenting, one can avoid assenting (or dissenting).

(6) Hence, one can avoid falling into error.

Now there are of course very serious difficulties with this position deriving from the notion of an infallible mark of truth, as postulated in premises (2) and (3). Intellectual history of recent centuries makes it very difficult to suppose that an individual's ability to conceive something could ever supply any kind of lasting standard of truth, if we assume any interpersonal consistency condition at all. And there is, I think, no way to interpret the *clearly and distinctly* condition that will altogether overcome this problem. Descartes may have *just known* that he had a more distinct perception of geometrical propositions than his housekeeper or even than Beeckman; but Leibniz, Newton, Euler and Riemann provide a different sort of challenge. In addition, the argument fails to make clear whether the conclusion that we can avoid error is of much interest from a scientific point of view: as far as the argument goes, I might never have any clear and distinct perceptions and hence avoid error only at the cost of assenting to nothing at all. (Though of course Descartes thinks he has already shown that we don't have to worry about this.)[14] For present purposes, however, I want to set aside this objection. I want to ask whether a position incorporating premiss (5) would be acceptable, assuming the criterion of clear and distinct perception could be maintained.

First, note that (5) apparently does not commit one to the claim that judgment is a matter of bare acts of will being directed to what is (or is not) evident. It is clear that 'can' in propositions (3), (4) and (6) should be read 'it is in one's power to,' and I see no reason why it should not be so read in premiss (5) as well. One can have this much of Descartes's objective without taking judgment to be directly dependent on will in the sense previously criticised. For example, it might be within my power to avoid assenting to p just because it's within my power to concentrate my attention, whenever I think of p, on the fact that my evidence is inadequate; in so far as I do this it follows, perhaps, as a matter of psychological necessity that I do not judge that p. This sort of story shows, I think, how one could hold that it is 'within our power' to 'withhold assent' without being committed to any particular view about the nature of judgment. Descartes's unfortunate theory of judgment is merely consistent with the argument sketched above; it is not entailed by it.

One may feel though that premiss (5) is still vulnerable to certain objections not very different from some of those discussed above in connection with the account of judgment. For doesn't it at least imply the existence of some kind of acts of assent (dissent), some kind of *judgings*—and isn't it at best questionable whether there are any such things? (Or, more generally, are the concepts of inner assent or dissent sufficiently clear and distinct?) Let us try to avoid this objection by putting the problem in still simpler terms. Is it always within our power to avoid forming an opinion when we perceive that the evidence for or against the proposition in question is less than adequate? It seems to me the answer is as follows: it is *empirically implausible* to suppose that our belief-formation is within our power to this extent. Therefore, I'm inclined to say that (5) is probably false, regardless of what we make of the 'clear and distinct perception' criterion. Nevertheless it is not *preposterous* in the way that the rejected theory of arbitrary acts of will is (surely) preposterous. And it is not (to repeat) inconsistent with Descartes's normal treatment of sensory prejudice.

If these observations are correct, it may be necessary to conclude after all that God *is* a deceiver in the restricted sense at issue in the Fourth Meditation. That is, He has *not* made me such that it is within my power always to control my assent; there are times when I just cannot help believing against the evidence, or despite the lack of evidence. This would not in itself entail that He is a deceiver in the sense that seems to be at issue in the Third Meditation. That is, it would not entail that He made me subject to deception in my most evident perceptions. (Sometimes Descartes himself seems to suppose that this is all that we should really require.¹⁵) However, historical considerations make even this weaker vindication seem untenable.

One more observation should be made, in conclusion, on Descartes's behalf. The Christian account of sin, on which he tries to model his theory of error, is surely in itself an idealization, considered in relation to our actual experience. The alleged dependence of our actions on our free will need not be taken to imply that a certain perverse determination is required in order to sin, or even that our experience tends to show that we always can avoid sinning if we only make up our minds to do so. So perhaps Descartes should say simply that his account of error makes it no less consistent with God's goodness, than sin is on the traditional theory of action. And whether or not this claim is strictly true, it does seem correct that the rationality of our belief-structure can to a *considerable extent* be influenced by matters within our control: by reflection, mental discipline, and so forth. This seems to be the element of truth in the Fourth Meditation (and it is something that, surely, Spinoza himself absolutely accepts).

A final caution. In considering the question whether judgment and action are comparably voluntary, we must carefully distinguish the concept of voluntariness *as control*, from that of first-order wants. Judgment is *un*like action in *not* involving desires on the first level. If when we say sin is voluntary we mean, say, that I eat the apple because I want or desire the apple, we cannot transfer the voluntariness of sin to judgment. I don't judge that the apple is red because I want to, or because I want it to be the case that the apple is red. The parallel can be maintained at all only in so far as 'sin is voluntary' means 'it is within our power not to sin.' But this, I have been suggesting, is just the perspective from which Descartes's Fourth Meditation argument has most interest and plausibility.

2 Consciousness

'Thought' enjoys a peculiar epistemological status in Descartes's system, as is evident from passages we have already considered from the central parts of the *Meditations*. I have occasionally characterized this status as 'epistemological transparency,' intending to suggest that we can, according to Descartes, somehow know our thoughts through and through, unproblematically. In this section I will explore Descartes's views about the epistemology of thought in a little more depth. This will prove a more complicated subject than one might at first suppose. I will argue that in the end the doctrine of epistemological transparency cannot be reconciled with other central features of Descartes's philosophy, including the conception of 'confused perception,' and his treatment of innate ideas.

The notion of epistemological transparency includes the two following theses, which are often supposed to lie at the heart of Descartes's philosophy of mind:

(1) My knowledge of my own mental states is certain and infallible; my judgments about them cannot be erroneous.

(2) There is nothing in my mind of which I'm not in some manner conscious.

There can be little doubt that Descartes did hold both these theses in some sense or other.

Consider, first, the evidence that he held (1). The Second Meditation tells us that 'I think' is indubitable, and ultimately includes under 'I think' a long enumeration of more specific mental activities: I will, affirm, deny, imagine, seem to sense, etc. Further, the certainty of 'I think' is casually extended to judgments about particular *cogitationes*: I seem to feel heat, see light, hear sound. The Third Meditation goes even further. It introduces, with hardly a nod to the 'Deceiver,' complex classifications and analyses of the ideas and other 'thoughts' that are 'in me' (AT VII, 35; HR I, 158). Thus, while Descartes can doubt the existence of all sorts of things, he regards as beyond doubt the fact that he has the 'ideas of' those sorts of things. He distinguishes ideas into three classes, according to their apparent cause or source: invented by him, apparently innate and apparently 'adventitious' (AT VII, 37–8; HR I, 160). He distinguishes his ideas or perceptions into clear and distinct and otherwise. He distinguishes mental states into ideas 'properly so called' and thoughts compounded out of an idea and 'another form' as in the cases of fearing lions, loving God and so forth (AT VII, 37; HR I, 159). And he implies that all mental states can be analyzed on this model. He makes confident determinations of the 'objective reality' of his ideas. As to freedom of will, it is not explicitly affirmed in the *Meditations* until after the proof of God; however, in the *Principles* the will is declared to be free even before the *cogito* is considered! (AT VIII–1, 6; HR I, 221). One could go on, but the point should be clear. Descartes does not merely exempt 'sense data judgments,' or simple recognition of what's 'going on in our mind' at a given moment, from the power of the hypothetical Deceiver. He is prepared to elaborate the major part of his philosophy of mind before dealing with the question whether a Deceiving God might exist.

This shows once again how far Descartes is from giving the Deceiver Hypothesis the full force that seems, logically, to be implicit in it. It is consistent with the view expressed above, that the principal sources of 'Cartesian doubt' are Descartes's scientific realism and his commitment to the dependence of the eternal truths on God's will. For neither of these two underlying aspects of his philosophy have direct bearing on the status of judgments about thought. It is also, of course, consistent with the view that Descartes *just found* thoughts to be 'so close and so interior to our soul,' that we can't make a false observation about them. (Cf. AT XI, 348; HR I, 343)

It is perhaps not quite clear whether or not holding proposition (1) by itself commits one to holding proposition (2). If (1) is interpreted as denying just the possibility of *error* with respect to one's own mental states it might be compatible with *ignorance* of some of them. This would be possible if, in the particular case of mental states, one could always tell when one is ignorant (so that ignorance would not lead to error). Proposition (2) is, in any case, clearly assumed in the Third Meditation, and stated explicitly elsewhere. In the Third Meditation, after the initial proof of God's existence, Descartes tries further to establish that God is necessary not only to provide him initially with the idea of God, but also to maintain him in existence. Accordingly he argues (rather quaintly to be sure) that if he had the power to maintain himself in existence he would be conscious of it:

> Thus I must now ask myself, whether I have any power, by which I can bring it about that the very I [*ut ego ille*], who now am, also will be a little later: for, since I am nothing else except a thinking thing, or at least since I am now concerned only with that precise part of me which is a thinking thing, if any such power is in me, I would without doubt be conscious of it. But I experience none to be, and from this itself I know most evidently that I depend on some other entity diverse from me. (AT VII, 49; HR I, 168–9)

In the Second Replies and in the *Principles* (I, 9) he *defines* thought in terms of consciousness or immediate consciousness. It is 'that which is in us in such a way that we are immediately conscious of it' (AT VII, 160; HR II, 52; cf. AT VIII–1, 7–8; HR I, 222). In the First Replies he says he can 'affirm as certain that there can be nothing in me of which I'm in no way conscious'—as long as he is only considering himself as a thinking thing (AT VII, 107; HR II, 13). In replying to Arnauld he says this proposition is 'self-evident' (AT VII, 246; HR II, 115). In confirming this reply, in a letter to Mersenne, he writes:

> As to [the proposition] . . . *that nothing can be in me, that is, in my mind, of which I am not conscious*, I have proved it in the *Meditations*, and it follows from the fact that the soul is distinct from the body and that its essence is to think. (AT III, 273; PL 90)

The remark to Mersenne is a little curious since 'the fact that the soul is distinct from the body' isn't supposed to be established until the *Sixth* Meditation; yet the principle in question is assumed in the Third. But probably Descartes has here simply telescoped the two ideas that (a) in so far as I am considered merely as a thinking thing, there is nothing in me of which I am not conscious; and (b) *I am*, most basically, a substance of which 'the whole nature and essence is only to think.'[16] In the Third Meditation Descartes should be arguing that in so far as he is merely a thinking thing he does not have the power to maintain himself in existence. He does not need the conclusion that *he is* essentially only a thinking thing to make this particular point.

There is, then, ample justification for ascribing to Descartes both (1) and (2). On the other hand, as a number of scholars have demonstrated in recent years, there is also ample reason to deny that he held to either of these propositions consistently, or in an unqualified form.[17] But before considering the other side of the issue I would first like to take up, in a preliminary way, an important question of interpretation. The question is, how should we understand the relation *between* (1) and (2)? What relation, in other words, should we suppose to obtain between the 'consciousness' mentioned in (2) and the 'indubitable knowledge' mentioned in (1)?

It is hard to know what being conscious of x could be, if it did not in *some* way involve having knowledge of x —knowing that x exists or occurs. And it is clear that Descartes does regard the concepts of consciousness and knowledge as, at least, closely connected. When he says in the Third Meditation that he could not fail to be conscious of having the power to maintain himself in existence if he did have it, he clearly means he could not be *ignorant* of such a power. To similar effect, the French version of the *Meditations* and *Replies* generally gives *'avoir connaissance de'* [*mes pensées*] for the Latin *'esse conscius.'* But should the 'consciousness' of (2) be read as the *certain and indubitable* knowledge of (1)? If so, the first principle leads to a relatively strong reading of the second, viz:

(2′) There is nothing in my mind of which I don't have certain and indubitable knowledge.

But then we are in a position to argue that Descartes is also committed by (1) and (2) to a much stronger position than (2′), namely:

> (3) My cognitions and judgments concerning my own mental states can never involve error *and* there is never any internal or intrinsic feature of my own mental states of which I am ignorant. (The phrase 'internal or intrinsic' is intended to rule out certain relational features, such as 'occurring to me 10 minutes after you thought of the sun.')

For suppose I have a thought or idea *I* which has feature *F*. Then *F*, by virtue of being an internal or intrinsic feature of something (formally) in my mind is *itself* 'something in my mind.'[18] It will follow that I must be conscious of *F* and hence, by the supposed entailment, have certain and indubitable knowledge of it.

But could I not have certain and indubitable knowledge of, *and* be in error concerning, something in my mind (as I might have both genuine knowledge of, and false beliefs concerning something in my living room)? Only, it seems, if I can know certainly and be in error concerning the very same *proposition about it*. Thus, suppose *F* is the precise degree of clearness and distinctness possessed by my idea or perception *I*. Then, according to our hypothesis I must be conscious of, and have indubitable knowledge concerning, the precise degree of clarity and distinctness possessed by this idea or perception. But how could my possessing 'certain knowledge of the precise degree of distinctness of my idea' be compatible with my not knowing *what* the precise degree *is*? There seems to be no way of establishing that I might not know the truth value of any proposition concerning (exclusively) internal features of my thoughts that would be compatible with the principles stated above. And if I do *know* the truth values of these propositions, can I also be in error concerning them? Now perhaps the answer is yes. Perhaps, for example, there is more than one 'way' of knowing that p; if so, we could know that p in one way, while being in ignorance or error about it in some other way. In fact, Robert McRae has held that this is precisely Descartes's position: that a distinction between types of knowledge or ways of knowing enables Descartes to allow that we may be in ignorance or error concerning 'things in us,' consistently with the principle that we are conscious of everything in us.[19] But before considering this view, we should first take note of some of the evidence that Descartes does *not* consistently adhere to (3)—at least in an unqualified form.

There is much to show that Descartes does think we can be ignorant of much that is in us as thinking things. For example,

Descartes begins the Third Meditation with the objective of making his thinking self more 'known and familiar' to himself.[20] In the Fifth Meditation he points out that certain of his ideas, such as that of a triangle, contain features which he had not 'in any way previously thought of' when he imagined a triangle (AT VII, 64; HR I, 180). This fact is used to establish a distinction between ideas he might have invented, and those which, representing 'true and immutable natures,' could not depend on him. This distinction is a crucial step toward the Fifth Meditation's presentation of the Ontological Argument. (Thus the proposition that we cannot be ignorant of what is in us, *and* the proposition that we need not be aware of all that is in our ideas, *both* figure in Cartesian arguments for the existence of God!) Further, in a letter Descartes remarks that it is 'the most perfect method of demonstration: to draw out of an innate idea something that was indeed implicitly contained in it, but which I did not at first notice in it' (AT III, 383; PL 104). (In another letter, discussed below, Descartes seems to indicate that we need not 'notice' a given innate idea at all.) Finally, Descartes's whole theory of the distinction between confused and distinct ideas, and hence his general theory of knowledge and error, depend on the possibility of our failing to discern intrinsic features of our ideas. Thus, for example, Descartes's idea of the wax changed from being obscure and confused to being clear and distinct 'according as my attention is more or less directed to the elements which are found in it, and of which it is composed' (AT VII, 31; HR I, 155). The difference between having a confused idea of x and having a distinct idea of x is drawn in terms of our *awareness or perception* of what is in the idea, rather than in terms of what *is* in the idea.[21]

Descartes also thinks we can make erroneous judgments about our ideas and mental states. For example, we may fail to notice of a simple idea that it is simple, and erroneously suppose that it contains something hidden from us (AT X, 420; HR I, 42); we may think an idea or perception is clear and distinct when it is not (AT VIII-2, 352; HR I, 438); we may—as discussed at length above—mistakenly suppose an idea is objectively real when it is not.[22]

There are three principal distinctions in Descartes's writings that can help us to rationalize his failure to accept (3) in an unqualified form. There are: a distinction between actual and potential consciousness; between implicit and explicit knowledge; and between reflective and non-reflective cognition. (The last two are both connected in some way with the concept of 'attention' which comes to the fore in the wax passage just quoted.) Professor McRae believes, I think, that these distinctions—or more exactly the latter two—are sufficient to provide Descartes with a coherent over-all theory concerning knowledge and ignorance or error concerning 'what is in us.' In my opinion this position is overly optimistic: Descartes's theory is not in the end satisfactory. But before taking up this issue directly, I want first to deal briefly with an important terminological issue.[23]

Analysis of Descartes's philosophy of mind is generally complicated by the fact that there is no great consistency in his use of the central term 'idea.' Sometimes he speaks of 'thoughts or ideas' as if the two terms were synonymous. In one place, as we've seen, he says ideas in the strict sense are a subclass of his thoughts—those that are 'like pictures of things' *simpliciter*, without attitudes of fearing, affirming, etc. attached. This is apparently consistent with his statement in the *Meditations*' preface that 'idea' can be understood *either* as an 'operation of understanding' or as 'the thing represented by this operation' (which need not 'be supposed to exist outside the mind' (AT VII, 8; HR I, 138).[24] Elsewhere, however, an idea is said to be 'that form of a thought by the immediate perception of which I am conscious of that thought' (AT VII, 160; HR II, 52). And in this usage 'idea' has no specific connection with understanding or representation. We are conscious of *every* thought—where 'thought' is used in its usual broad Cartesian sense. And to be conscious of a thought is just to be aware of its 'idea':

> I claim that we have ideas not only of all that is in our understanding but also of all that is in the will. For we cannot will anything without knowing that we will it, nor could we know this without an idea; but I do not hold the idea is different from the action itself. (AT III, 295; PL 93)

> I use the term idea for whatever is immediately perceived by the mind, so that when I will and fear, since I at the same time perceive that I will and fear, that same volition and fear are numbered among my ideas. (AT VII, 181; HR II, 67–8)

(Note that Descartes seems to treat 'be conscious of,' 'know that,' and 'perceive that' as equivalent for purposes of expressing this claim.) When Descartes says an idea is the 'form of a thought,' he seems to mean just the determinate nature of that particular thought—e.g. fearing-a-lion.[25]

In the usages so far mentioned, the term 'idea' is tied rather closely to the notion of a mental *act*, an occurrent thought. However, when Descartes speaks of an idea as an *object in* the mind, what is represent*ed* ('the thing represented by the operation of the understanding') he is of course not restricting the term to mental acts. Thus, when I think of God, the idea of God is in some sense the object of my mental act.[26] In some passages, Descartes goes so far as to say that having an idea of God is to 'have the aptitude to perceive [the idea] explicitly,' though we may never notice it even after the thousandth reading of the *Meditations*; or to have 'the faculty of knowing him,' even though one may never 'distinctly represent this idea' to himself.[27] In such contexts the notion of 'idea' is tied to mental latency, rather than mental acts.[28] So perhaps Descartes wants to hold that we are invariably conscious of our mental acts, and of our ideas considered as either forms or objects of such acts; however, there are also 'in us' certain mental latencies, also referred to as 'ideas,' of which we are *not* conscious. Thus, we have in us the faculty to know God: i.e. we 'have,' in one sense of 'have,' the idea of God. However, we do not know we have this faculty, we 'have not noticed the idea in us.' We have not 'had' the idea in the sense of having had an actual thought in which it figured as form or object. The same distinction might also apply to the features or elements of our ideas which 'we do not at first notice in them,' even when we do become actively aware of the ideas in question.

This suggestion receives some support from Descartes's espousal of a distinction between actual and potential consciousness in the Fourth Replies. Arnauld had objected to the Third Meditation's assumption that we are conscious of everything that is in our minds. He commented:

> Who does not see that many things [*multa*] may be in the mind, of which the mind is not conscious? The mind of an infant in its mother's womb has the power of thought; but he is not conscious of it. I pass over innumerable similar [instances]. (AT VII, 214; HR II, 92–3)

Now Descartes does hold that an infant in the womb is actually thinking and hence actually conscious; hence, the first part of his reply to Arnauld is merely a repudiation of the example:

> [T]here can be in us no thought, of which, at the very same moment that it is in us, we are not conscious. Wherefore I do not doubt that the mind begins to think as soon as it is infused into the body of an infant, and is at the same time conscious to itself of its own thought, though afterwards it does not remember that, because the specific forms [*species*] of these thoughts do not inhere in the memory. (AT VII, 246; HR II, 115)

157

But having thus taken care of Arnauld's example, Descartes goes on to introduce a distinction between actual and potential consciousness:[29]

> But it has to be noted that, while indeed we are always in actuality [*actu*] conscious of an act or operation of the mind; [we are] not always [conscious of its] faculties or powers, except potentially; so that when we dispose ourselves [*nos accingimus*) to using any faculty, immediately, if that faculty is in the mind, we are actually conscious of it; and thus we can deny it is in the mind if we are unable to be conscious of it. (AT VII, 246–7; HR II, 115)

Unless being 'potentially conscious,' then, is being 'in some manner conscious,' it is not strictly Descartes's position that we are in some manner conscious of all that is in us. Nevertheless, even with this concession to potential consciousness Descartes's position is still much more extreme than, for example, the claim of some contemporary philosophers that a condition of something's being 'in our mind' is that we *can become* conscious of it.[30] I want to maintain it is still too strong for Descartes's own purposes. For what Descartes says to Arnauld is, in effect, that we cannot fail to discover a faculty, if it is in us, as soon as we try to use it. Taken with the conception of ideas as faculties, this does give some sense to Descartes's talk elsewhere of discovering ideas in us, or discovering what is contained in our ideas. What it cannot help us understand is how someone could fail to 'perceive' his idea of God, even after a 'thousandth reading' of the *Meditations*, or how there could be slow learners in geometry. It cannot, in general, help us with the notion that we might *have trouble* converting our confused ideas or perceptions to distinct ones. I believe that the same type of difficulty arises in connection with Descartes's other distinctions—those having to do with attentive and non-attentive knowledge or consciousness.

Besides the distinction between actual and potential consciousness, Descartes also espouses, in certain writings, a distinction between express or explicit and implicit knowledge. In the *Conversation with Burman* he deals with the problem of the dependence of the *cogito* on a general principle in these terms:

> Before this conclusion: 'I think therefore I am,' one can have knowledge of the major premise 'Everything that thinks is,' since it is in reality prior to my conclusion and my conclusion depends on it. And thus, in the *Principles*, the author says it precedes [the conclusion], since implicitly it is always presupposed and precedes; but I do not always expressly and explicitly know [*cognosco*] that it

precedes; and I know [*scio*] my conclusion before, because that is I attend only to what I experience within myself, that is, 'I think therefore I am,' but I do not thus attend to that general notion, 'whatever thinks, is'; for, as pointed out previously, we do not separate those propositions from the particulars [*singularibus*], but rather consider them in [the particulars]. . . . (AT V, 147; B 4)

(In the *Principles* Descartes had remarked that in calling the *cogito* 'the first and most certain proposition' in philosophical inquiry he had not meant to deny 'the necessity of prior knowledge of what thought, certainty, or existence are, and that *in order to think it is necessary to exist*, and other matters of this sort. . . .' Burman had inquired how this might be consistent with Descartes's statement elsewhere that one 'learns' general principles from particulars.) Descartes does not in this passage (as reported by Burman) say anything specifically about *consciousness*. However, since Descartes here (and in the *Principles*) ascribes epistemological priority to the general principles, it seems the 'implicit' knowledge in question must be *actual knowledge*. (Whereas it seems unlikely that we are supposed to have actual knowledge of a faculty which we have never tried to use, and of which we are hence only potentially conscious.) Descartes seems to be denying, not so much that we are actually conscious of the general principle, as that we are *heeding* it, are attentively conscious of it. A similar sort of distinction occurs in the *Search After Truth*. There Polyander is made to say:[31]

I can state for certain that I never doubted what doubt is, although I only began to know [*cognoscere*] it, or rather to direct the mind to it [*mentem in id intendere*], at the time when Epistemon desired to call it in doubt. (AT X, 524; HR I, 325)

Again, Polyander does not *quite* deny that he 'knew what doubt is': as Descartes's spokesman in the dialogue has just remarked, 'To know what doubt or thought are, it is sufficient to doubt and to think' (*ibid.*). And it is extremely unlikely that Descartes meant him to be denying that he was formerly *conscious of* doubting: for this would be in straightforward contradiction with the claim that we are conscious of all our mental acts.

I am suggesting then that explicit knowledge for Descartes requires *attention*, whereas attending to x is *not* a necessary condition of being actually conscious of x. Thus, the distinction between implicit and explicit knowledge is *not the same as* the distinction between actual and potential consciousness. Above I have suggested that Descartes's remarks about our possible ignorance of our innate idea of God could be interpreted through the latter distinction. Notice now that they could alternatively be understood in terms of the distinction between implicit and explicit knowledge. In the passages quoted Descartes says we need not 'notice' or 'represent distinctly' this idea—which *may* be the same as saying that we might not attend to it, or attend to all that is 'in it.' (Similarly, he represents the wax to himself distinctly, 'according as I attend more or less to those things of which [the perception of it] is composed' AT VII, 31; HR I, 155.) Finally, very similar language is found at the beginning of Meditation V, where Descartes expounds the innateness of the ideas of nature 'considered as the object of pure mathematics' (AT VII, 63ff; HR I, 179ff). He mentions that he can 'distinctly imagine the quantity, which philosophers commonly call continuous [*continuam*], or the extension of this quantity, or rather of the thing with quantity, in length, breadth, and depth.' He numbers in it 'various parts,' he assigns 'to these parts various magnitudes, figures, locations, and local motion, and to these motions various durations.' He continues:

> Not only those things, thus regarded in general, are completely known and perceived [*perspecta*] by me, but besides I also perceive when I attend many particulars about figure, about number, about motion, and the like, the truth of which is so open and consonant with my nature, that when I first uncover [*detego*] them, I seem not so much to learn [*addiscere*] something new, as to recollect [*reminisci*] of them what I already knew before, or to turn for the first time toward those things which formerly were indeed in me, although I did not previously turn the eye of the mind to them [*licet non prius in illa obtutum mentis convertissimem*]. (AT VII, 63–4; HR I, 179)

Here again, the crucial issue is attending, or turning the mind toward. One could suppose that Descartes means he was at first only potentially conscious of his innate ideas of geometry and kinematics. Or, noting that he seems to ascribe to his past self implicit knowledge of these things ('what I already knew before') we might take him to be saying that he had been (only) non-attentively conscious of his innate ideas.

In the Sixth Replies Descartes introduces a distinction between 'reflective knowledge' and that 'internal cognition [sc. of our thought] which always precedes reflection.' This distinction is very close to, if not identical with, that between explicit and implicit knowledge; however, the way that Descartes presents it raises a new and different issue. Here again the topic is the *cogito* and its general principle:

It is indeed true that *no one can be sure that he thinks or that he exists, unless he knows what thought is and what existence*. Not that this requires reflective knowledge [*scientia reflexa*] or [knowledge] acquired by demonstration, and much less knowledge of reflective knowledge, by which one knows that he knows and further [knows that] he knows that he knows, and so *ad infinitum*. Such knowledge could never be had about anything. It is completely sufficient that one knows it by that internal cognition which always precedes reflection, and which, concerning thought and existence, is innate in all men; so that, while perhaps overwhelmed by prejudices and attentive to the words rather than their signification, though we can feign [*fingere*] that we do not have it, we cannot nevertheless really lack it. When, therefore, anyone notices that he thinks and that it thence follows that he exists, although perhaps he never previously asked what thought is, nor what existence, he cannot nevertheless fail to know of each sufficiently to satisfy himself on this score. (AT VII, 422; HR II, 241)

This notion of an 'internal cognition' is, I take it, the same that Descartes introduces elsewhere when he says we are conscious of our own mental acts by means of an idea, 'but I do not hold that the idea is different from the action itself' (AT III, 295; PL 93). It is a question of what Ryle has labeled, with disparaging intent, the doctrine of the 'self-luminousness of consciousness.'[32] The texts suggest that Descartes holds all our mental acts are self-luminous;[33] that (mere) self-luminousness corresponds to implicit knowledge; and that to form explicit knowledge of 'what is in us' we must reflect on our thoughts and ideas. To 'reflect on them' is evidently the same as to attend to them, or turn the 'eye of the mind' to them. The passage just quoted from the Sixth Replies also strongly suggests that reflection involves an 'external' as well as an internal cognition of what is or occurs in us.[34]

It seems to me that Descartes's distinction between internal cognition and reflective (or attentive) consciousness is a plausible and valid one up to a point. It is after all commonplace to say, 'he doesn't know the gun is loaded'; 'she wasn't aware of his intentions'; but distinctly peculiar to assert: 'He doesn't know he (himself) has decided to shoot'; 'She wasn't aware of her (own) intentions.' And yet we surely don't want to say that the man has necessarily *had the thought* 'I have decided to shoot,' nor that the woman has necessarily articulated her intention 'to herself.' Neither is it necessary that either has focused attention on his or her decision or intention—

although it is certainly in some sense possible to do this. I would go farther and claim (in agreement with Descartes) that, for example, her awareness (non-reflective) of her own intentions does not reduce to her ability (if asked) to explain or state her intentions. In the first place, she may be aware of her intentions but, for one reason or the other, not able to do this. Second, the fact that she is aware of her intentions is (I would say) non-tautologically the reason she can explain or state them—assuming she can.

The real problem with Descartes's position lies, I believe, in the suggestion that *an act of attention* is all that is needed to make our implicit knowledge explicit, combined with the view that we have (at least) implicit knowledge of our innate ideas and what is 'in' them. This implies that ignorance and error are purely a question of inattention, and are never in any case absolute—at least with respect to our own mental 'acts,' and subjects such as geometry and kinematics, which are supposed to be innate. Now, Professor McRae apparently sees no difficulty here. He writes:[35]

> We have implicit knowledge of everything present to consciousness, and any part of this implicit knowledge can be rendered explicit by the direction of attention upon it. In defining clear and distinct perception Descartes says, 'I term that clear which is present and apparent to an attentive mind. . . . But the distinct is that which is so precise and different from all other objects that it contains within itself nothing but what is clear.' Explicit knowledge, that which we get from attending to what we are conscious of as being in ourselves is, then, the *clear and distinct perception* of what we are pre-reflexively conscious of. Error can arise, according to Descartes, only when we allow ourselves to assent to what is not clearly and distinctly perceived. Accordingly, it follows that we *can* be mistaken about what is occurring in the mind, in spite of the fact that there is nothing in the mind of which the mind is not conscious. Moreover we can be ignorant or partially ignorant of what is in the mind in so far as ignorance is identified with lack of explicit knowledge.

Now I believe that McRae's analysis is said to be textually sound. A letter to Voetius of May 1643 provides especially direct support for his interpretation. Descartes is responding to the objection that his proofs of God's existence will have value only for those who already know that He exists, since 'they depend only on notions innate [*ingenitus*] in us.' Descartes replies:[36]

> But it must be noted that all things, the cognition of which is said to be placed in us by nature, are not thereby expressly known by us;

but only are such, that without any sense experience, we can
know them from the powers of our own mind [*ex proprii ingenii
viribus, cognoscere possimus*]. Of which sort are all of the truths of
Geometry, not only the most obvious, but even the others,
however abstruse they may seem. (AT VIII–2, 166–7)

He goes on to cite the *Meno*, where Socrates interrogates a boy in such
a way as to bring it about that the boy 'brought out of his own mind
certain truths, which he had not previously noticed to be in it.' The
knowledge of God is of the same sort,

> and when you infer from it . . . that there is no one who is
> speculatively an Atheist, that is, there is no one who altogether
> fails to know [*omnino non agnoscat*] that God exists, you were not
> less silly than if, from the fact that all Geometrical truths are in the
> same way innate in us, you had said there is no one in the world
> who does not know [*nesciat*] Euclid's elements. (*Ibid.*, 167)

But notice how the emphasis has subtly shifted. The clear implication
of this passage is that one doesn't really have knowledge at all until
one has explicit knowledge. Implicit knowledge is assimilated to
(merely) potential knowledge: we 'can know' the truths of
geometry from the resources of our own minds. I have argued above
that *this* construal of the implicit-explicit distinction will not do for
the comments on the role of the general principle in the
cogito—passages on which McRae particularly insists. If 'whatever
thinks exists,' 'what thought is,' etc. are epistemically prior to 'I
think therefore I am' they must be (in *some* sense) *known* before it; it
is not enough to hold they are know*able* from the resources of our
mind at the time we are considering the *cogito*. It seems even clearer
that this interpretation will not do for the distinction between
knowing our thoughts by an internal cognition, and attentively
reflecting on them. If implicit knowledge is what I have of my
decisions, intentions, etc. when I'm not actually reflecting or
focusing my attention on them, it is hardly what I, as a
non-mathematician, have of even the simplest theorems of Euclidian
geometry—let alone the most 'abstruse.' I have held Descartes is
correct in supposing I'm normally 'aware' of the former, even
without reflection. But this is to say I in some sense do know
them—not merely that I can.

A related difficulty arises from Descartes's insistent suggestions
that the difference between implicit and explicit knowledge is a
matter of noticing, attention or reflection. (Even in speaking of the
Meno to Voetius, he says the boy at first 'did not notice in himself'

the truths of geometry.) It seems plausible to hold that I may obtain explicit knowledge of my own thoughts when I direct my attention to them. But this is also tied to the important Cartesian tenet that my *cogitatio* judgments are certain and indubitable. It does *not* provide a way of understanding how I can be in error or even (strictly) ignorant of 'what is in me.' By the same token, the metaphor of 'attention' does not provide a good way of understanding the difference between apprehending and not apprehending geometrical or metaphysical truths. It is not the case that merely attending to our confused ideas is supposed to be sufficient for us to 'understand them distinctly.' There is a *dis*analogy here between our ideas generally and our 'thoughts' specifically that the 'attention' metaphor misleadingly glides over. It may be the case that we are always in some sense aware of our thoughts, and can gain explicit knowledge of them automatically, by a mere act of attention. But, as Descartes's remarks to Voetius make perfectly plain, it is 'silly' to suppose we are in the same sense aware of all the features of our innate ideas. Similarly, an act of attention is *not* sufficient to apprehend all that is contained in the latter—or in initially 'confused' ideas generally. *That* is why ignorance and error are possible. I conclude that Descartes does not provide a coherent account of how we are both 'conscious of all that is in us' and possibly ignorant of mathematics and metaphysics. Nor does the metaphor of 'attention' really help to explain what it is to pass from a confused to a distinct idea or perception—given that this is a process involving effort and analysis (and the possibility of error requires that it be so).

One final question. Descartes, as we saw in Chapter II, ridicules Gassendi's demand that he provide an understanding of mind 'beyond the vulgar,' some kind of 'chemical analysis' of thought. One may ask whether Descartes's position on this point depends on his doctrine of the transparency of 'what's in us.' The answer, perhaps, is that the supposed transparency of thought would provide an adequate basis for the reply to Gassendi, since it seems to preclude the possibility of thought having a hidden structure. However, the theory of innate ideas, in requiring a limitation on the transparency doctrine, also dictates one sort of qualification on Descartes's reply to Gassendi. In so far as we are unaware of our innate ideas our thought does, it seems, have a hidden structure in one sense. The mysteriousness of the infinitary capacities of our reason, which are stressed in the Second Meditation and the *Discourse*, may provide another, related sense in which the structure of our minds is 'hidden.' Descartes's stress on the doctrine that we are conscious of all that is in us may be partly intended as a way to avoid responsibility for a science of thought. If so, it is partly foiled by his failure to come fully to terms with his own observations concerning both our rational capacities, and the widespread human ignorance of God, metaphysics and geometry.

V

True and Immutable Natures

1 Res extensa

The Fifth Meditation continues the treatment of matter begun in the Second. Here for the first time Descartes introduces the idea of *res extensa* as preceding that of particular bodies. He continues to set aside the question whether bodies exist, and to consider only which of his ideas of them may be distinct. This procedure is, according to the title of the Meditation, sufficient to determine 'the essence of material things.'

> I distinctly imagine the quantity, which philosophers commonly call continuous, or the extension of this quantity, or rather of the thing with quantity [*rei quantae*], in length, breadth, or depth. . . . (AT VII, 63; HR I, 179)

As in the *Principles*, although somewhat less explicitly, Descartes goes on to indicate that this idea of extension includes that of divisibility into parts; size, figure, location and motion are attributed to the results of division:

> I number in it various parts, and assign to these parts various magnitudes, figures, situations and local motions, and to each of these motions various durations [*quaslibet durationes*]. (*Ibid.*)

As the First Meditation moved from particulars to 'the simple and most universal things' in the generation of hyperbolic doubt, Descartes now moves from the universal to 'particulars' in setting forth his new claims to certainty concerning matter. To cite again a passage considered above in connection with the notion of 'attention,'

And not only those things that are thus regarded in general are completely known and perceived by me, but besides in attending I perceive also innumerable particulars concerning figure, concerning number, concerning motion, and the like, the truth of which is so open and consonant with my nature, that, when I first uncover them, I seem not so much to learn something new, as to recollect of them what I already knew before. . . . (AT VII, 63–4; HR I, 179)

Descartes goes on to present a theory of 'true and immutable natures,' which seems intended to provide a grounding for an *a priori*, non-conventionalistic mathematical science, as well as a sort of underpinning for his version of the ontological argument. I will consider some of the difficulties in this theory in a moment. But first I would like to call attention to a point that is often overlooked, concerning Descartes's conception of the attribute-mode relation in the case of *res extensa*.

A thinking substance, Descartes tells us, must always be exercising thought.[1] And it must, evidently, be exercising thought in some mode or other (if not in several at once): it must be willing *or* imagining *or* understanding *or*. . . . (The 'or's' are of course non-exclusive: I can be perceiving and desiring, perceiving and denying, imagining and fearing, and so forth at a given time.) Furthermore, a thinking substance must at any given time, be having some *specific* volition, act of imagination or understanding, etc. It must, then, be very determinately modified. However, there seems to be no parallel sense in which *res extensa must* be determined by some mode of extension or other. Two points are relevant here. First, *res extensa* as a whole is characterized by Descartes as indefinite, unlimited: it cannot be ascribed a particular size or shape.[2] Second, while *res extensa* is necessarily potentially divisible, there is no evidence that Descartes regards it as necessarily divided. It seems rather to be his view that God introduced motion and division by, so to speak, an act separate from the bare creation of *res extensa*.[3] It is true that for Descartes any particular body must have at a particular time a determinate size, figure, motion and location: but it necessarily has these determinations in virtue of being a *part*, not in virtue merely of being extended.

This observation has an important corollary. Descartes cannot base his version of the primary–secondary quality distinction on the claim that something's having size, figure, etc. is *entailed* by its being extended, whereas its having color, odor, warmth, etc. is not. In other words, the kind of argument used in the *Principles* to show that the latter qualities are not essential to matter will work for *every* quality except extension (and those 'transcendental' qualities that characterize any type of substance whatsoever).[4] The most that is deducible *a priori* is that matter *can* have parts, and that any *part* of matter must have a determinate size, figure and motion. Now the latter observation might perhaps help elucidate the claim that figure, size, situation and motion are clearly and distinctly perceived in bod*ies*—but only where these qualities are understood as determinables. To arrive at the claim that a given body's figure, for example, at a given time is distinctly perceived 'in it' ('I assign to these parts various magnitudes . . .'), we seem to need also the stipulation that if a given determinable is clearly and distinctly perceivable in O, the determinates of that quality are also potentially objects of clear and distinct perception.[5]

2 *Immutable natures and fictitious ideas: a critique*

It is evident that the Fifth Meditation is expounding the possibility of a science of nature that is in a sense *a priori*. Descartes has not yet accorded any truth to the deliverances of sense experience, and has not yet affirmed the existence of any corporeal entity. Further, the innumerable particulars of figure, motion, etc., concerning which he now claims certain knowledge are said to have been already present to his mind, or 'drawn from it.' It is a question, then, of the innate science described in Part V of the *Discourse*:

> I have . . . observed certain laws which God has so established in nature and of which He has imprinted such notions in our minds, that, after having reflected sufficiently on the matter,[6] we cannot doubt that they are exactly observed in all that exists or that occurs in the world. Further, in considering the consequences of these laws, it seems to me that I have discovered a number of truths more useful and more important than all that I had formerly learned or even hoped to learn. . . . [In the treatise on the World] I described . . . matter and tried to represent it in such a way, that it seems to me that there is nothing in the world more clear and intelligible, excepting what has just been said of God and the soul: for I even supposed expressly that there was in it none of these forms or qualities which are debated in the Schools, nor generally anything the knowledge of which is not so natural to our souls that one could not even pretend to be ignorant of it. Further, I explained what are the Laws of Nature, and, without resting my reasons on any other principle than the infinite perfections of God,

I tried to demonstrate all those of which one could have any doubt. . . . (AT VI, 41–3; HR I, 106–8)

But while the science of Meditation V is in this sense *a priori*, it does not follow that it is strictly a science of pure intellect, or of mind in separation from body. Very significantly, Descartes begins his exposition with the following words:

I *distinctly imagine* the quantity which philosophers commonly call continuous, or the extension of this quantity . . . in length, breadth, or depth. . . .

Professor McRae has argued that Descartes actually regards the idea of extension as derived from the *senses*. I believe this is incorrect.[7] What is clear is that for Descartes geometrical physics does appeal to the representation of extension in *imagination*. Now Descartes in fact believes that imagination requires a corporeal basis, an image on the brain.[8] In the *Rules* this seemingly led him to conclude that we cannot distinctly represent extension in abstraction from the conception of an existing body.[9] Further, since we require an image in our brain to form a distinct conception of extension, we cannot claim to have a conception of extension that does not presuppose corporeal *existence*. In the *Meditations*, however, Descartes treats it as (just barely) conceivable that we might have the power of imagining without having a body.[10] Thus, while Descartes will in the end hold that our distinct imagination of extension does involve our body, he in effect suggests this is a contingent rather than a necessary truth. The distinct idea of extension brought forward in Meditation V is not there 'known' to depend on input from the body, but in fact does so.

It is in this light, perhaps, that we should understand Descartes's remark in the First Meditation that arithmetic and geometry 'scarcely care' whether their objects exist in nature or not. Since we *in fact* rely on the brain, which actually instantiates the simple natures of extension, figure and so on to form completely distinct ideas of these entities, it would be false to say it is completely unimportant to corporeal science whether anything extended exists. But since, according to Meditation V, one can commit oneself to the truth of mathematical 'ideas' without (logically) committing oneself to the existence of any body, the connection between mathematics and physical existence is epistemically tenuous.

In this light also we must understand some of Descartes's first remarks about knowledge of 'true and immutable natures'—entities which have an 'external' reality independent of his mind, even if there exist no physical objects that 'have' them. For these entities, which he seems to take as the immediate objects of mathematical reasoning, are first introduced with reference to 'imagining a triangle.'

> And what I here think is most worthy of consideration is that I find in me innumerable ideas of certain things which, even if perhaps they exist nowhere outside of me, nevertheless, cannot be said to be nothing; and although they are in some way thought by me at will, they are nevertheless not formed [*finguntur*] by me, but have their [own] true and immutable natures. Thus when, for example, I imagine a triangle, even if perhaps such a figure nowhere exists outside my thought, and never existed, there is really nevertheless a certain determinate nature, or essence, or form of it, immutable and eternal, which is not made [*efficta*] by me, and does not depend on my mind; as appears from the fact that various properties can be demonstrated of this triangle, as that its three angles are equal to two right angles, [or] that its largest angle is subtended by its largest side, and the like, which whether I wish or not I now recognize clearly, even though I did not in any way think of them before, when I imagined a triangle, and hence were not made [*effictae*] by me. (AT VII, 64; HR I, 179–80)

In so far as a triangle is imagined it does exist outside his 'thought'—namely in his brain—although Descartes does not yet 'know' this. Of course, as Descartes will point out at the beginning of Meditation VI, there are figures, such as the chiliagon, which can be understood but not distinctly imagined. And we must surely assume that they too have their 'true and immutable natures.'[11] Yet it seems unlikely Descartes would hold that our ability to carry out clear and distinct deductions with reference to these 'unimaginable' entities is independent of our ability distinctly to *imagine* continuous quantity. On the other hand, there is no suggesting that the *reality* of the essences depends on anyone's ability to imagine.

It is important, accordingly, to distinguish two issues, in considering whether or not Descartes is a 'Platonist' in the philosophy of mathematics; namely:[12]

(1) Are the objects of mathematical science dependent on the existence of bodies for their reality? and

(2) Does our mathematical knowledge depend in any degree on our having a body (or does it rather derive directly from pure understanding)?

For Descartes the answer to the first question would appear to be 'no'—at least in the mature philosophy. Further, Descartes presumably means to hold that geometrical essences strictly depend only on the will and understanding of God, and not at all on any finite minds that may think of them. In this ontological respect Descartes's position seems at least quasi-Platonic. On the other hand, Descartes's answer to the second question seems to be 'yes'—in the *Meditations* as well as in the *Rules*. Even in the later work, our ability to develop a systematic science of body is not presented as independent of our ability to form corporeal images (the *verae ideae* of the *Rules*)—despite the fact that Descartes now stresses also the *limitations* of imagination, with respect to the conceptions of infinite variability, very complex figures and so forth.[13] Doubtless imagination is only an aid, which helps us understand or grasp truths about immaterial entities (the 'immutable natures') by presenting to our mental vision some kind of physical exemplar of these objects. Still, the prominence accorded the notion of imagination in Meditation V (and the beginning of Meditation VI) would suggest that it is far from being an *incidental* aid. Hence I think it would be a mistake to portray Descartes as a Platonist with respect to mathematical *science*.

Whether or not the position developed in Meditation V can strictly be described as 'Platonist,' it is clearly both anti-conventionalist and anti-empiricist. The true and immutable natures are, as Kenny stresses, *given*, and not by the senses.[14] What shows they are not derived from sense, according to Descartes, is that there are many of them 'of which there can be no suspicion that they ever came into my mind through the senses.' What shows they are given, not invented, is that many things can be demonstrated of them that I did not at first think of when I thought of them. Or, as Descartes says a little later in connection with the claim that existence is contained in the nature of God,

> [F]rom the fact that I cannot think of God except existing, it follows that existence is inseparable from God, and that he really exists; not that my thought brings this about, or imposes any necessity on any thing, but on the contrary because the necessity of the fact itself, that is of the existence of God, determines me to this thought: for I am not free to think God without existence (that is the most perfect being without the most perfection), as I am free to imagine a horse either with or without wings. (AT VII, 67; HR I, 181–2)

The point seems to be twofold: a true and immutable nature has implications which I did not *foresee* (which were hence not *put in* it by my will), and which I am not *free to separate from it*, once I notice them—which are not in any sense *dependent* on my will.

Descartes may be right that considerations of unforeseen and unwilled consequences of his ideas show that these ideas are not wholly within the control of his invention. But does this implication, as Descartes suggests, provide a basis for a conception of *a priori* real predication? Can we conclude that 'from this alone that I can draw out the idea of some thing from my thought, whatever I clearly and distinctly perceive as pertaining to that thing really does pertain to it?' Or, more basically, do the criteria Descartes mentions of true and immutable natures really provide the distinction between 'real' and invented ideas? Between, that is, the idea of something 'drawn from his thought,' and a merely invented idea?

Suppose I define the term 'Onk' as meaning 'the first non-terrestrial life-form to be discovered by man.' Is it possible this concept will have implications I did not at first perceive in it, but cannot, on reflection, deny of it? It seems so. For in defining 'Onk' I may very well not have reflected on the question of what are the necessary conditions for something's being a life-form. But having done so, I see that reproduction and ability to assimilate nourishment are necessary conditions;[15] hence that 'Onk has reproductive potential' and 'Onk assimilates nourishment' are necessary truths—*velim nolim*, as Descartes might say. But does 'Onk' pick out a true and immutable nature? If it does, some (at least) of Descartes's examples of factitious ideas would too. For just as I can say that Onk is a life-form without having reflected on all the implications of something's being a life-form, so I can, for example, speak of a hippogryph as part-horse without having reflected on certain implications of the predicate 'part-horse.'[16]

3 Immutable natures and the ontological argument

Descartes tries to enlist the conception of true and immutable natures as a bulwark for the ontological argument. He wants to hold that only true and immutable natures can be used in deductions that derive real predications from concepts. This is supposed to forestall certain kinds of counter examples, that would tend to show that the ontological argument if sound could be readily adapted to prove the existence of myriads of things, things of which we clearly do not want to say that *their* existence can be proved *a priori*. However, for reasons just suggested, the notion of unforeseen and unwilled consequences will not establish the desired bulwark. Thus, Caterus argues that the concept of an existent Lion 'includes existence essentially'; it does not follow that this 'complex' exists (AT VII, 99–100; HR II, 7–8). Similarly, Caterus reasons, even if the concept of the supremely perfect being includes existence essentially, it does not follow that this essence exists. In reply, Descartes distinguishes between true and immutable natures, and 'fictitious ones due to a mental synthesis,' arguing that the concept of a supremely perfect being falls in the former category and that of an existent lion in the latter (AT VII, 117, HR II, 20). But there is no good reason to suppose that the *Meditations'* criterion of unforeseen and unwilled consequences will be sufficient here. Just as the concept of Onk has implications I did not at first notice in it, so the concept of an existent lion may too.

In fact, in replying to Caterus Descartes offers a different criterion for distinguishing true and immutable natures from factitious ones. An idea contains a true and immutable nature if and only if it cannot be analyzed into its parts 'not merely by abstraction but by a clear and distinct mental operation.'

> For example, when I think of a winged horse, or a lion actually
> existing, or a triangle inscribed in a square, I easily understand that
> I can also on the contrary think of a horse without wings, or a lion
> as not existing, and of a triangle without a square, and so forth,
> and that hence these things have no true and immutable natures.
> But if I think of the triangle or the square (I here do not speak of
> the lion or the horse, because their natures are not wholly
> perspicuous to us), then certainly whatever I recognize as being
> contained in the idea of the triangle, as that its angles are equal to
> two right, etc., I shall with truth affirm of the triangle; and [I shall
> affirm] of the square whatsoever I find in the idea of the square;
> for even though I can understand a triangle, abstracting from the
> fact that its three angles are equal to two right, yet I cannot deny
> that of it by any clear and distinct operation. . . . (AT VII, 117–
> 18; HR II, 20)

But if I can think of a lion without existence, cannot I not equally think of a figure with angles but not a *tri*angle? The notion of an existing lion, and that of a triangle seem to be equally analyzable. And in fact in the above paragraph Descartes does not so much deny this as simply change the subject in the middle. Rather than denying that the idea of triangle can be analyzed, he points out that it has certain necessary implications. But so, one must repeat, does the idea of an existing lion.

Neither of Descartes's two criteria for distinguishing immutable natures will really do. The criterion of having unforeseen implications is too weak: it will admit Onk, winged horses and other ideas Descartes would consider factitious. The criterion of being not distinctly analyzable is too strong, since it excludes even simple geometrical figures. We know Descartes *wants* to say that mathematics deals with a certain sort of entities that are given to the mind independently of the senses, and 'impose their necessities upon us.' However, he does not succeed in providing a criterion for recognizing this class of entities.

But even if Descartes's second criterion, that of unanalyzability, is too strong with respect to mathematical entities, it might still, perhaps, help defend the ontological argument. We might try to maintain, that is, that existence can be affirmed of a thing on the basis of the thing's essence, when and only when existence is necessarily connected with the other properties of the essence. This is in fact the move that Descartes tries to make in the continuation of the First Replies (AT VII, 118; HR II, 21).

Now there are two ways of understanding the suggestion that existence is non-trivially entailed by the properties that define the essence of God. In the Fifth Meditation Descartes's idea seems to be that existence, or necessary existence, is necessarily connected with the property of being 'most perfect,' although we might not at first notice that it is. This is so because existence, or necessary existence, is itself a 'perfection' (AT VII, 65ff; HR I, 180ff). However, this way of looking at the matter seems to leave open the door to the classic objection that 'ontological arguments' can be generated for an indefinitely large class of entities: most perfect islands, most perfect bodies, most perfect lions. The trick is simply to make existence implicit rather than explicit in specifying the essence by means of the term 'most perfect.' In the First Replies, in any case, Descartes seems to give up on this line and to try a quite different one. He argues that in the case of God, and only in the case of God, existence (or necessary existence) is entailed by his other specific perfections, in particular the perfection of omnipotence. Thus, in the case of a 'body of the highest perfection,' 'existence does not arise from the other corporeal perfections, because it (existence) can equally well be denied and affirmed of them' (AT VII, 118; HR II, 21). Necessary existence ('which is here alone in question') can in fact be denied of this body; for 'when I examine this idea of body I see there is no force in it by which it produces or preserves itself.' The case of God is quite different:

But if we attentively consider whether existence belongs to a being of preeminent power, and what sort of existence, we shall be able clearly and distinctly to perceive in the first place that possible existence at least belongs to it, as it does to all other things of which there is a distinct idea in us, even of those things which are composed by a fiction of the understanding. Further, because we cannot think of [God's] existence as being possible, without at the same time, taking heed of His immense power, knowing that he can exist by His own force, we hence conclude that He really exists and has existed from all eternity; for by the natural light it is most evident [*notissimum*] that that which can exist by its own force always exists. And thus we understand that necessary existence is contained in the idea of a being of pre-eminent power, not by a fiction of the understanding, but because it belongs to the true and immutable nature of such a being that it exists. . . . (AT VII, 119; HR II, 21)

(This line of argument, though a radical departure from the Fifth Meditation, is foreshadowed in the Third, where Descartes writes: 'the unity, simplicity, or inseparability of all things which are in God is one of the principal perfections which I understand to be in Him' (AT VII, 50; HR I, 169).)

Kenny has offered an ingenious and interesting defense of this argument. Kenny feels Descartes has suppressed a crucial premiss; namely, the premiss that *omnia appetunt esse*, everything desires to exist.[17] His point, I take it, is that it is not evident to the light of nature that whatever can exist by its own power does exist, unless it is first evident that everything wants to exist. Kenny defends the latter principle against the objection that 'pure objects' or non-existent essences cannot be ascribed desires. In his rather poignant example, a non-libidinous satyr wouldn't be a satyr at all.

But is ascribing the desire to exist to possible objects really analogous to ascribing libidinous desires to possible satyrs? Well, we can ascribe to a possible satyr, for example, the desire to exist in a way analogous to the ascription of libidinous desires. We can say, for example, that a satyr, if it existed, would desire to exist. That is, it would like existing, and want to continue to exist. But this must be distinguished from ascribing to a possible entity *qua* possible the desire to become actual.

A similar distinction must, I think, be recognized with respect to the 'power to exist by one's own force.' To say that God, considered as possible, has the power to exist by His own force, could mean either of two different things. It could mean first that any existent entity that is God has the power to exist by its own force. (Similarly, anything that is Pegasus has the power to fly.) Or it could mean that

God, considered as possible, has the power to make Himself actual. The latter suggestion, although not the former, crosses the bounds between possibility and actuality.

But what could it mean to say that something has the power to exist by its own might, if not that it, considered as possible, has the power to make itself actual? Well, it might mean: has the power to maintain itself in existence; and indeed Descartes sometimes speaks of God's power to exist with this signification in mind. Now even if we suppose God might coherently be ascribed this sort of power, it does not follow that He can coherently be ascribed the 'power to exist by His own force,' in the sense of the power to 'make Himself actual.' The case here is closely parallel with that of the desire to exist.

It does not seem to me that God can be ascribed the power to make Himself actual. I even think this follows from Descartes's own principles. To say that God has the power to actualize Himself, is to say that His omnipotence, considered as a possible entity, is sufficient to bring about the actual existence of itself. This is to say that something considered merely as possible can have an actual effect with the same degree of formal reality as itself. And this seems a clear violation of Descartes's principle that for every effect there must *exist* a cause with as much reality as the effect.

Descartes's causal argument for the existence of God turns, as we have seen, on the latter principle. My claim is that this principle is violated by the final form that Descartes's ontological argument (if that term is still appropriate to the argument from omnipotence) assumes. Now Kenny holds that the ontological argument and the *cogito* cannot both be sound. [18] I have criticized this position above, arguing that the interpretation of the *cogito* that it assumes cannot be correct. On the basis of the foregoing analysis, however, I would like to propose an alternative inconsistency. The *causal* and the ontological arguments cannot both be sound.

VI

Mind, Body and Things Outside us

1 Introduction

In Meditation VI Descartes concludes his argument for the 'real distinctness' of mind from body that he had begun in the Second. He also argues that our sense experiences must be caused by really existing physical objects, and that they can give us, to a very limited extent, knowledge of these objects. Finally, he discusses at some length the nature of the union of the human mind with 'its' body. These are the topics with which the present chapter will be concerned.

Before analyzing in detail Descartes's argument for the independence of mind from body, I would like to establish in a general way the nature of his dualism, in relation to present-day discussions of the mind–body issue.

2 Cartesian dualism

We have already noted above that the Sixth Meditation opens with a discussion of the difference between imagination and understanding. Imagination involves not merely comprehending or conceiving something (say a geometrical figure), but also intuiting it as if present to the sight of the mind. In imagining a pentagon, for example, I must make a special mental effort to apply the vision of my mind to each of its five sides, and the area enclosed within them. The experience of imagination, Descartes believes, provides some reason to affirm the existence of body:

[F]rom the faculty of imagining, which I experience myself to use when I reflect about these material things, it seems to follow that

177

they exist; for considering more attentively what imagination may be, it appears to be nothing else than a certain application of the faculty of cognition [*facultatis cognoscitivae*] to a body intimately present to it, and hence existing. (AT VII, 71–2; HR I, 185)

Further, imagination unlike understanding is not required 'for myself, that is to say for the essence of my mind;' without it I would be the same as I am. This too suggests that it 'depends on something different from me.'

And I easily understand that if some body exists to which the mind is so conjoined that it can apply itself as to inspect it at will, it could be that in this way it imagines corporeal objects; hence that this mode of cognition differs only in this from pure understanding: that the mind, when it understands, in some way turns to itself, and views [*respiciat*] some of the ideas that are in itself [*illi ipsi insunt*]; when it imagines however, it turns to the body, and views [*intueatur*] something in [the body] conforming to the idea, either understood by itself or perceived by the senses. (AT VII, 73; HR I, 186)

Since this is the 'best explanation' he can think of for imagination, the phenomenon of imagining makes it likely that body exists. The conclusion, however, is so far merely probable: imagination, Descartes tells us, will not yield a demonstrative proof of the existence of body.

The significance of this distinction between imagination and understanding for Descartes's dualism is brought out well in the Fifth Replies, where Descartes responds to Gassendi's 'materialist' objections. Gassendi, for example, had commented:

In order to prove that you are of a diverse nature [from the brutes], (that is, as you contend, an incorporeal nature), you ought to put forth some operation in a way different than they do, if not outside the brain, at least independently of the brain: but this you do not do. For you yourself are perturbed when it is perturbed, and oppressed when it is oppressed, and if something destroys the forms of things in it, you yourself do not retain any trace. (AT VII, 269; HR II, 145)

Descartes answers:

I have . . . often distinctly showed that the mind can operate independently of the brain; for certainly the brain can be of no use to pure understanding, but only to imagination or sensing. And although, when something strongly strikes the imagination or

senses (as is the case when the brain is perturbed), the mind does
not easily free itself to understand other things, we nevertheless
experience that when the imagination is less strong, we often
understand something completely different from it: as, when
while sleeping we notice that we dream, the imagination is indeed
necessary for dreaming, but only the understanding is necessary to
notice that we dream. (AR VII 358–9; HR II, 212)

In a similar vein, Descartes denies Gassendi's claim that the mind
develops or deteriorates with the body, arguing that Gassendi cannot
prove it:

[F]or, from the fact that it does not act as perfectly in the body of
an infant as in that of an adult, and its actions can often be
impeded by wine and other bodily things, it only follows that as
long as the mind is joined to the body, it uses the body as its
instrument in those operations in which it is usually occupied, not
that it is rendered more perfect or less perfect by the body. . . .
(AT VII, 354; HR II, 208–9)

According to Descartes, the mind may be distracted, impeded or
limited in its operations by the condition of the body (cf. also AT VII,
228; HR II, 103). But he seems to allow no connection at all between
the mind's *basic capacity* for pure intellection or ratiocination and
anything that does or could occur in the brain or other parts of the
body.

The contrast between strictly intellectual acts and mental acts
involving reference to physical states is found already in Descartes's
early work, *The Rules for the Direction of the Mind*. In a rather
well-known passage in Rule XII he writes:

That power by which we are properly said to know things is purely
spiritual, and not less distinct from the whole body than blood
from bone, or hand from eye . . . it is one and the same power
which, if it applies itself along with imagination to the common
sense is said to see, touch, etc.; if to imagination alone as [the
latter] is clothed in different forms, it is said to remember; if to the
imagination as fashioning new forms there, it is said to imagine or
conceive; *finally if it acts alone it is said to understand.* (AT X,
415–16; HR I, 38–9; emphasis added)

And the contrast is still present, although perhaps somewhat muted,
in Descartes's last published work, *The Passions of the Soul*. (Cf.
e.g., Part I, 47: AT XI, 364ff; HR I, 352ff.) Similarly, in letters of the
late 1630s and early 1640s we find other aspects of the contrast

spelled out. In a letter to Mersenne of 1639 Descartes contrasts the knowledge the soul gains 'by reflection on itself' in the case of intellectual matters, with that it derives from reflection 'on the various dispositions of the brain to which it is joined, whether these result from the action of the senses or from other causes' (AT II, 598; PL 66). And in letters of 1640 he also espouses a contrast between corporeal and spiritual memory:

> [Concerning the folds of memory,] I do not think that there has
> to be a very large number of these folds to serve for all our
> memories, in that a single fold will do for all the things which
> resemble each other, and that besides the corporeal memory,
> whose impressions can be explained by these folds of the brain, I
> judge that there is also in our understanding another sort of
> memory, which is altogether spiritual, and is not found in animals,
> and it is this that we mainly use. (AT III 143; cf. III, 48; PL 76; cf.
> 72)

It follows, I think, that Descartes's own position on the mind–body distinction is rather dramatically different from the view that frequently passes for 'Cartesian dualism' in contemporary discussions of the mind–body issue.[1] The gist of the latter position—frequently mentioned as a principal alternative to the various forms of materialism—is that mental events *are not identical* with events in the body (brain, or whatever). This conclusion is based on the claim that *any* mental event (understood as a conscious experience) is conceptually distinct from any physical event. The claim is meant to apply even-handedly to all conscious experience, sensations no less than acts of intellect (although sensations tend to be the favored example). This distinction of mental and physical events may or may not be then taken to entail a distinction of substances—or 'logical types of subject'[2]—although careful scholars do note that this implication was important to Descartes. It is, in any case, entirely compatible with the conception of 'Cartesian dualism' reflected in these discussions to suppose that *every* type of mental occurrence, from twinges of pain to metaphysical reflection—has a *corresponding* or *correlated* type of physical occurrence. Hence, this contemporary understanding of 'Cartesian dualism' does not maintain that the search for a neurophysiological account of 'pure thought' is in any sense more chimerical than the search for a neurophysiological account of sensation.

It is true that Descartes's own principal argument for the mind–body distinction is itself a conceivability argument that does not cut in any obvious way between acts or powers of *understanding*, on the one hand, and any other type of *cogitationes*, or cognitive powers, on the other hand. We will consider this argument below. However, the replies to Gassendi and other passages do require us to conclude that Descartes regarded his mind as *essentially* only intellect, and denied corporeal correlates of purely intellectual acts, capacities and powers. Bodily states are not merely not *identical* with mental states: they are not even *relevant* to a subclass of such states. Thus, in imagining and in certain kinds of remembering the mind is said to 'utilize' or 'turn to' impressions existing in the brain; and in the experiences of sensations and passion the mind is affected by changes in the body's organs and may even become aware of itself as united or 'intermingled' with the whole body. In these sorts of mental occurrences 'some understanding is comprised'—this is a necessary condition of their *being* mental occurrences—but because of the dependence of the thoughts on physical states or occurrences they cannot be construed as 'pure understanding.' But a person doing metaphysics, or thinking about God, or reflecting on the mind itself, *is* exercising pure understanding—assuming, at least, that he has the true, non-physical notions of God, the mind and so forth. Pure understanding is carried on independently of all physical processes; any physiological study will necessarily be irrelevant to it. There is hence a very fundamental contrast, from the scientific point of view, between the exercise of pure understanding on the one hand, and all other mental occurrences on the other. For Descartes, of course, was firmly committed to the possibility of providing physiological accounts of the various emotions, sensations and patterns of reflex behavior, as well as of imagination and what he calls the corporeal memory. Much of his life's research was directed to developing just such accounts.

As I have said, the principal argument for the mind–body distinction in the *Meditations* does not obviously support this robust form of dualism, as opposed to the relatively pallid but less discredited view that tends to go under the name of 'Cartesian dualism' today. It is worth asking, therefore, what Descartes did think supported it—and also what motives he might have had for accepting and indeed insisting upon such an 'unscientific' conception of the operations of the human organism. (I will defer till later the question whether Descartes did in the last analysis suppose that his conceivability argument separated *all* mental states from physical states.)

Now it is natural to point out that 'the cerebral basis of human intelligence' is little enough understood in the twentieth century; it seems no wonder that a seventeenth-century figure should refuse to

181

credit such a notion at all. Further, Descartes did not have the opportunity we have had to observe the development of computer technology—and even in our own times this development has been met with various forms of self-serving resistance and denial: 'machines will never be able to_____the way human beings do,' etc. True, but we must notice (and I don't think this is usually sufficiently recognized) that Descartes stands alone among the major philosophical thinkers of the seventeenth century in denying both the possibility that thought inheres in material substance, and the possibility of any form of mind–body parallelism. Hobbes, Spinoza and Leibniz all accepted some form of either materialism or parallelism—for reasons, partly, of scientific seriousness. Locke came closer to embracing Descartes's dualistic interactionism, but was far less doctrinaire, and expressed a variety of doubts and reservations concerning the proposition that *matter cannot think*.[3] As we have seen, even a less bold and creative thinker such as Gassendi was defending a version of materialism against Descartes; in fact, even Descartes's *minor* critics objected that for all he had really shown, thought could still be a property of body.

For somewhat similar reasons, theological considerations cannot be regarded as fully explanatory either. On the strength of their published works, Spinoza and Leibniz were far more deeply concerned with the problem of personal immortality than was Descartes, yet both of these men accepted a more or less parallelistic position concerning the relation of mental states to states of the brain or body. It is true that Descartes seems to have been more centrally concerned even than Leibniz to gain acceptance for his views among the established political and theological powers of the age. Yet it is impossible to believe that the enormous range and variety of Cartesian pronouncements concerning the independence of intellect from body, including all those we have already cited, could have been dictated by this type of prudence or hypocrisy.

Descartes's position as a scientist provides a much more plausible explanation for his insistence on the complete immateriality of the operations of the understanding. A *motive* for his dualism may perhaps be found in the universalist pretensions of his physics, briefly touched on above. For example, he claims, or boasts, at the end of the *Principles* that 'there is no phenomenon of nature that has been omitted from this treatise' (IV, 199: AT VIII–1, 323; HR I, 296). Yet he must have perceived that the accounts of human behavior he was able to provide did not go beyond the level, roughly, of reflex action. To deny that reason has any corporeal basis would be a necessary condition of reconciling his ambitions with his limitations. A *reason* for his dualism may be found in his commitment to mechanistic explanation in physics, together with the perfectly creditable belief that human intelligence could never be accounted for on the available mechanistic models.

The latter view is only briefly indicated in the *Meditations*, when Descartes stresses that the limited representations of the imagination are not sufficient for knowing the wax. It is much more fully developed in a now-famous passage in the *Discourse on Method*. Here Descartes indicates that two aspects of human behavior tend to show that our actions must be governed by some non-mechanistic principle. The first of these, relating to our use of language, has been particularly stressed by Noam Chomsky, who is largely responsible for the celebrity of the passage in our time.[4] Descartes writes:

> [Machines] could never use words or other signs in composing them as we do to declare our thoughts to others. For we can easily conceive a machine's being constituted so that it utters words, and even that it utters some à propos of corporeal actions, which cause some change in its organs; for instance, if it is touched in a certain place it will ask what we wish to say to it; if in another place it will exclaim that it is being hurt, and so on; but not that it arranges words differently to reply to the sense of all that is said in its presence, as even the most moronic man can do. (AT VI, 56–7; HR I,116)

Chomsky takes Descartes to be referring here to the 'creative aspect of language use.'[5] If Chomsky means by 'creative' *innovative* (e.g., the ability to invent and understand sentences different from any one has previously heard), it is not entirely clear that his reading of the passage is correct. What Descartes seems to be saying is that we could not imagine a machine sufficiently complex to have an appropriate verbal response to each of the enormous range and variety of occurrences to which we human beings do respond verbally. And this does not seem to be quite the same as pointing to a peculiarly 'innovative' feature. What is clear, in any case, is that Descartes is maintaining that an immaterial soul must be invoked to 'explain' human language use, because a strictly mechanistic account is inconceivable.

The second consideration is, superficially, much less convincing:

> And . . . although [machines] can do certain things as well as or perhaps better than any of us, they infallibly fall short in certain others, by which we may discover that they did not act from knowledge, but only from the dispositions of their organs. For

while reason is a universal instrument which can serve for all sorts of occasions, these organs have need of some particular disposition for each particular action. (AT VI, 57; HR I, 116)

Or, as Descartes elaborates the point with reference to animals:

It is . . . a very remarkable fact that although there are many animals which exhibit more skill than we do in some of their actions, we at the same time observe that they do not manifest any at all in many others. Hence the fact that they do better than we do, does not prove that they are endowed with mind, for in this case they would have more than any of us, and would do better in all other things. It rather shows that they have none at all, and that it is nature which acts in them according to the disposition of their organs. . . . (AT VI, 58–9; HR I, 117)

The underlying assumption here seems to be that if you do something, A, better than I do, and do it from reason or knowledge (and assuming perhaps that I also do A 'from knowledge') then you will also excel me in every other activity (or at least in every other activity that I perform 'from knowledge'). That is, if you excel me in bridge you will also excel me in chess—and in literary criticism, landscape architecture, in solving differential equations and in the resolution of moral dilemmas or social predicaments. And this assumption is at best very implausible: even in those activities deemed most rational or reason-guided we exhibit varying degrees of specialization, knack and skill.

But I think we must assume that Descartes is speaking hyperbolically in this passage. His point, surely, is only that if animals used something like human reason to accomplish their various remarkable feats, then they should show qualities of adaptability, and learning abilities, far beyond any they actually exhibit.[6] Conversely, the adaptability and educability of human beings, including their linguistic competence, cannot, according to Descartes's reasoning, be supposed capable of explanation on mechanical principles alone. Or rather, in Descartes's own words, 'it is morally impossible that there should be sufficient diversity in any machine to allow it to act in all the occurrences of life in the same way as our reason causes us to act.' This implies, at least, that it is morally impossible that we ourselves should turn out to be only very complex physical mechanisms.

The passage from the *Discourse* provides motivation for Descartes's dualism by suggesting he had reflected—perhaps more systematically than his contemporaries—on the possibility of a mechanistic account of human behavior. It suggests he had concluded that such an account was impossible, in view of the complexity and 'diversity' that would be required in such a machine. If this was his reasoning he must be given credit for, at least, an admirable realism concerning the state of the art and the difficulty of the problem—in contrast, for example, with the unabashed mechanistic optimism of Hobbes (or, as Chomsky might point out, of latter-day behaviorists).[7]

One can make considerable sense, then, of Descartes's espousal of a quite 'robust' form of dualism, with reference to his understanding of the available forms of materialist explanation. It appears, however, that Descartes thought he also had another way of proving the truth of this position, one that appears in the Sixth Meditation.

We have noticed that Descartes answers Gassendi with the statement:

> I have . . . often distinctly showed that the mind can operate
> independently of the brain; for certainly the brain can be of no use
> to pure understanding, but only to imagination or sensing. (AT
> VII, 358; HR II, 212)

Now in the Fifth Replies Descartes sometimes does make reference to the *Discourse* and other works, as well as the *Meditations*. However, this statement about the lack of a cerebral basis for 'pure understanding' pretty clearly does *not* have reference to the arguments from the *Discourse* that we have just considered. Rather, Descartes seems to be referring to the discussion of understanding and imagination at the beginning of the Sixth Meditation. And so the question is simply this: does Descartes really suppose that the phenomenological considerations that are there in question provide a reason for maintaining that 'the brain is not at all involved in pure understanding'? I do not see how we can avoid the conclusion that he does. (What he hesitates about in that passage is not this 'negative' conclusion, but rather the legitimacy of concluding that the body *is* involved in our acts of imagination.) Pure understanding involves neither the sensations or affects that are 'caused' in the mind as a result of its close union with the bodily organs, nor 'corporeal images' that might be presented on a surface of the brain, as if on a blackboard. Ergo, the brain (or body) is not at all involved in pure thought. For what task would there be left for it to perform?

3   The Epistemological Argument

I have tried to show that Cartesian dualism, as Descartes himself understood it, differs in both content and motivation from the view sometimes called 'Cartesian dualism' in later discussions of the mind–body problem. The differences derive, especially, from his conception of the possibilities and limitations of mechanistic physical explanation, and his peculiar contention that 'brain can be no use to pure understanding'—as opposed to the faculties of imagination and sense, which are more dependent on body. On the other hand, when he finally tries to establish, in Meditation VI, that the mind is 'really distinct from the body,' Descartes places greatest stress on an argument that does not seem to entail his own 'robust' form of dualism. This argument, which I will call the 'Epistemological Argument' for the distinctness of mind from body, is presented in the Sixth Meditation—and, in somewhat different versions, in various other works. Descartes's Epistemological Argument consti- tutes the principal bridge between historical Cartesianism and contemporary (i.e. twentieth-century) discussions of the mind–body relation. In this section I will develop an interpretation of the argument that seems to me both more adequate to the texts, and less subject to obvious criticisms, than those commonly found in the literature.

First I will present a preliminary account of the Epistemological Argument, based on Descartes's presentation in the Sixth Meditation. I will explain briefly why certain common objections to Descartes are not in fact relevant to this argument; and examine some related criticisms by two of Descartes's contemporaries which appear more relevant. Finally, I will try to show that Descartes both understands the significance of the latter objections and succeeds in replying to them in a reasonably cogent manner (in a way that acknowledges, however, the need for some revision in the original statement of the argument). In developing the last point I shall also return to the issue of Descartes's intentions in the Second Meditation, with respect to the *cogito* reasoning. I believe that once we combine a careful reading of Descartes's replies to his critics, with a careful reading of parts of the Second Meditation, we will end up with a more compelling account of the Epistemological Argument than is generally current.[8] Also, we will see why Descartes continued to maintain the soundness of his argument in the face of objections that some recent, as well as seventeenth-century, philosophers seem to regard as conclusive.

Let me begin by recalling those aspects of the Second Meditation reasoning that provide the foundation for the Epistemological Argument. Having used the Deceiver Hypothesis in the First Meditation to bring into 'doubt' the existence of body, Descartes has argued in the Second Meditation that this 'doubt' does not extend to his own existence. He has then considered what attributes can be ascribed with certainty to himself at this stage of his reasoning. He has concluded that even certain properties traditionally associated with the soul or vital principle—for example, nutrition—must be presently excluded as part of the doubt of body. There is only one, he's found, that is not called into question on this basis:

> To think? Here I find it: thought [it] is; this alone cannot be separated from me. . . . I do not now admit anything except what necessarily is true. I am therefore strictly only a thinking thing, that is mind, or soul, or understanding or reason. . . . I am however a true and truly existing thing; but what sort of thing? I have answered, a thing which thinks. (AT VII, 27; HR I, 151–2)

As we have observed above, however, Descartes goes on to cancel the implication that he can know at this stage of the argument that only thought and nothing corporeal pertains to his nature. On the other hand, he is *not* at this point of the argument restricting himself to just the non-committal conclusion, 'as far as I now know I am a thinking thing and only a thinking thing.' For instance, he is implicitly claiming to know, not merely that he thinks, but that thought pertains to his nature or essence: it 'cannot be separated from me.' Also, he explicitly maintains that reasoning concerning the indubitability of his own existence (the *'cogito* reasoning') has brought him to the conclusion that he is a *true and truly existing thing (res vera et vere existens)*. The importance of this statement should soon become clear.

The Second Meditation contains at least two other assertions that turn out to be important to the Epistemological Argument. First, there is Descartes's claim to have a *clear and distinct* idea of himself as a thinking thing (apart from any concept of the corporeal). He begins to hint at this point immediately after the statements already cited, and (as we have already seen) it is made explicit at the end of the Meditation.

> What however shall I say of this same mind, or of myself? For so far I do not admit that there is in me anything except mind. What, I ask, [of] I who seem to perceive this wax so distinctly? Do I not then know myself not only much more truly, much more certainly, but even much more distinctly and evidently? (AT VII, 33; HR I, 156)

Second, there is the claim that he has a distinct conception of the wax as an extended thing—which conception is separate from that of thought. In other words, the distinctly perceived nature of a body contrasts with the distinctly perceived nature of the self. Or, as Descartes says elsewhere, 'nothing at all is included in the concept of the body, that belongs to mind; and nothing in the concept of mind, that belongs to body.'[9] This point is further developed, as we have seen, in the affirmations concerning *res extensa* at the beginning of Meditation V.

It is very important to notice that prior to the Sixth Meditation Descartes does express his discoveries about self and matter in terms of clear and distinct perceptions. For of course it is his explicit position that *only* clear and distinct perceptions or conceptions will suffice as the basis for positive affirmations about the nature of a thing. Thus, Descartes observes in responding to one of his critics:

> [I]t must be noted that this rule, *whatever we can conceive, can be*, while it is mine, and true, as long as it is a matter of clear and distinct conception, in which the possibility of the thing [or state of affairs: *rei possibilitas*] is contained, because God can bring about anything that we clearly perceive to be possible; nevertheless it must not be made use of rashly [*temere*], because it easily happens that someone who thinks he rightly understands some thing, nevertheless does not understand it, being blinded by some prejudice. (AT VIII–2, 351–2; HR I; 437–8; cf. AT III, 215; PL 80)

Difficulties with the notion of clear and distinct perception should not cause us to overlook the fact that Descartes did not think his argument would work without it.[10]

Besides the discussion of *res extensa*, the intervening Meditations have contributed the 'proofs' of God's existence and benevolence, intended to establish that Descartes can 'trust' those perceptions he recognizes to be most evident. With this result, the stage is fully set for the conclusion the Second Meditation by itself would not permit.[11]

Let us now turn to the Epistemological Argument itself. The Sixth Meditation begins with the observation that God is capable of bringing about or making the case whatever I am capable of clearly and distinctly perceiving: 'And I never judged that anything could not be brought about by him, except for the reason that it was impossible for me to perceive it distinctly' [*propter hoc quod illud a me distincte percipi repugnaret*] (AT VII, 71; HR I, 185). The first application of this principle is to establish the possible existence of 'physical things conceived as the object of pure mathematics'—since previous Meditations, and particularly the Fifth, have held these to be distinctly conceivable. The second application—after the consideration of imagination and a summary of his doubts of the senses—is in the Epistemological Argument.

> Because I know that all that I clearly and distinctly understand can be brought about by God as I understand it, it is enough that I can clearly and distinctly understand one thing apart from another [*unam rem absque altera*], for me to be certain that one is different from another, because they can be placed apart [*seorsim poni*] at least by God; and it doesn't matter by which power this is done, in order for us to judge them to be different; and thus, from this very fact, that I know I exist, and that meanwhile I notice nothing else at all to pertain to my nature or essence, except this alone that I am a thinking thing, I rightly conclude that my essence consists in this one [thing] that I am a thinking thing. And although probably (or rather, as I will afterward say, certainly) I have a body, which is very closely conjoined to me, because nevertheless on the one hand I have a clear and distinct idea of myself, in so far as I am only a thinking thing, not extended, and on the other hand I have a distinct idea of body, in so far as it is only an extended thing, not thinking, it is certain that I am really distinct from my body, and can exist apart from it. (AT VII, 78; HR I, 190)

To begin discussion of the argument I will simply propose a provisional reading, which seems to me natural:

(1) If A can exist apart from B, and vice versa, A is really distinct from B, and B from A.

(2) Whatever I can clearly and distinctly understand can be brought about by God (as I understand it).

(3) If I can clearly and distinctly understand A apart from B, and B apart from A, then God can bring it about that A and B are apart (separate).

(4) If God can bring it about that A and B are apart, then A and B can exist apart (and hence, by (1), are distinct).

(5) I am able clearly and distinctly to understand A apart from B, and B apart from A, if there are attributes ϕ and ψ, such that I clearly and distinctly understand that ϕ belongs to the nature of A, and ψ belongs to the nature of B, and I have a clear and distinct conception of A which doesn't include ψ, and a clear and distinct conception of B which doesn't include ϕ.

(6) Where A is myself, and B is body, thought and extension satisfy the above conditions on ϕ and ψ, respectively.

(7) Hence, by (5), (6), (3), and (4), I am really distinct from body (and can exist apart from it).

What, if anything, is wrong with this argument? Let me first mention some commonly heard objections to Descartes's position on the distinctness of mind that are not in fact effective against it.[12]

Sometimes Descartes's mind–body dualism is taken to rest on (or partly on) the so-called 'argument from doubt'—which is universally recognized to be fallacious. The argument from doubt is supposed to go something like this:

> My mind (or self) is distinct from all body. For something true of all body (that I can doubt it exists) is not true of myself (mind). But A and B are the same only if everything true of the one is true of the other.

And this argument is subject to a familiar sort of counter-example. Thus, suppose someone confronted with a masked personage reasons:

> I cannot doubt that the masked person in front of me exists; I can doubt that movie star R.R. exists (he might have suddenly died, or have somehow been 'created' by camera tricks; the name just might not satisfy conditions on successful reference); therefore the masked person in front of me is not R.R.

We all know we cannot solve ordinary identity problems in this way. But we need not dwell here on the problems with this argument, for (I trust) it is perfectly obvious that the argument I have quoted from the Sixth Meditation is not a version of it. In fact, I am inclined to believe that *all* attributions to Descartes of the 'Argument from Doubt' are erroneous: in a reply to Arnauld Descartes even indicates he is perfectly aware of the fallacious nature of such arguments (AT VII, 225; HR II, 101).[13] In any case, the concept of doubt figures nowhere in the argument from the Sixth Meditation we have quoted. Granted, there seems to be *some* direct connection in Descartes's mind between his inability to doubt his own existence while doubting the existence of body, and the ultimate conclusion that mind and body are distinct. But this connection must be understood in some other way than that represented by the disastrous 'Argument from Doubt.'

According to another objection, Descartes's argument can show at best that mind and body are possibly or potentially distinct (would be distinct if God should choose to separate them)—not that they *are* distinct. This objection fundamentally misses Descartes's point. Descartes holds that 'two' things *are* really distinct if it is *possible* for them to exist in separation. On this view actual *distinctness* does not entail actual *separateness*.

A third common criticism of Descartes's treatment of the

distinctness of mind derives from the claim that, under sufficient conditions of ignorance, one can conceive almost anything. Thus, the fact that we can conceive that p does not entail that p is even possible: all that follows (at best) is that we have not yet noticed any contradiction in p. But, as our previous discussion indicates, Descartes would turn this objection aside by pointing out that his argument is not based on mere conceivability, but on clear and distinct conceivability. One cannot ignore this crucial distinction without radically misunderstanding his position.

I do not wish to claim that the appeal to the distinction between clear and distinct perception and mere perception raises no problems of its own. It raises, of course, the important question of how one recognizes clear and distinct perceptions—and indeed what exactly they are. The underlying worry here is a fundamental one, and has already emerged at several crucial points in my analysis of Descartes's arguments. Thus, I have not been able to suggest a satisfactory 'Cartesian' answer to the challenge: how can we rule out the possibility that advances in science will reveal that our present conceptions, however 'evident' they seem, depend on a certain *ignorance* of the facts of the matter? Surely Descartes was in serious error about certain facts of the mind–body relation—for example with reference to the function of the brain in 'understanding.' Why shouldn't these be supposed to vitiate his claim to clear and distinct perceptions? I will briefly return to this critical problem later. Now, however, I wish to take up a criticism of Descartes's use of the notion of distinct perception in the Epistemological Argument that is, unquestionably, more directly relevant than the objections previously discussed.

In the first set of *Objections*, Caterus finds fault with Descartes's attempt to reason from the fact that *A* and *B* are distinctly and separately conceived to the conclusion that *A* and *B* can exist apart. He implies that Descartes may have overlooked the finer points of the scholastic theory of 'distinctions' on which his argument relies.[14] Caterus writes:

> Here I match the learned man against Scotus, who says that for it
> to be the case that one [thing] is conceived distinctly and separately
> from another, a distinction of the sort called formal and
> objective—intermediate between a real [distinction] and one of
> reason—is sufficient. And thus he distinguishes God's justice from
> His mercy; for, he says, they have concepts [*rationes*] formally
> diverse before all operation of the understanding, thus that even

191

then the one is not the other; and nevertheless it does not follow: justice can be conceived separately from mercy, therefore can also exist separately. (AT VII, 100; HR II, 8)

Caterus here does not exactly follow Descartes's 'clear and distinct conception' terminology; nevertheless he has put his finger on a problem that Descartes must come to terms with. For Descartes himself holds that such 'simple natures' as extension, figure and motion can each be clearly and distinctly conceived in itself; yet at the same time they are *not* really distinct; figure cannot exist apart from extended body, and so forth. (See especially *Rules for the Direction of the Mind*, Rules xii and xiv: AT X, 410ff; HR I, 35ff.) In his doctrine of simple natures Descartes appears to be squarely committed to the negation of the principle that what can be clearly and distinctly conceived in separation can *exist separately*.

Descartes replies to Caterus by stressing a distinction between *complete* and *incomplete* beings.

As to the matter of formal distinction . . . I briefly say that it does not differ from a modal one, and extends only to incomplete beings, which I have accurately distinguished from complete [beings], for which distinction it indeed suffices that one [being] is conceived distinctly and separately from another by intellectual abstraction from a thing inadequately conceived, not however so distinctly and separately that we understand one or the other [being] as if an entity in itself [*ens per se*] and distinct from all others. But for the latter to be the case a real distinction is always required. (AT VII, 120; HR II, 22)

Descartes goes on to give precisely the sort of example we would expect, in view of the doctrine of simple natures. Thus, he says,

The distinction between the motion and the figure of the same body is a formal one; and I can quite well understand the motion apart from the figure, and the figure apart from the motion; and I abstract both from the body: but nevertheless I cannot understand motion completely apart from a thing in which the motion is, nor the figure apart from a thing in which the figure is, nor motion in a thing in which figure cannot be, or figure in a thing incapable of motion. (*Ibid.*)

The same point, Descartes says, applies to the example brought forward by Caterus. With these cases Descartes contrasts the mind–body case:

But I completely understand what body is [French version: that is to say I conceive of a body as a complete thing] merely by thinking that it is extended, figured, mobile, etc., and denying of it all those things which pertain to the nature of the mind; and vice versa I understand the mind to be a complete thing, that doubts, understands, wills, and so forth, although I deny that any of those things contained in the idea of body are in it. (AT VII, 121 (cf. IX-1, 95); HR II, 22-3)

The gist of the passage seems to be that we can conceive body and mind not only *distinctly*, but *as complete things*, while denying of each whatever pertains to the nature of the other. Justice and motion, on the other hand, while perhaps capable of being understood distinctly 'in separation,' are not thereby capable of being understood 'completely'—i.e., as complete beings.

I do not know what passage or passages Descartes may have in mind when he says he has 'accurately distinguished' complete from incomplete beings. Certainly this distinction does not seem to be made explicit in the *Meditations*.[15] Further, we have seen that the argument as Descartes states it begins with the unrestricted claim that: 'It is enough that I understand one thing clearly and distinctly apart from another, to know that one is different from another, for they can be placed apart, at least by God. . . .' This statement must now be rephrased. In order to be able to conclude that A is different from B in the relevant way—i.e., *really* distinct—one must be able to conceive A clearly and distinctly and *completely* (as a complete being) apart from B. Also, we can now see that Descartes's further statement in the argument, that he has a clear and distinct conception of himself in so far as he is 'only a thinking thing, not extended,' must be given a different reading than that reflected in premiss (5), above. He must be saying *both* that the concept of himself as a thinking thing comprises no notion of extension, *and* that in thus conceiving himself as a thinking thing he clearly and distinctly conceives of himself as a complete being.

An interesting feature of this reply to Caterus should be noted. Consider the two following statements:

(1) A and B can be distinctly conceived separately from each other.
(2) A and B can be distinctly conceived as being separate from each other.

According to the former proposition, one can form a distinct conception of *A* without thinking of *B*, and vice versa. According to the second proposition, one can form the distinct conception *that A exists without B* (and vice versa). While the original formulation of the Epistemological Argument seemed to be using (1), it turns out that (2) is what Descartes really needs. And part of what Descartes is saying in reply to Caterus is that the two propositions are *not* equivalent: while (2) entails (1), (1) does not entail (2). Yet Descartes's reply is not restricted to amending his words to make this point clear. Rather, Descartes introduces into the argument the following proposition, which is a *sufficient condition* for (2), but also stronger than (2):

(3) *A* can be conceived as a complete being apart from *B* (and vice versa).

Presumably he does this because he wants to base the claim that (2) *on* some claim about the way *A* and *B* are individually or respectively conceived.

In the Fourth Objections, Antoine Arnauld picks up on Descartes's remarks to Caterus about the need for 'complete knowledge' as a basis for the mind–body distinctness argument. Arnauld reads this as an acknowledgment that the argument will go through only if our knowledge of ourselves as thinking things is, demonstrably, complete in the sense of being exhaustive. He further observes that nothing in the *Meditations* seems to bear at all on this problem except the argument in the Second Meditation that one can be certain of one's own existence as a thinking thing while doubting or denying the existence of body. But, he concludes,

all I can see to follow from this, is that a certain notion of myself can be obtained apart from [the] notion of body. But it is not yet quite clear to me that this notion is complete and adequate, so that I am certain that I am not in error when I exclude body from my essence. (AT VII, 201; HR II, 83)

According to Arnauld, then, Descartes is not entitled to conclude that extension does not belong to his essence, merely from the observation that he clearly and distinctly perceives that thought is essential to him while he 'notice[s] nothing else to pertain to [his] nature.' For perhaps in perceiving himself as a thinking thing, he is perceiving, so to speak, only *part* of his essence. Arnauld is in effect taking issue, specifically, with the following statement from the Epistemological Argument—which signals the transition from the conclusions of the Second Meditation to those of the Sixth:

194

From this very fact, that I know I exist, and that meanwhile I notice nothing else to pertain to my nature or essence, except this alone that I am a thinking thing, I rightly conclude that my essence consists in this one [thing] that I am a thinking thing. (AT VII, 78; HR I, 190)

Here Arnauld adduces the case of a man who clearly and distinctly conceives that a given triangle is right-angled, yet lacks a perception of the proportion of sides to hypotenuse. Because his knowledge of the triangle is in this respect incomplete, the man is able to doubt, and even deny, that the sum of squares on the sides is equal to the square on the hypotenuse. According to Arnauld, this man would be in a position to reason, in a way parallel to Descartes, that since the clear and distinct idea of a right triangle does not include the notion of Pythagorean proportion, God can make a right triangle with some other proportion among the squares. This conclusion, however, is false.[16] So the Epistemological Argument must be invalid.

Arnauld has misunderstood Descartes's use of the distinction between complete and incomplete knowledge in his reply to Caterus. (This is not entirely Arnauld's fault: Descartes's language in the First Replies was tricky and misleading.) However, clearing up the misunderstanding is not sufficient to dismiss the objection. Descartes recognizes both these points, and therefore his reply has two parts. Let us now consider it.

Descartes rightly takes Arnauld's main question to be: 'Where did I begin to demonstrate how it follows from the fact that I know nothing else to belong to my essence . . . except that I am a thinking being, it follows that nothing else does truly belong to it?' (AT VII, 219; HR II, 96). And he answers:

Surely where I have proved that God exists . . . who can do all that I clearly and distinctly know to be possible. For although much exists in me which I do not yet [at this stage of the *Meditations*] notice . . . *yet since that which I do notice is enough for me to subsist with this alone*, I am certain that I could have been created by God without other [attributes] which I do not notice. (AT VII, 219; HR II, 96–7)

Hence, these other attributes may be judged not to belong to my essence since 'none of those [properties] without which a thing can exist is comprised in its essence.' (There is a suspicion of 'could-can' sloppiness in the Latin, which I won't try to evaluate here.) Descartes further explains that when he spoke, in the First Replies, of the need for 'complete knowledge,' he did *not* mean exhaustive knowledge of the subject—as Arnauld seems to have assumed. (He observes that while we might sometimes *have* complete knowledge in this sense, we could never know that we have it.) Rather, he meant 'knowledge of a thing sufficient to know it is complete,' i.e. 'endowed with those forms or attributes, which are sufficient that from them I recognize that it is a substance.' He concludes:

> Mind can be perceived clearly and distinctly, or sufficiently so for it to be considered a complete thing, without any of those forms or attributes by which we recognize that body is a substance, *as I think I have sufficiently shown in the Second Meditation*; and body is understood distinctly and as a complete thing without those which pertain to mind. (AT VII, 223; HR II, 99–100; emphasis added)

He goes on to observe that Arnauld's triangle example is not effective against him, since it 'differs from the case at hand' in making no use of the notion of 'complete knowledge' in the sense that Descartes originally intended.

As I said above, Descartes's reply to Arnauld should be viewed as having two parts. On the one hand Descartes points out that, contrary to Arnauld's understanding, he had not meant to claim in the First Replies that the Epistemological Argument requires a complete knowledge in Arnauld's sense, i.e. a knowledge of all the properties that follow or flow from the essence with which one is concerned. On the other hand, he also now tries to make clear why a complete knowledge in Arnauld's sense is not required, why a 'complete knowledge' in Descartes's originally intended sense is sufficient. Arnauld's basic objection was that for all Descartes knows, some other attribute, such as extension, might be necessarily implicated in his essence together with the known attribute of thought; the only way of eliminating this possibility is to establish that one knows *all* the properties of the self. *Descartes's position, however, is just that since he recognizes that thought is sufficient 'for me to subsist with it alone,' he thereby knows no other attribute is necessary. To claim that thought and extension are different, and that either is sufficient to determine a complete or true thing, is already to deny the possibility of some 'hidden' necessary dependence of a thinking thing on the attribute of extension.* Thus a 'complete knowledge' in Descartes's originally intended sense is sufficient for the Epistemological Argument to go through.

We may now obtain a clearer understanding of the intended relation between the Second Meditation and the Sixth—indeed Descartes seems finally to make this relation explicit in the important passage I have quoted from the reply to Arnauld. The *cogito* reasoning and its immediate sequel are intended to establish, precisely, that 'mind can be perceived clearly and distinctly, or sufficiently so for it to be considered a complete thing, without any of those forms or attributes, from which we recognize that body is a substance. . . .' I think this explains, for example, Descartes's insertion into the Second Meditation of the statement that he knows he is a true and truly existing *thing*, merely in conceiving himself as *thinking*. The role of the Epistemological Argument in the Sixth Meditation is merely to establish that the perception of the mind argued for in the Second Meditation (clearly and distinctly perceived as a complete thing in virtue of having the property of thought) is sufficient ground for the conclusion that the mind is *really* a distinct thing. What is primarily needed, besides the conclusions of the Second Meditation, is the validation of clear and distinct perceptions as reliable guides to reality.

I think these observations also help one understand Descartes's notorious tendency—in works other than the *Meditations*—to move without visible transition from *cogito ergo sum* to *sum res cogitans*.[17] The *cogito* reasoning is supposed to show that we can clearly and distinctly conceive the self as a complete entity, or *ens per se*, merely in conceiving it as *thinking*. But, providing only that our clear and distinct perceptions are reliable guides to reality, and extension is a property distinct from thought, this amounts to saying that we need only thought, and not extension in order to exist. And *this* is to say that we are only thinking things.

Discussion of the objections of Caterus and Arnauld has shown the need for some changes in the analysis of the Epistemological Argument offered above. I suggest, finally, the following reading:

(1) If A can exist apart from B, and vice versa, A is really distinct from B, and B from A.

(2) Whatever I clearly and distinctly understand to be possible can be brought about by God.

(3) If I clearly and distinctly understand the possibility that A exists apart from B, and B apart from A, then God can bring about that A and B *do* exist in separation.

(4) If God can bring it about that A and B exist in separation, then A and B can exist apart and hence, by (1) they are distinct.

(5) I can clearly and distinctly understand the possibility of A and B existing apart from each other, if: there are attributes ϕ and ψ, such that I clearly and distinctly understand that ϕ belongs

to the nature of A, and that ψ belongs to the nature of B (and that $\phi \neq \psi$), and I clearly and distinctly understand that something can be a complete thing if it has ϕ even if it lacks ψ (or has ψ and lacks ϕ).

(6) Where A is myself and B is body, thought and extension satisfy the conditions on ϕ and ψ respectively.

(7) Hence, I am really distinct from body and can exist without it.

It seems to me, then, that Descartes's argument is stronger and much more carefully thought-out than his critics—contemporary or later—have generally recognized. It is surely time to put behind us the idea that it rests on nothing more than a dumb mistake, such as we find in the notorious 'Argument from Doubt.' Descartes's replies to his critics' objections to the argument are in general sharp and apposite—not in the least unworthy of a first-rate philosophical intelligence. Nevertheless, the problem of 'clear and distinct conception' still confronts us. How can I know that my ability to conceive myself as a thinking thing, independently of any corporeal attributes, may not actually derive from an *ignorance* of 'what thought is'—however distinct the conception may seem and however 'intimate' my apprehension of thought seems to be? As I've indicated before, I think the answer has to be that strictly speaking *I cannot know that*—especially since it appears perfectly manifest that not all the evidence is in. We simply do not have a very thorough understanding of human cognition, from any point of view, and there is no way of knowing what empirical and conceptual shocks may lie ahead. This notion, however, has implications that are not restricted to Descartes's argument. There is no reason that I can think of to suppose that recent essentialists' appeals to intuition are on any firmer ground than Descartes's appeals to distinct perception. In general, *most* current positions on the mind–body issue take out 'futures' on scientific progress in one way or another. And in fact the materialists' predictions of the 'reduction' of mind to matter, or of the 'elimination' of mentalistic categories, are not clearly more secure than anti-materialists' complacency about their own intuitions of the *difference* of mind and body, or the 'irreducibility' of the one to the other.

There is another serious objection to Descartes's position, that has been touched on above in connection with the *cogito* reasoning. It has to do with the possibility of knowing oneself *as a particular* on Cartesian principles. Thus, Descartes claims that through the *cogito* he knows *himself* distinctly as *a* thinking thing; and he goes on to

198

conclude, through the Epistemological Argument, that *he is only* a thinking thing, *a* substance of which the whole nature is only to think. He also implies, as we have noted, that in thus knowing himself, he knows himself as a continuing identical entity. It is, surely, natural to suppose that when Descartes uses 'I,' and speaks of knowing himself, he is conceiving himself as a particular entity, in distinction from other actual or possible selves. (Indeed, in treating the mind–body union—a topic to be considered below—Descartes makes explicit the point that there is only one mind per body: he even holds that the mind of a man individuates his body (AT IV, 166–7; PL 156–7). The problem is, first, that Descartes provides no account at all of what individuates souls, or distinguishes one from another; and, second, that the possibility of knowing oneself as a particular seems ruled out by the doctrine that we apprehend only general attributes like 'thought' and 'extension,' and *infer* from them to a *'res'* which is their subject. The Cartesian system seems to leave no basis at all either for claiming that one *res* continues from moment to moment as the subject of (what we're inclined to call) 'my' consciousness; or for denying that there is only one *res*, which is the subject of all thought (both 'yours' and 'mine').

I have suggested above that a partial solution might be found, if we could charitably interpret Descartes as not *really* meaning to deny that we are aware of substances as particulars, but only that we are aware of substances naked of attributes. Apart from textual issues, however, this suggestion has a disadvantage that has not been previously mentioned here. For it would seem to reduce knowing oneself as a particular self to being aware of a *thing*, without placing any restrictions on the properties of that thing, except that they be mental. But this is to dissociate both self-identity and consciousness of self-identity from the obvious sorts of psychological continuities, such as memories, beliefs, interests, attitudes and so forth. Even if Descartes could be saved from inconsistency by such a move, he would not be left with a very plausible theory.

To make his position at all plausible, I think, Descartes would have to introduce a principle that would not be easy to justify. He would have to hold that mental substances may after all be identified and distinguished according to the psychological or phenomenological features they 'exhibit.' Thus, while I am 'only a thinking thing' (i.e. not essentially extended), and you are 'only a thinking thing,' nevertheless we can claim we are different thinking things on the grounds that we have (or think we have) different and incompatible thoughts, memories, attitudes and so forth. Similarly, my memories *would* after all be relevant to my belief that I have continued in existence for a while as an identical self (as surely they are!). (Note that the suggested principle is addressed only to the question, 'What possible grounds could you have for supposing there is one and only one *res cogitans* for each human body that gives signs of intelligence?' It would be a *further* question whether or not the answer the principle provides has implications for the metaphysical issues of *what it is to be* a particular self (say me), or what I essentially am.)[18] To deal in detail with this problem would, however, take us farther beyond the actual Cartesian system than is warranted here.

4 Sensation and the Epistemological Argument

A final, curious question about the Epistemological Argument is whether Descartes, in saying he clearly and distinctly conceives himself as merely a thinking thing, means to be enunciating the first or the second of the following two propositions.

(1) I can clearly and distinctly conceive myself as a pure understanding, while excluding any corporeal attributes;

(2) I can clearly and distinctly conceive myself as having all the conscious experiences I do, in exclusion of any corporeal attributes.

A present-day 'Cartesian dualist' would, as we've noted, probably hold (2). For him or her pains and twinges and other sensations are just as 'distinctly conceivable' independently of the body as any 'higher' mental operation. And there is some reason to think that Descartes himself would accept this. According to the Second Meditation, for example, he does not need to know that he has a body in order to know with certainty that he seems to feel heat, see light and hear sound—i.e. have the 'sensations' of warmth, light and sound. And this would seem to be all he needs to claim that the having of such sensations is conceptually distinct from having a body. However, this consideration is not conclusive. For it is not entirely clear that Descartes does ultimately hold that having a sensation is clearly and distinctly conceivable apart from the supposition of corporeal attributes. As we will see in a moment, Descartes believes that sensation rightly regarded gives us incontrovertible proof of the existence of bodies, and of our own embodiment. Further, in the Epistemological Argument he seems to be concerned only with the question of his *essence*. And he makes it very clear that he does *not* regard the 'faculties' of sense and imagination as belonging to his essence as *res cogitans*. One relevant passage has already been cited:

I consider that this power of imagining which is in me, is different

200

from the power of understanding, in that it is not requisite to the essence of myself, that is of my mind; for although it were separated from me, there is little doubt I would remain nevertheless the same thing I now am. . . . (AT VII, 73; HR I, 186)

Still more significant is the fact that *after* Descartes states the Epistemological Argument—in the course of which he asserts, 'I rightly conclude that my essence consists in this one [thing], that I am a thinking thing'—he continues:

Besides I find in me the faculties of certain special modes of thinking, that is the faculties of imagining and sensing, without which I can clearly and distinctly understand myself a whole, but not vice versa, them without me, that is without an intelligent substance in which they are. . . . (AT VII, 78; HR I, 190)

This is already sufficient to show, I think, that the Epistemological Argument of Meditation VI is not intended by Descartes to make any *claim* that he can clearly and distinctly conceive his *sensations*, for example, independently of anything physical. This argument is concerned only with the isolation of Descartes's essence as a thinking thing—and this, as we have seen, means *intellectus purus*, pure understanding.

For all that, Descartes might still be ready to agree (with present-day versions of 'Cartesian dualism') that every one of his experiences or *cogitationes is* clearly and distinctly conceivable apart from any physical occurrence or bodily state. He could, in other words, be prepared to agree to this proposition, despite the fact that it is not strictly relevant to his demonstration that he is essentially only a thinking thing, and does not have any physical properties essentially. (In other words, it is not relevant to the *core* of *his* form of 'Cartesian dualism.') But is there even this much agreement?

We have seen that Descartes does not believe it possible conclusively to demonstrate the existence of body or brain from the experiences of *imagination*. The supposition of physical traces in the brain, which the mind 'inspects,' merely provides the 'best explanation' of imagination that he is able to produce. It seems safe to conclude, then, that for Descartes there is no *contradiction* in supposing that my phenomenal states of imagination occur although no body exists. And this means (I take it) that the experiences of *imagination* can be clearly and distinctly conceived in separation from anything physical. With sensation the situation is far less clear. But to see this we must consider the role of sensation in the arguments concerned with the existence of body and personal embodiment.

201

5   The evidence of the senses

At last, in the middle of the Sixth Meditation, Descartes affirms that 'corporeal objects exist.' However, his treatment of the truths of the senses, as opposed to their fallaciousness, is curiously vague and sketchy.

In recapitulating his reasons for doubting the senses Descartes has remarked that his past judgments concerning sensible objects have merely been 'taught him by nature,' since

> I persuaded myself they were constituted in a certain way, before I had considered any reasons by which this was proved. (AT VII, 76; HR I, 188–9)

Apart from the 'teachings of nature,' however, Descartes does find a reason for supposing that sense experiences proceeded from a corporeal world external to his mind: sensory ideas came to him independently of his will, and were in a certain way more distinct than the ideas he was conscious of causing himself. However, he goes on to observe that he has come to mistrust 'nature,' and also that he cannot yet rule out the possibility that he has himself an 'unknown faculty' that produces the ideas of sense.[19] The resolution of the problem is provided by his present knowledge of God:

> Now, however, that I begin better to know myself and the author of my origin, I do not indeed think that all that I seem to have from the senses is to be rashly admitted; but neither should all be called in doubt. (AT VII, 77–8; HR I, 189–90)

In considering God's benevolence in the Fourth Meditation Descartes maintained that such a benign creator could not have given him a faculty that would lead him into error if he used it rightly. The partial vindication of the senses, however, is made to rest on a different principle: that God would not allow me to fall into any error which he did not give me the power to correct. This principle is needed to affirm the existence of material objects, since Descartes apparently wants to hold back from saying their existence is clearly and distinctly perceived.[20] Thus, God has given me a 'great propensity to believe' that my sense ideas are caused by physical objects, and 'no faculty to recognize' that they are caused by Him or 'some other creature nobler than body.' These considerations together with God's benevolence allow us to deduce, so to speak, that our sense ideas really are caused by physical objects.

> I do not see by what reason it would be possible to understand him not to be a deceiver, if [the ideas of sense] were produced

202

[*emitterentur*] otherwise than by corporeal things, (AT VII, 80; HR I, 191)

Descartes's statement here is cautious. And he goes on to stress that the objects do not perhaps exist just as he comprehends them by the senses, 'for this comprehension by the senses is in many respects very confused and obscure.'

[B]ut at least all those things are in them, which I clearly and distinctly understand, that is all things, generally regarded, that are comprehended in the object of pure Mathematics. (*Ibid.*).

So far, then, the truths of the senses have been restricted to one: that bodies exist. Our clear and distinct knowledge of the material world is so far restricted to the *a priori* science of geometry. And from this point of view we have knowledge of bodies only 'generally regarded'—not as particulars. In the sequel Descartes groups together judgments that are only particular, such as that the sun is of such a shape and size, with the 'less clear' perceptions of light, sound and pain. He announces 'hope' of attaining truth even concerning these. He goes on to affirm that there is 'something true in' the notion that he has a body, that is harmed when he feels pain, that needs food when he is hungry, and so on. Certain further truths concerning embodiment are put forward, which we will consider below. But concerning the senses as sources of reliable cognition, very little further is said. What is said comes down, I think, to the following three propositions:

(1) The senses reliably inform me that there are other bodies external to my own that interact with it.
(2) By and large (though not without exception) the senses are reliable guides to what is beneficial and harmful to my body in the physical world.
(3) There is something in bodies corresponding to the variations in my sense perceptions of color, odor, sound, etc., and from which these various perceptions come, but not necessarily similar to them (*varietates iis respondentes, etiamsi forte iis non similes*).

These meager conclusions lead one to wonder whether Descartes can be ascribed a theory of sense perception at all, in the ordinary philosophical sense.[21] It would certainly be misleading to call him either a causal realist or a representative realist, as far as the evidence of the Sixth Meditation goes: the claimed connection between ideas and things is too tenuous, too nearly void of cognitive significance.

Sense perception, Descartes says, arises from the union of mind and body, and has significance mainly with respect to the preservation of the latter. Thus 'Nature,' understood specifically as what arises from the union of mind with body, can teach me what to pursue and what to flee,

> But it does not appear that it teaches us besides that we should conclude anything from those sense perceptions concerning things posited outside of us, without a previous examination by the understanding, because to know the truth about them seems to pertain to the mind alone, but not to the composite. (AT VII, 82–3; HR I, 193)

This leaves us with a puzzle. It is certain Descartes wants to hold that 'perceptions' of color, odor and so forth are to be classed as 'sensations,' like pain; that is, they have very little objective cognitive significance. But what about the perception of what Locke will call primary qualities? Well, we know that Descartes recognizes that the senses are not consistently reliable guides to shape, figure and so on: towers that look round in the distance look square close up, as he has just pointed out in the Sixth Meditation. On the other hand, as we have seen above, he does claim in the *Principles* that perceptions of extension, figure and motion have *some* kind of objectivity that distinguishes them from mere sensations (see Chapter III, Section 2). Perhaps the 'examination by the understanding' is meant to establish first, which of our sense perceptions have some internal claim to objective significance; and second, which of *these* were obtained under acceptable conditions of observation (the tower not too far off, etc.). Perhaps sense perceptions, thus doubly cleansed, may be counted as clear and distinct. Perhaps. What we must recognize is that Descartes, as his rationalism permitted, was much less explicit on this point than, for example, Locke. He was correspondingly inexplicit about what kinds of judgments we can make with certainty concerning the 'particulars' of sense.

6 *The body which by a certain special right I call mine*

As we've seen, Descartes presents the fact of his own embodiment as, so to speak, the first particular certainty of sense. Throughout the Sixth Meditation, and in other works, Descartes stresses that the real distinctness of mind and body does not prevent them from existing in a tight and intimate union. Among the manifestations of this union are the facts that rational deliberation and decision can affect what a person physically *does*, and that a person's conscious experience reflects in more or less dramatic ways the needs of his body and the impacts of other physical things upon it. As the very lengthy discussion of the Sixth Meditation shows, Descartes was deeply preoccupied with various problems connected with mind–body union. In particular, the theodicy of the *Meditations* evidently requires him to explain how bodily appetites can be so treacherous: the dropsical man desires to drink, and poisoned food can taste good. The answer to *this* problem is that the mind, being by nature indivisible, can 'operate' only in one small part of the brain (presumably he means the pineal gland). The body, on the other hand, is divisible and extended; peripheral changes can be communicated to the brain, and ultimately the mind, only by certain pathways, or 'intervening parts.' In the nature of the case, there is no way of excluding the possibility that the intervening parts may be changed in a way *normally* caused by specific peripheral stimulations when the usual causes are in fact absent. In such cases the brain, alas, will get a false message. But body being body, and mind being mind, there is just no way that God could have arranged things otherwise. At the same time Descartes insists that 'the whole mind is united to the whole body,' and that the mind is 'as if inter-mixed' [*quasi permixtum*] with the body. (Cf. AT VII, 83ff; HR I, 194ff.)

From the very beginning the issue of mind–body union has been regarded as a point of maximum vulnerability in Descartes's philosophical system. I want to argue that Descartes's account is afflicted with a fundamental ambivalence between two incompatible conceptions, neither of which he is willing to relinquish.[22] I call these the 'Natural Institution' theory and the 'Co-extension' theory. Both are reflected in the preceding paragraph, and are found side by side in the *Principles* and the *Passions* as well as in the Sixth Meditation. But before explaining this view in more detail, I will recapitulate some of the traditional objections to Descartes's philosophy that arise from the concept of mind–body union.

1 Problems of causal interaction

From Descartes's time to the present his critics have interpreted his system as a form of dualistic interactionism that fails to provide answers to crucial questions concerning the 'how' of interaction between substances of distinct types. Princess Elizabeth wondered how an immaterial thing, which could not be conceived either as extended or as in physical contact with any body, could be supposed to cause physical movement. In reply, Descartes chooses to interpret her remarks as a confession of a growing personal difficulty in conceiving herself as a single person, and tactfully suggests that she spend less time on philosophy (AT III, 690ff; PL 140ff). Leibniz and later critics have insisted that Descartes's views concerning the intervention of mind in nature are predicated on an overly lax conception of the fundamental conservation principles of physics.[23]

2   Location problems

From the *Meditations* we learn that the mind is both restricted to a small part of the brain and 'sort of intermingled' with the whole body. The potential for contradiction here is more fully realized in other texts. In the *Passions of the Soul*, Descartes makes the following assertions concerning the mind (*l'âme*): (a) it is united to all the parts of the body together, and cannot be said to exist in any one to the exclusion of others (I, 30); (b) it exercises its functions immediately only in the pineal gland, and has its 'principal seat' there (I, 31); (c) it radiates throughout the body from the pineal gland by means of the animal spirits (I, 34); (d) the mind has no relation to 'extension or dimensions or other properties of the matter of which the body is composed' (I, 30). (AT XI, 351ff; HR I, 345ff.) To Elizabeth, on the other hand, he remarks that the mind can be thought of as having extension—that this is nothing else than to conceive it united to the body. But, he tells her, we must bear in mind that the extension we thus attribute to mind differs from corporeal extension in that it does not exclude other corporeal extension from its location (AT III, 694; PL 143). Is it, then, correct or incorrect to say that the mind is extended throughout the body? If it is in some sense correct to say this, why should Descartes also say that it exercises its functions directly only in the pineal gland?

3   Substantial union or 'one whole' problem

Since Descartes's dualism commits him only to the view that mind and body are *potentially* separate, it isn't clear why he should see any difficulty in holding both that mind and body are conceived as distinct substances, and that they are conceived as presently conjoined. He in fact says as much, in replying to a question of Arnauld's (AT VII, 228; HR II, 102-3). Nevertheless, in correspondence with Elizabeth he comes up with the following startling assertion:

> [I]t does not seem to me that the human mind is capable of conceiving quite distinctly and at the same time both the distinction between mind and body, and their union; because to

do so, it is necessary to conceive them as a single thing [*une seule chose*], and at the same time [*ensemble*] to conceive them as two things, which is self-contradictory [*qui se contrarie*]. (AT III, 693; PL 142)

It is hard to see how to avoid interpreting this statement as an overt admission on Descartes's part that his position on the mind–body relation is self-contradictory.[24] But what could motivate him to make such a statement, given that all he seems officially committed to is the view the mind and body are capable of existing apart? Why should he not say that we must conceive them as two things in this sense, while also (quite consistently) conceiving them as temporarily constituting one thing as a result of their present conjunction?

I won't try to deal with all of these problems directly. However, I do think the distinction between Natural Institution and Co-extension theories helps to throw light on them. I will suggest also that the Natural Institution theory is philosophically resourceful and relatively intelligible. It is therefore an interesting question why this theory does not seem completely to satisfy Descartes—why he keeps trying to combine it with the seemingly distinct and seemingly almost ineffable Co-extension theory. I will begin by considering the Natural Institution account, as Descartes presents it.

When Descartes asserts in the Sixth Meditation that the mind is 'immediately affected' not by all parts of the body, but only by a small part of the brain, he is not relying only on *a priori* considerations about the nature of mind (cf. AT VII, 86; HR I, 196). He is also relying on observations that it is necessary and sufficient for our having certain experiences that the brain be affected in the appropriate ways. It is on the other hand neither necessary nor sufficient that the peripheral sensory organs or intervening nerves be in any particular state. Typically, when 'the nerves are contracted in the foot' the contractions bring about contractions in the intimate parts of the brain, 'and excite in them such motion as is instituted by nature to affect the mind with a sensation of pain as if existing in the foot' (AT VII, 87; HR I, 197). But the same motion will create the same sensation of pain whether or not it is ultimately caused by an actual contraction in the nerves of the foot, or is rather brought about by tampering with the nervous system at some intermediate point. Moreover, Descartes goes on to insist, it is only by the natural institution of God, and not by any intrinsic relation, that this particular motion in the inmost part of the brain brings about this particular sensation—the sensation of pain in the foot. He writes:

when the nerves that are in the foot are moved violently and more than is usual, that movement of them, passing through the medulla of the spine, to the inmost parts of the brain, there gives a sign to the mind to sense something, namely pain as if existing in the foot [*dolorem tanquam in pede existentem*], by which the mind is excited to remove the cause of the pain, as harming the foot, so far as it can. Of course the nature of man could have been so constituted by God that that same motion in the brain would exhibit something else to the mind: namely, either itself [i.e. the motion], in so far as it is in the brain, or in so far as it is in the foot, or in some other intermediate location, or finally anything else at all. . . . (AT VII, 88; HR I, 197)

According to this account, then, the mind is affected in the same way, or has exhibited to it the same thing, whenever the brain is in a particular type of state; that is, it has the same sort of experience, regardless of the actual physical origin of the brain-state. This is to say, I should think, that the mind has no direct contact with parts of the body remote from the brain, no way of knowing (immediately) whether there is in fact damage being done to the foot, or merely a malfunction in the intervening nervous structure. Further, there is no necessity, independently of God's decision to associate one thing with another, for a particular sort of brain state to give rise to a particular state of mind or experience. The brain state in question, which gives rise to a sensation of pain 'as if in the foot,' *could* have given rise instead to a vivid visual impression of movement in the brain itself, 'or finally anything at all.' Most interesting of all is Descartes's description of what the mind senses, as a result of the 'sign' given to it by the brain—namely 'pain as if existing in the foot.' The sensation the mind feels has a location, but it is an 'as if' location. The mind experiences a tendency, one might almost say, to assign pain to the foot. The 'location' of the sensation is merely a function of the *mind's locating* the sensation—and where it locates it, or tends to locate it, will depend on what God has determined a particular change in the brain should mean to the mind. (It is, incidentally, not at all clear that the intrinsic intentionality Descartes here assigns to sensation is compatible with the views expressed elsewhere, and discussed above, that we make the error of assigning sensations to bodies only because of the material falsity or obscurity of the ideas of sense, or their association with more 'objectively real' perceptions.)

A very similar analysis of the mind's location is offered in the *Principles*. Descartes there again remarks that the mind has its 'principal seat in the brain' and it is there that the mind perceives (IV, 189; AT VIII-1, 315; HR I, 289). He again stresses that motions in the body cause the mind to have thoughts which do not give us 'any image of' the occasioning motions.

> It is clearly proved . . . that the mind senses what happens in the individual members of the body by means of the nerves, not in so far as it is in the individual members, but only in so far as it is in the brain. . . . (AT VIII-1, 319; HR I, 293)

The ascription of pains to the foot or hand, therefore, must involve a sort of *double* illusion. Pains are not in the body at all, but in the mind. And the mind is not in the foot or hand, but in the brain. (Cf. *Principles* I, 46 and 67; AT VIII-1, 22, 33; HR I, 237, 247.)

Descartes's theory of sensation, as I've so far expounded it, was obviously motivated by a combination of scientific and common-sensical considerations. The mind must be said to perceive 'in the brain,' since if it perceived 'in the limbs,' for example, we should be able directly to distinguish cases of peripheral stimulation from cases of intermediate nervous disorder, and this we cannot do. (In fact, as Descartes loves to point out, we are unable directly to distinguish cases of actual damage to the foot from cases of nervous discharge in the leg when the foot has been amputated.) The connection between a particular type of mind state and a particular type of brain state is said to be arbitrary, or depend on divine institution, for, I imagine, the simple reason that Descartes could not see any way of establishing an *intrinsic* connection between the two. The prevailing tendency *to ascribe pains* to our feet and hands is said to be deluded for the reason that pains are after all *sensations*, and feet and hands are nothing but bits of *res extensa*, and assigning sensations to *some* bits of *res extensa* is just as intelligent as assigning them to any other bits—say to the chalk or the blackboard. (This is, of course, an overly popular way of stating Descartes's point. For it is supposed to follow from his principles that ascribing *colors* to the blackboard or the chalk is just as bad a mistake as ascribing pains to them.) Now we must consider Descartes's departure from this account.

When in the Sixth Meditation Descartes first 'concludes' that he is not *just* a mind, he observes that there is 'some truth in' the idea that he 'has a body, which is hurt when I feel pain, which needs food or drink when I experience hunger or thirst, and the like . . .' (AT VII, 80; HR I, 192). Descartes goes on from this passage to make an assertion from which we have previously quoted only a phrase or two. It is perhaps his best-known statement about embodiment.

209

Nature teaches through these sensations of pain, of hunger, of thirst, etc., that I am not only present in my body as a sailor is present in a ship, but that I am very tightly joined to it and as if mixed through [*permixtum*] so as to compose one thing with it. For otherwise, when the body is injured, I, who am nothing but a thinking thing, would not feel pain on that account, but would perceive this injury by the pure understanding, as a sailor perceives by sight if something in the ship is broken; and when the body needs food or drink, I would expressly understand this fact, not have confused sensations of hunger and thirst. For certainly these sensations of thirst, hunger, pain, etc., are nothing else than certain confused modes of thought arising from the union and so to speak intermixture [*quasi permixtione*] of the mind with the body. (AT VII, 81; HR I, 192)

Does the talk in this passage of the 'intermixture' of mind with body imply a different conception of the mind–body relation than that expounded in the 'Natural Institution' passages? I will argue later that when Descartes talks of the 'intermixture' of mind with body he generally is invoking a different conception of their union. But first I want to point out that the considerations Descartes adduces in the passage just quoted can mostly be accommodated within the Natural Institution theory. Descartes's position is, first, that unembodied mind would be a pure intellect or pure understanding. Whatever it knew about it would know by reason alone (and perhaps this means it would have no knowledge that was not clear and distinct). It is not clear to what extent Descartes has really reflected on what it would be like to know about particular states of affairs 'by pure understanding'; obviously the sailor analogy is unhelpful in this respect, since the sailor does rely on sense perception for knowledge of the state of his ship. In any case Descartes is also holding, second, that in the *having of sensations* an embodied mind experiences a more direct or close connection with its own body than it experiences with other bodies when it perceives them (even though visual perception too requires the 'having' of a body). Now, forgetting for a moment the talk of 'intermixture,' let's see what might be made of all this from the point of view of the Natural Institution theory.

The Natural Institution theory will allow us to *say*, obviously, that we are more closely united with our bodies than a sailor with his ship. But it will give a very particular explanation or account of this 'close union.' On the Natural Institution view, the difference between 'our' relation to 'our own' bodies, and our relations to other bodies is that certain changes in our bodies (especially advantageous and

210

disadvantageous changes) frequently result in motions in our brains that, by God's institution, give rise to particular sort of experiences in the mind that the mind tends to locate in the body itself. Similar changes in other bodies, on the other hand, do not lead to these types of motions in *our* brains, and do not result in any experience that we tend to locate as an experience in the remote body affected. Since it is part and parcel of the Natural Institution theory that a given motion in the brain could give rise to just any experience, and that the tendency to locate experiences is itself the result of natural institution, we will of course have to say it is a purely contingent matter that we feel pains 'as if in the hand' or 'as if in the foot,' but not 'as if in the blackboard' or 'as if in the hull of our ship.'

On the Natural Institution theory, then, it would seemingly be wrong to say that we experience sensations in different parts of our bodies *because of* a state of affairs designated as the close or intimate union or intermingling of mind with body. Rather, what we call the close union or intermingling of this mind with this body is nothing but the arbitrarily established disposition of this mind to experience certain types of sensations on the occasion of certain changes in this body, and to refer these sensations to (parts of) this body.[25]

But now we can also begin to see why it is not possible to ascribe to Descartes consistent adherence to the rather austere Natural Institution conception of embodiment. For in the passage we have just been considering Descartes is surely saying that one has sensations of a certain sort, in response to changes in a certain body, *because* one is united with that body—not that having sensations of a certain sort, etc. is what *it is* to be united to that body: 'For certainly these sensations of thirst, hunger, pain, etc., are nothing else than certain confused modes of thought *arising from the union* and so to speak intermixture of the mind with the body.'

It is useful to notice that when Descartes departs from the austere Natural Institution conception of embodiment, he actually introduces not one but two ideas that seem to be incompatible with it. First, as we have just seen, he implies there is a 'something' called the mind–body union that has some kind of unique explanatory function. Second, he implies that this union in some sense involves the extension of the mind throughout the body—as opposed to some sort of exclusive location of the mind in the vicinity of the pineal gland.

There are, I think, three principal texts which demonstrate most clearly Descartes's inability to rest content with the Natural Institution conception of the mind–body union: they are the Replies to the Sixth Objections, the *Passions of the Soul* (pt I), and the correspondence with Elizabeth. *The Passions of the Soul* show Descartes trying to maintain simultaneously and very explicitly both the Natural Institution and the Co-extension views of embodiment. Article 30 of Part I of the *Passions* reads in part:

> the soul is truly joined to the whole body, and one cannot properly say that it is in some one of [the body's] parts to the exclusion of others. . . . (AT XI, 351; HR I, 345)

And Article 31 reads in part:

> although the soul is joined to the whole body, there is nevertheless in the body a certain part in which the soul exercises its functions more particularly than in all the others. (AT XI, 351–2; HR I, 345)

This part, of course, turns out to be the pineal gland. From the pineal gland, Descartes explains, 'the soul . . . radiates into all the rest of the body by means of the [animal] spirits, the nerves, and even the blood . . .' (AT XI, 354; HR I, 347). Yet despite this 'radiation' of the soul or mind throughout the body it turns out that we feel passions, for example, just because of the natural institution of a connection between a particular state of the pineal gland (normally resulting from antecedent physiological changes) and a particular mental occurrence. Thus, in explaining how the passion of fear is brought about in the soul, Descartes writes:

> For from the fact alone that these spirits enter into these pores [of the brain] they excite a particular movement in this gland, which is instituted by nature to make this passion felt by the soul. And because these pores are principally related to the little nerves that serve to contract or enlarge the orifices of the heart, this makes it the case that the soul feels [the passion] principally as in the heart. (I, 36: AT XI, 357; HR I, 348)

There are, it may be noted, certain differences between the *Passions of the Soul* and the *Meditations*, with respect to the ways in which the Natural Institution view and the Co-extension view are respectively presented. Descartes makes explicit in the *Passions* that there is a physiological *reason* why a particular movement in the inner brain gives rise to an experience that is referred to the heart. He does not stress in the *Passions*, as he does in the *Meditations*, that the connection between this brain state and this experience (of fear as if in the heart) is purely arbitrary and contingent, that it could have been anything else at all. (Yet there is no reason, on the other hand, to suppose that he gives up the view.) More significant, I suppose, is the fact that Descartes gives in the *Passions* a very different sort of *reason* for the Co-extension conception than the one suggested by the sailor-in-his-ship passage of the *Meditations*. In the *Passions* he does not appeal to the experience of sensation to justify the claim of co-extension or intermingling; rather he cites the fact that the body is an integral whole, and the soul, which is indivisible, relates to it *as* a whole (I, 30). Once again, though, it is not made very clear how the considerations mentioned are supposed to constitute an argument for some sort of accommodation between the Co-extension and the Natural Institution conceptions: '*although* the soul is joined to the whole body, there is *nevertheless* in the body a certain part in which the soul exercises its functions more particularly. . . .'

In the Sixth Replies and in the correspondence with Elizabeth, Descartes mentions neither the pineal gland nor the theory of Natural Institution, and seems in effect to go whole-hog for the Co-extension view. In both texts he says that the relation of mind to body should be thought of on the model of the relation of gravity (or weight) to body on the old Scholastic system of thought (AT VII, 441f and III, 667; HR II, 255 and PL 139). This seems to mean, in particular, that we should conceive the mind as extended throughout the body, but not in such a way as to occupy a set of locations to the exclusion of other extended things. Further, the extension of the mind through-out the body is not supposed to preclude the presence of the *whole* mind in *every* distinguishable part of the body. He explains in the Sixth Replies that when he had formerly accepted the Scholastic view, according to which gravity is a real quality of bodies, he had believed

> that there was as much gravity in a mass of gold or of some other metal a foot long, as in a piece of wood ten feet long; and I believed that all that same [gravity] could be contracted within a mathematical point. But I also saw that while it remained coextensive with the heavy body, it could exercise its force at any point of the body, because from whatever part that body was hung by a rope, it pulled the rope with all its gravity, exactly as if this gravity was only in the part touching the rope, and was not also distributed through the others. And in no other way [*nec alia ratione*] do I now understand mind to be coextensive with the body, the whole in the whole, and the whole in any of its parts. (AT VII, 442; HR II, 255)

In the Sixth Replies, and more expansively in the correspondence with Elizabeth, Descartes indicates that everyone has a *direct and immediate experience* of the mind–body union; it is this direct experience which is apparently supposed to ground the conception of mind as coextensive with the body, 'the whole in the whole, and the whole in any of its parts.' In fact, Descartes explains, it is this immediate experience of the mind–body union, of the coextensiveness of mind with body, that originally gave rise to the erroneous conception of gravity on which the Scholastics rely! (AT III, 667–8; PL 139).

Elizabeth found this explanation less than satisfactory as a response to her original question about the 'how' of mind–body interaction. 'I must confess,' she writes,

> that . . . the life I am constrained to lead does not permit me
> enough time at my disposal to acquire a habit of meditation
> according to your rules. . . . [T]his will serve, I hope, as an excuse
> for my stupidity in being unable to understand the idea by which
> we should judge how the soul (unextended and immaterial) can
> move the body, in terms of the notion which you previously had of
> gravity. . . . (AT III, 684)

Subsequent commentators have, of course, tended to sympathize with Elizabeth's 'stupidity.' But the interesting question, I think, is simply why Descartes should feel impelled to get involved in the obfuscating talk about gravity, or about coextensiveness, in the first place. Why should he not, in other words, be prepared to rest content with the Natural Institution conception of mind–body interaction and union? The arguments that he offers, in the *Passions* and elsewhere, seem uncompelling.

Now one good reason might be that the conception can be construed as having unorthodox implications with respect to the unity of man. Descartes's replies to the theologian Arnauld show that Descartes had hoped in the *Meditations* to avoid the unacceptable conclusion that a person is 'a spirit that makes use of a body.' (Cf. AT VII, 227; HR II, 102.) Also, he stresses to Regius that one must be careful to affirm that the unity of mind and body is real, true and substantial—and exhibited in sensation.[26] To be sure, the Natural Institution theory is not totally inadequate to these purposes. A mind experiencing sensations as a result of natural institution is not a mere spirit (not, at any rate, a pure understanding), and not a mere affector of its body (it is also affected *by* the body). Yet the Natural Institution theory does in one very clear sense imply that the union of mind and body that constitutes a man *is* a unity *per accidens*. For it is an explicit tenet of this theory that the particular relation between a given human mind and its body is the result of mere correlation by Divine fiat of certain states of one with certain states of (part of) the other. This consideration might provide a temptation (if not a reason) to slide toward the Co-extension view. For as Descartes's language

[margin note:] What about HR II 208-9 (MDW p. 179)?

frequently suggests, that theory, obscure as it is, suggests a 'tighter,' 'closer,' or 'more intimate' connection between mind and body. Also, its very obscurity helps to make it less vulnerable to theological objection.[27] (Interestingly, however, this issue of orthodoxy does not seem to be expressed or even implicit in either the Sixth Replies or Descartes's letters to Elizabeth.)

Some people have suggested to me that Descartes might be unable to rest with his Natural Institution conception because of the difficulty of rationalizing causal relations between distinct sorts of substances (the difficulty pointed out by Elizabeth). Now I would agree that the Natural Institution theory, according to which sensations are said to 'arise from' brain movements, is in apparent conflict with some of the things Descartes says about causation. In particular, it is in apparent conflict with his various espousals of the 'like cause, like effect' principle.[28] But it is not clear that this consideration has much explanatory value in the case at hand. It is true that, in response to Elizabeth's question about causation, Descartes spontaneously moves to talk of direct experience of the mind–body union, which he seems to take as equivalent to direct experience of mind–body interaction. This move may suggest that he is trying to evade questions about the 'how' of interaction by presenting the mind–body relation as a simple unanalyzable notion. But if this is the idea behind Descartes's move, it appears to be a deluded one. For the move to co-extensiveness does not, after all, put him in a position either to deny interaction between distinct sorts of substances (indeed, this is explicitly reaffirmed), or to reconcile the supposition of interaction with other assumptions about causation. And if Descartes is going to take refuge in the brute fact of interaction, it seems he should not need such apparatus as the 'gravity' pseudo-concept in order to do so. Thus, while problems about causal interaction between distinct substances might indeed provide genuine philosophical reasons for not being quite satisfied with the Natural Institution theory, it is not clear that these problems provide good reasons for preferring the Co-extension theory. We should bear in mind, also, that Descartes does not just *drop* the Natural Institution conception—as might be expected if he had come to believe it rested on unacceptable assumptions about causality. For as we have noticed this conception is still present in the *Passions of the Soul*, which is of a later date than the correspondence with Elizabeth—and was in fact Descartes's last published work.

One possibility, of course, is that Descartes was subject to confusion in thinking about the mind–body relation, and that this confusion, together perhaps with concern to conform to the 'unity of man' tradition, is the main factor underlying his espousal of apparently disparate theories. In particular, Descartes may have been subject to the confusion of thinking he did have direct experience of the mind–body union in himself, while forgetting that on the Natural Institution theory, *no such experience is possible*. According to the Co-extension theory (on my interpretation) we experience the co-extensiveness of mind throughout the body (the whole mind is united to the whole body), and (perhaps by this very fact) experience something called the mind–body union. According to the Natural Institution theory, on the other hand, all we can experience, with respect to the body, are sensations which we (considered as minds) refer to various parts of the body (feet, hands, etc.). On this latter view the unity itself, which involves essentially a special correlation between brain states and sensations, cannot be fully experienced. In effect, all we can experience is one side of it.

Willis Doney and Ronald de Sousa have suggested to me independently that perhaps Descartes's slide into the Co-extension theory arose from considerations such as those more recently brought against Cartesian dualism by such philosophers as Ryle and Strawson. Thus, Ryle seems correct when he says the strict form of Cartesian dualism entails that whenever I am carrying out any normal activity, such as giving a lecture or driving a car or running for the bus, there are two distinct subjects involved—my mind and my body—and two distinct series of events, my 'thoughts' and my physical motions.[29] If some of what Ryle says about Descartes is caricature, this seems at any rate to be purely literal interpretation. Ryle's refutation of this theory consists more of ridicule and defining it as a 'category mistake' than of logically exact argument. However, he is right: the idea *seems absurd*. Strawson similarly has maintained that one single entity, the human person, must be the subject of both mental and physical predicates.[30] Strawson has offered extensive and ingenious argument for this claim, deriving especially from considerations of reference and re-identification. (Also, he has accorded to his opponents more logically scrupulous treatment than Ryle.) Strawson's arguments are not unchallengeable; the central argument of 'Persons,' in particular, seems to turn on a claim only obscurely defended in a footnote.[31] Again, however, there is something overwhelmingly plausible and sensible about his general position—and, correspondingly, something implausible and incredible about the two-subject view, considered in relation to human action. Perhaps Descartes himself could not altogether avoid noticing this, and his response was talk of 'co-extension,' of 'one whole,' of the mind–body union as a third thing?

This is an interesting suggestion, and for all I know could be correct. However, I'm afraid my response is to feel that Descartes should have stuck to his guns. The attempt to accommodate Rylean intuitions within a dualistic system—if that is what is at issue—has resulted not in an improved theory but a self-contradictory and incoherent one. As Descartes in effect remarks to Elizabeth, mind and body are either two things or not two things. To suppose they both are two things and are not two things is unacceptable. Descartes may think the law of non-contradiction is in some sense contingent; he has not said it is false.

Apart from the issues so far considered, other objections to the Natural Institution theory can be raised within the context of Descartes's system. I will present two of these. I see no reason to think, though, that Descartes himself ever considered them, and no reason to suppose they are behind his drift into 'co-extension' talk. The first has to do with the sorts of 'errors' we make about our sensations on Descartes's account.

According to the Natural Institution theory, experiencing pain is in crucial respects just like having 'a sensation of' color. In both cases, the following process is supposed to occur. At the end of a chain of bodily movements, a certain state occurs in the brain, which, as a result of arbitrarily established laws, gives rise to a certain 'sensation' in the mind. In both cases the sensation is in some sense referred outside the mind. Thus, the mind experiences color 'as if in the rose' and pain 'as if in the foot.' In both cases the mind may be said to represent or exhibit something to itself as external (color as if in the rose; pain as if in the foot). In either case, there is really no such a thing as color in the rose or pain in the foot.

The trouble with this account is that it provides no room for recognizing an important *dis*analogy between perceiving colors and experiencing pains. When we see colors in roses we have no inclination to attribute experiences or sensations to roses, but when we feel pains in our foot we do tend to say that there is a feeling—a sensation—in the foot. This distinction is obviously crucial to the notion of *being embodied*—as opposed to just consciously perceiving or representing (seeming) states of bodies. While the distinction in question is not obviously incompatible with a Natural Institution account of embodiment, Descartes's exposition of this account leaves us with nothing on which to hang the distinction. To this extent it must be regarded as defective.

The second point of objection to the theory is even more serious. It arises from the fact that Descartes wants to use the experience of sensations such as pain as a basis for justifying the claim that the 'mind' with which he is still identifying himself at the beginning of the Sixth Meditation actually does 'have a body.' This is one of the things he is trying to accomplish in the 'sailor in his ship' passage that we have already quoted. Similarly, in Principle II of Part II of the *Principles* Descartes explains that we know that 'a certain body is more tightly conjoined to the mind than other bodies,'

> from the fact that we clearly notice that pain and other sensations occur without our foreseeing them; of which the mind is conscious they do not arise from itself alone, nor pertain to it from the fact alone that it is a thinking thing, but only from the fact that it is united to a certain other thing, extended and mobile, which thing is called the human body. (AT VIII-1, 41; HR I, 255)

But *how* does the experience of pain demonstrate that the body of man is closely united to the mind? In the *Meditations* Descartes argues that our sensible perceptions must be caused by bodies, since we have a strong disposition to suppose that they are, and God would be a deceiver if this disposition were misleading us—e.g. if He were Himself the cause of our sensible perceptions. But if this line of reasoning shows anything, it shows only that there are bodies that act on our mind; it does not by itself serve to show that we are embodied, 'have bodies.' One is inclined to suppose, therefore, that the latter conclusion must be based on our particular disposition to assign pains, and other experiences that we consciously have, to various parts of some particular body—namely, the one we call ours. But the problem here, of course, is that Descartes also wants to hold that this disposition to assign sensations to various parts of the body should be resisted—that in so far as we succumb to it we commit the *error* of ascribing experiences to matter. It is, at best, hard to see how our unjustified tendency to ascribe experiences to parts of what we call our body could justify us in calling this thing our body. (It is, in addition, hard to see how our having such a disposition, as a result of divine institution, is compatible with God's not being a deceiver but that, I think, is a separate issue.)

In summation, I want to hold that the Natural Institution theory is Descartes's best account of embodiment, in the sense that it is far more intelligible than the Co-extension view, and it is possible to see the reasons he had for holding it. I have done what I could to account for his holding the Co-extension view too. Finally, I've tried to offer some reasons for believing that the Natural Institution view is not in itself satisfactory—or at any rate is not shown to be satisfactory within the context in which Descartes sets it.

In conclusion, I would like to return briefly to the well-known objections to Cartesian dualism from the point of view of the problem of mind–body union—the objections that I mentioned at the outset.

1 Causality

The Natural Institution theory attributes the effect of body on mind ultimately to an *ad hoc* arrangement on the part of God. As far as I know, there is nothing Descartes directly says in this connection that would help significantly with any difficulties one may find in the notion of interaction between distinct sort of substances. It is worth noting, though, that in the *Meditations* Descartes does suggest that the interaction in the body–mind direction may be interpreted as something like the reading of a *sign*.[32] This metaphor cannot, of course, be regarded as dramatically elucidatory. But it does help a little to free the theory from the impact model of basic causal relations that Elizabeth rightly found unintelligible when applied to immaterial substances.

2 Location

According to my reading Descartes gives two different accounts of the mind's location because he has two different theories of embodiment. These theories are not compatible, despite being sometimes expressed in close conjunction with each other. The Natural Institution theory, incidentally, does not seem strictly to entail that the mind is located in the center of the brain. What it entails, I think, is that the mind is directly affected only by the brain, or pineal gland. As we've seen though, Descartes does seem to make the inference from the causal to the locational claim.

3 'One whole' problem

If Descartes held consistently to the Natural Institution conception, he should, I think, have said that to conceive mind and body as united is just to conceive of mind as subject, at a given time, to experiencing certain sorts of sensations in response to certain movements in the brain; and the brain as subject to certain movements as a result of certain thoughts or volitions in the mind. To conceive of mind and body as distinct, on the other hand, would be to conceive of mind as capable of existing as pure intellect, no longer subject to experiencing sensations. There does not seem to be any outright contradiction between these two conceptions—whatever other objections they may have to face. (Contradiction arises when we try to combine the Natural

219

Institution account with the obscure if 'intuitive' Co-extension theory.)

This suggestion does, of course, require a certain constraint on the interpretation of the Epistemological Argument. In discussing the argument above I left open the question whether 'conceiving my mind apart from body' should be taken to mean 'conceiving any and all of my present mental states apart from any physical state,' or rather 'conceiving my understanding or intellect apart from any physical state.' If then mind–body union is to be explicated in terms of the having of sensations, the mind–body distinctness must evidently be understood in terms of the possibility of the mind existing without sensations. But as I indicated above, Descartes does seem to set up the Epistemological Argument as if he had the latter alternative in mind. If so, his views must again be sharply distinguished from those of contemporary philosophers troubled by the 'mind–body problem.' For these philosophers tend to regard sensations such as pain (or orange after-images) as the very paradigm of mental states conceivable apart from the body.

Conclusion

It is a commonplace of the history of philosophy that Descartes initiated the modern era by placing the critique of knowledge at the forefront of philosophical inquiry. That is, he accorded the questions 'How can I know?' and 'How can I be certain?' priority over questions about the nature of reality. However, if the interpretation presented in this book is correct, this view is at least partly misleading: Cartesian doubt is very much in the service of certain fundamentally metaphysical convictions about God, self and nature. This is not to deny that the 'doubt' is historically significant—even momentous. For example, to the extent that the metaphysical views in question are 'new' ones, and to the extent that they run counter to commonsense assumptions, the thrust of the doubt is truly revolutionary, and hence in a certain sense 'real.' Also, since the views in question involve a severe circumscription of the powers of sense, and a less damning but still significant circumscription of reason, the 'doubt' of the *Meditations* does have some genuine epistemological implications. The error would be to suppose that epistemological issues take precedence, in Descartes's philosophy, over a general metaphysical vision of reality, and commitments to a special conception of what the world is like and how it works.

There are a number of respects in which Descartes's system, for all its anchoring in methodic doubt, fails to manifest a new critical spirit with respect to the human 'faculty of knowledge.' The 'possibility' of metaphysics does not seem to have been genuinely problematic for Descartes, nor does he show any lasting reservations about the possibility of a given individual arriving once and for all at a true and close-to-adequate scientific system. The idea of science as an ongoing inquiry, where all systems are provisional and the greatest genius is still restricted in his vision by the limitations of his time, was obviously no part of Descartes's conception of himself and his work. Cartesian skepticism is, after all, swiftly dispelled by the Divine guarantee—which readily confirms reason over sense, and Descartes's light of nature over two thousand years of philosophical, theological and scientific 'prejudice.' Descartes's casual treatment of the central and crucial notion of 'distinct idea'—of which I have frequently complained—itself reveals how far he must have been from wrestling with tough epistemological problems of justification, of understanding, of interpersonal and intergenerational confirmation.

There is another, more 'philosophical,' respect in which Cartesian skepticism may be misjudged, in the light of subsequent philosophical history. There is some tendency today, reading history backwards, to interpret Descartes's enterprise in terms of the empiricistic ideaism of Berkeley, Hume and Mill, thus giving his 'skepticism' very potent force. It is true that Descartes advanced the view that knowledge of our own sensations, together with knowledge of our other 'thoughts,' is immediate and unproblematic, and prior to knowledge of physical existence. But it is surely ironic that this aspect of his position should have achieved its historical influence in nearly complete abstraction from his metaphysics of substance, from the doctrine of distinct ideas, and from Descartes's extensive questioning of the cognitive significance of sensation. It is really hard to imagine a work more sharply opposed to empiricistic phenomenalism than Descartes's *Meditations*.

There are, to be sure, observations about the limitations of human reason to be found in Descartes's writings—and not merely in connection with the creation of the eternal truths doctrine. In Rule viii Descartes indicated that some problems may be humanly unsolvable—and that it's to the scientist's advantage to be aware of this fact (AT X, 392–3; HR I, 22–3). There is—especially in the *Discourse* and the *Rules*—a firm stress on the importance of method, of order, of starting with 'the simplest things,' of not over-reaching oneself in one's scientific inferences or conclusions. In the *Principles* Descartes even exhibits brief willingness to entertain the idea that his scientific system is only 'morally' certain (*Principles* IV, ccv: AT VIII-1, 327–8; HR I, 301). It is clear that Descartes attributes his philosophical success to his 'method'—and that methodological self-consciousness is bound up with some degree of awareness of epistemological complexity. On the other hand, in the next Principle Descartes explains, characteristically, that all the conclusions of his scientific text are 'even more than morally certain,' because they are grounded in distinct perceptions, and God is not a deceiver. The question of certain knowledge has been raised—and answered. The fact that the question has endured for three hundred years, and the answer hardly at all, should not be accorded disproportionate significance in interpreting Descartes's intentions.

Notes

Note: Full bibliographical information on all works cited is provided in the Bibliography, except for those few works that appear on the Abbreviations list at the front of the book.

Chapter I General Doubt

1 This point is also made by L. J. Beck, *The Metaphysics of Descartes*, pp. 22ff. (It has been a commonplace in French scholarship for many years.) In what follows, however, I make more polemical use of the point than Beck does.

2 '[A]ll of Philosophy is like a tree, of which the roots are Metaphysics, the trunk is Physics, and the branches which come out of this trunk are all the other sciences, which reduce to three principal ones, namely Medicine, Mechanics, and Morality [*la Morale*]. . . .' (AT IX-2, 14; HR I, 211).

3 See, for instance, the letter to Huygens, 24 July 1640, AT III, 102–3, as well as the letter to Mersenne previously cited. Hiram Caton has maintained that Descartes's metaphysics and theology were *nothing but* a screen for the introduction of his physics; that Descartes didn't 'actually believe' the 'pious' views about God and the soul presented in the *Meditations* and other works. I find Caton's defense of this position totally unconvincing. Cf. *The Origin of Subjectivity, passim*, and 'Will and Reason in Descartes's Theory of Error,' *Journal of Philosophy*, vol. lxxii, 1975, pp. 87–104, especially pp. 98ff. Compare Charles Mark's critique in his review of *Origin*, *Philosophical Review*, July 1975, pp. 457–60. A position somewhat like Caton's was previously advanced by Charles Adam. For a powerful defense, against Adam and others, of what I consider the correct perspective, see A. Boyce Gibson, *The Philosophy of Descartes*, pp. 50ff.

4 See for instance AT I, 181–2; PL 19; and AT I, 350; PL 31.

5 References are provided in Chapter III, §3.

6 See Beck, *op. cit.*, p. 18. In the 'Synopsis' of the *Meditations*, however, Descartes maintains that immortality is in principle demonstrable from the indestructibility of substance (AT VII, 13; HR I, 141).

7 Descartes does say the *Meditations* were written according to the 'analytic' method of proof, or method of discovery. See Beck, *op. cit.*, Ch. II, §2, for details. He also tells Burman that the causal proof of God was presented before

the ontological proof 'because the author discovered the two proofs in such a way' that the former came first (AT V, 153; B 12). *Given* Descartes's notion that there is such a thing as *the* order of discovery my statement in the text may be too strong. (But compare the remarks to Regius cited in §9, below.) For a searching discussion of the 'autobiography' issue in relation to the *Meditations*, see F. Alquié, *Descartes*, pp. 3–11.

8 Beck has a good discussion of this point (*op. cit.*, II, §2).

9 The philosophical significance of this issue is demonstrated by Nicholas Rescher's article, 'The Legitimacy of Doubt,' *Review of Metaphysics*, 2 December 1959, pp. 226ff. Rescher's severe criticism of Descartes would not be possible on an adequate conception of Descartes's project of 'attacking principles.' It can also be argued (though I will not try to do so here) that G. E. Moore's 'common sense' attacks on Descartes overlook (or implicitly deny) Descartes's conception of ordinary beliefs as founded on 'principles.'

10 Kenny, pp. 19–20.

11 *Ibid.*, p. 20.

12 Several passages in the *Replies* also make explicit the point that methodic doubt is intended to detach the mind from the senses, thus clearing the way for correct conception of mind, body and God. See *Replies* II, AT VII, 130; HR II, 31; *Replies* III, AT VII, 171–2; HR II, 60–1; and *Replies* VI, AT VII, 440ff; HR II, 253ff. The latter passage provides an especially clear and full account of the objectives and doctrines of the *Meditations*, in relation to pre-existing 'prejudice' concerning mind and body. (God is not mentioned in this context.)

13 The distinction between the goal of certainty *per se* and the aim of 'withdrawal from sense' was pointed out long ago by Etienne Gilson in *Etudes sur le rôle de la pensée médiévale dans la formation du système cartésian*, p. 185.

I borrow the term 'scientific realism,' as well as the distinction (used later) between the scientific and the manifest image, from Wilfrid Sellars. See for instance 'Scientific Realism or Irenic Instrumentalism' in *Philosophical Perspectives*, pp. 337–69, and 'Philosophy and the Scientific Image of Man' in *Science, Perception, and Reality* pp. 1–40. In the latter article Sellars discusses the concepts of the scientific and manifest images in relation to Descartes.

14 Cf. DDM, pp. 17ff.

15 *Ibid.*, p. 18. In the passage Frankfurt cites, Descartes is saying that an act of will is sufficient for withdrawing assent from one's previous beliefs, provided one has a 'reason' for doing so. There is in the passage no suggestion that Descartes ever regarded the considerations advanced in the first sentences of the *Meditations* as providing an adequate reason.

16 Kenny, p. 21.

17 See G. E. Moore, 'Certainty,' in *Philosophical Papers*, pp. 227–51, esp. pp. 245ff; Norman Malcolm, 'Dreaming and Skepticism,' in Doney, pp. 54–79, and *Dreaming*, esp. pp. 101–7.

18 *Op. cit.*, p. 245. Cf. Moore's 'Proof of an External World,' in the same volume, p. 149.

19 DDM, pp. 42, 46.

20 W. H. Walsh, *Metaphysics*, p. 91.

21 DDM, pp. 49–50.

22 *Ibid.*, p. 53.

23 See Chapter III, §2, below.

24 See Alan Gewirth, 'The Cartesian Circle Reconsidered,' *Journal of Philosophy*, 8 October 1970, p. 677.

25 In Meditation V, Descartes seems to take it as important that there *are* such things as 'true and immutable natures' even though these may have nothing corresponding to them existing outside the mind. This point is also discussed below, in Chapter V.

26 See Malcolm, *Dreaming*, pp. 108ff, and Margaret MacDonald, 'Sleeping and Waking,' *Mind*, April 1953, p. 205.

27 It is of course possible that as a matter of fact a given individual has never had *this* experience, but for that matter it is also possible that a given individual has never come to believe that he has been deceived in dreams about the presence and nature of familiar sensible objects. The general consideration of what does or might well occur in dreams is what's important.

28 Descartes has meanwhile 'discovered' the criterion of clear and distinct perception, demonstrated that God is not a deceiver and concluded that 'material things exist.'

29 Pascal in one passage interprets the Dreaming Argument this way. Cf. *Pensées*, no. 434: in Penguin edition, ed. A. J. Krailsheimer, pp. 62–3.

30 *Loc. cit.*

31 I borrow this term, of course, from P. F. Strawson. By 'bounds of sense issue' I mean, for example, the question whether it *makes sense* to suppose that *all* our sense experience is in some way non-veridical, all the objects of sense in some way unreal.

32 See, for instance, AT VI, 112–14; Ols. 89–91.

33 Cf. DDM, p. 51. Sometimes (for instance on the same page) Frankfurt says that Descartes's point is that the Dreaming Argument can't be answered by materials which 'common sense' provides. This is true, however, only in so far as the 'solution' of Meditation VI does implicitly assume the criterion of distinct perception.

34 In the *Discourse* and the *Principles* Descartes doesn't introduce the 'connect-ability' criterion at all. He just argues that the problem of error is solved once we know that clear and distinct perceptions necessarily are true.

35 Cf. AT VII, 62ff; HR I, 178; and Chapter IV, below.

36 In the First Meditation Descartes suggests that considerations of dreaming fail to call into question mathematical knowledge (and the Deceiving God argument is ultimately needed) since,

> Whether I am awake or asleep, two and three joined together are five, and the square does not have more than four sides, and it does not seem possible that such perspicuous truths should incur the suspicion of falsehood. (AT VII, 20; HR I, 147)

This suggests that the consideration of dreaming is not supposed to bring in question mathematical knowledge since I *can't* 'only dream' that $2 + 3 = 5$, in the way that I can 'only dream' that I'm sitting by the fire, etc. However, if this is the intended point there are at least two obvious objections to it. One lies in Descartes's extension of the scope of the Dreaming Argument to *all* physical objects or composites: if, admittedly, I *can't* 'only dream' that $2 + 3 = 5$, Descartes has not given us any reason to suppose I *can* only dream that, say, I have a body. Second, assuming Descartes would allow we *can* dream that $2 + 3 = 7$, he seems to owe some reason why we are entitled to suppose that the latter mathematical judgment is false 'plutôt que l'autre.'

37 Cf. Kenny, pp. 33–4.

38 Descartes goes on to 'boast' that he actually doesn't suffer from bad dreams himself, but he doesn't retract the suggestion that we lack complete control over our minds when asleep.

It must be conceded, however, that *Principles* I, xxx contains a strong hint of the *Discourse* view: AT VIII-1, 17; HR I, 231–2 (but the HR translation is erroneous). I would, I suppose, be satisfied with the conclusion that Descartes's later writings show evidence of vacillation on the question whether we can avoid error in dreams—and that he should have dropped the *Discourse* position altogether, if only for reasons of elementary credibility.

39 Technically, Descartes's general position would seem to allow two alternative possible accounts of errors in dreams. It could be that the sleeping mind loses the capacity to distinguish its distinct from its confused perceptions. Or it could be that the will loses its 'freedom' to abstain from affirming what is not clearly and distinctly perceived. (Or, for that matter, both could be the case.)

40 *Descartes: Essais* . . . , pp. 143–75. At the beginning of the '*cogito* reasoning' in Meditation II, Descartes does refer to the possible deceiver as '*aliquis Deus, vel quocunque nomine illum vocem*' (AT VII, 24; HR I, 150).

41 I think Gouhier's observation is essentially accurate, and useful in understanding the rhetoric and organization of the first three Meditations. It may also have some deeper significance, because of the association (which I argue for in Chapter III) of the possibility of deception in mathematics with the doctrine of the creation of the eternal truths. One must concede, though, that the texts do not reveal any sharp distinction between the power hypothetically ascribed to the 'malignant spirit' and that genuinely attributable to God.

42 Cf. Kenny, p. 24.

43 Even if we should suppose, with Frankfurt, that at this point he is only thinking of those beliefs as supported by sensory evidence, we know that the uncertainty will remain, even after he comes to think of them as deliverances of intellect.

44 'Descartes' Evil Genius,' *Meta-meditations*, ed. Sesonske and Fleming, pp. 26–36.

45 Further evidence for my claim that 'indubitability' is not Descartes's central concern is found in the following consideration. If Descartes were only or mainly concerned to show that all his beliefs are in some measure doubtful, it would have been sufficient for him to argue for the weaker 'skeptical' conclusion that 'I may *sometimes* be deceived in what seems to me maximally certain.'

46 DDM, pp. 33–4.

47 DDM, p. 36.

48 DDM, p. 39.

49 *Ibid.*

50 Cf. DDM, p. 42.

51 DDM, p. 46.

52 DDM, p. 47.

53 DDM, p. 49.

54 I think there is no clear sense in which figure, for example, can be said to be 'given' in auditory or olfactory experiences, or even in the visual perception of an indefinitely extended plane of undifferentiated gray. Frankfurt cites Gueroult in support of his point; however, Gueroult seems to me to be saying something altogether different on the page cited (*Descartes selon l'ordre des raisons*, vol. I, p. 36).

55 DDM, p. 56.

56 See, for instance, DDM, p. 56.

57 As presented for example in *Rules for Direction of the Mind*, AT X, 417ff; HR I, 40ff: *Principles* I, 48ff; AT VIII–1, 22ff; HR I, 238ff. See also the beginning of Meditation V, and Chapter V, below.

58 Kenny, p. 23.

59 The question of the reality of someone's doubts on a certain subject should not be confused with questions of the reasonableness of preoccupation with that subject. Those who think philosophers waste their time on unimportant or unreal problems would not (or should not) deny that philosophical perplexity is *real perplexity*.

60 Haldane and Ross have Descartes saying at the end of Meditation VI that he need no longer fear that 'falsity may be found in matters every day presented to me by my senses' (HR I, 198). The Latin says he doesn't need to fear that such things 'are false' (*non amplius vereri debeo ne illa, quae mihi quotidie a sensibus exhibentur, sint falsa . . .*: AT VII, 89). The point, surely, is not that there is no falsity in the manifest image, but that waking experience does in some sense present to us real things.

61 DDM, p. 16; cf. Kenny, p. 24. Ruth Mattern has maintained (in an unpublished paper) that 'one can explain how the protagonist ends up with changes in his opinions without supposing that the hyperbolic doubt that begins the program involves "real" suspension of beliefs.' I think this is probably true, in the sense that we don't have to suppose that the Cartesian doubter doubts that he has a body in the way that a madman might. The 'doubt,' however exactly it should be characterized, is special in being controlled, purposive, voluntarily produced. What I'm concerned to maintain is that the doubt is supposed to be 'real' in the sense of having a sort of experiential significance for the thinker. To have my trust in the veridicality of the manifest image shaken is different from merely analyzing the conditions of being conclusively justified in believing that p. I believe that Descartes sees this shaking of trust in the senses (and even reason) as a precondition of having his philosophical viewpoint accepted—that is, as a precondition of the sort of change of opinion that is supposed to occur in the course of reading and reflecting on the *Meditations*.

62 Kenny, p. 24.

63 However, this suggestion would relate in a clear-cut way only to the extreme position beyond 'doubt,' where Descartes resolves to treat his former opinions as *false*.

64 It is, surely, an essential feature of Hume's skepticism (in so far as Hume may be interpreted as a skeptic) that we have no reason to believe that past regularities in the sequence of events will continue to hold up in the future. It would seem to follow from that that we have no reason not to jump off cliffs, refrain from eating and so forth. But such results do not follow from the Cartesian proposal that the manifest image might be altogether false.

Naturally, in so far as Cartesian doubt is supposed to be universal, it *should also* generate skepticism about continued regular sequences in the manifest image. However, Cartesian doubt is considerably less than universal in Cartesian practice (as later chapters should make clearer) and there doesn't seem to be any direct evidence that Descartes recognized Hume's problem.

Chapter II Knowledge of Self and Bodies

1 For instance, in the *Principles* (AT VIII–1, 9; HR I, 223); see also AT II, 37–8. It

228

is now widely appreciated how right Arnauld was in claiming Augustinian ancestry for Descartes's *cogito* reasoning. See AT VII, 197-8; HR II, 80, and (for instance) Rudolph Arbesmann's introduction to Denis J. Kavanagh's translation of Augustine's *Contra Academicos* (*Answer to Skeptics*), pp. xviii–xix. In fact many elements of Descartes's arguments have more or less close Augustinian parallels. A number of these have been pointed out and discussed by E. M. Curley, in *Descartes Against the Skeptics*. I do not think it is yet clear how recognition of the Augustinian influence should affect our reading of Descartes.

2 André Gombay, in his perceptive article, '"Cogito Ergo Sum"': Inference or Argument?' seems to suppose that Descartes must rely on 'Whatever thinks exists' as a premiss if he is to have 'entailing support' for his conclusion, *sum*. CS, pp. 71–86; see esp. pp. 77 and 83.

3 AT VII, 140; HR II, 38; AT IX–1, 205–6; HR II, 127 (in the latter passage the denial is, I think, clearly implicit).

4 AT V, 147; B 4.

5 See M. D. Wilson, 'Leibniz and Locke on "First Truths,"' *Journal of the History of Ideas*, July–September 1967, pp. 347–66.

6 Compare DDM, p. 98. I refer to Locke's and Leibniz's general positions on principles and instances—not on the *cogito* specifically.

7 Kenny, for example, stresses that for Descartes thought by definition involves consciousness and that 'everything we know involves a piece of conscious thinking' (Kenny, p. 60). But he also proposes an 'implicit knowledge' reading of the *cogito* passages (*ibid.*, p. 52).

8 DDM, p. 10.

9 See also the statements of Alquié cited below (notes 37–8).

10 DDM, p. 92.

11 DDM, p. 100; cf. pp. 105, 106. On p. 106 Frankfurt does note that 'immediately *following* the end of his discussion, . . . Descartes says: "But I do not yet sufficiently understand *what* I am, I who already necessarily am"' [emphasis added]. He dismisses this statement as 'misleading.'

12 In Latin: '*nihil nunc admitto nisi quod necessario sit verum. . . .*'

13 Doney, pp. 108–39.

14 *Ibid.*, pp. 114–15.

15 *Ibid.*, pp. 88–107.

16 In fact, Frankfurt doesn't discuss this objection.

17 Descartes is however open to an *ad hominem* objection here. For he does indicate in the *Rules* that deductive arguments are useless for advancing knowledge: one must 'already know' what is asserted in the conclusion in order to form the argument. Cf. AT X, 406; HR I, 32–3.

18 Viewed in one way, this is equivalent to the question, 'why should we regard "If I think, I exist" as immune to hyperbolic doubt?'

19 Doney, p. 113.

20 Kenny, p. 171. By 'valid' Kenny seems to mean 'sound': cf. *ibid.*, p. 58.

21 For example, in Meditations II and V Descartes clearly assumes that we can settle questions about the essence of body, or of geometrical entities such as triangles, prior to any determination of whether such things exist.

22 Doney, p. 114.

23 Kenny, pp. 50, 170.

24 Cf. *Principles* I, lii: AT VIII–1, 24–5; HR I, 240. Here the principle, 'Nothing has no attributes,' is again employed in the reasoning, and Descartes's language seems to confirm the interpretation I am suggesting. Having presented

the principle as a 'common notion,' he writes: '*Ex hoc enim quòd aliquod attributum adesse percipiamus, concludimus aliquam rem existentem, sive substantiam, cui illud tribui possit, necessariò etiam adesse*' [emphasis added].

25 Descartes says that we conclude ('*concludimus*') that a substance is present. (*Ibid.*)

26 Hence I disagree with Kenny's view that the principle 'Nothing has no attributes' is fundamentally important in clarifying the *cogito* reasoning. I also believe Kenny is wrong in suggesting that 'To think, one must exist' is a particular instance of this principle: certainly the one does not appear formally to be an instance of the other. Cf. Kenny, p. 50.

27 This point is illustrated by Kant in a famous footnote to the Third Paralogism, in the Dialectic section of the *Critique of Pure Reason* (A 364).

28 That is, as mentioned above, since 'I think' emerges as a sufficient condition of 'I exist,' 'I have a body' is not necessary. The relation of the *cogito* to the mind–body distinctness argument is discussed at more length later in this chapter, and in Chapter VI.

29 See A. J. Ayer, 'I think, therefore I am,' Doney, pp. 80–7, esp. p. 81.

30 Peter Geach and P. F. Strawson have argued (in different ways) that for 'I' to succeed in referring there must also be a public context of discourse. See Geach, *Mental Acts*, pp. 117–21; Strawson, *Bounds of Sense*, pp. 163–66. I take it that Geach, but not Strawson, would hold that 'I' genuinely refers only on those *occasions* when it's used in public discourse (as opposed to soliloquy).

31 A similar point has been made by E. M. Curley in *Descartes Against the Skeptics*. I take it the claim that the assumption in question is not trivial, is distinct from the Kantian claim that the unity of consciousness (apperception) is not epistemically posterior to isolated 'thoughts.'

32 Cf. Hintikka, *op. cit.*, Doney, pp. 118ff.

33 *Ibid.*, pp. 121ff.

34 Cf. H. G. Frankfurt, 'Descartes's Discussion of His Existence in the Second Meditation,' *Philosophical Review*, July 1966, pp. 329–56 (*passim*), and Kenny, pp. 42ff.

35 Feldman, 'On the Performatory Interpretation of the *Cogito*,' *Philosophical Review*, July 1973, pp. 361–2.

36 AT VII, 145–6; HR II, 42.

37 Alquié, *Oeuvres de Descartes*, vol. ii, p. 418.

38 *Ibid.*, p. 246.

39 Behind this sort of statement is a tacit assumption that we are not concerned with properties such as unity or duration that are attributable to every substance.

40 HR translates 'that obscure part of myself' for '*istud nescio quid mei*,' but this translation surely carries the wrong implication. In fact, '*nescio quid mei*' can be translated even less committally than I have done in the text as 'that [unspecified] part [or aspect] of me.'

41 *Principles* I, xlv: AT VIII–1, 21–2; HR I, 237.

42 Although it does hark back to the list of simples presented in Meditation I. As E. M. Curley has pointed out (*Descartes Against the Skeptics*, ch. VIII) *mutabile* cannot be translated 'movable'—contrary to several translators, and the passage from Burtt quoted below. (But see the passage from *Replies* quoted on p. 81.)

43 E. A. Burtt, *The Metaphysical Foundation of Modern Science*, p. 117.

44 In *Discoveries and Opinions of Galileo*, ed. S. Drake, pp. 274–5.

45 Compare Meditation II, where Descartes, in describing the notion he had

previously had of body, includes the idea that it was something perceived by touch, sight, hearing, taste or smell (AT VII, 26; HR I, 151).

46 Anthony Quinton, 'Matter and Space,' *Mind*, July 1964, p. 344.

47 Letter to Henry More, 5 February 1649, AT V, 268–9; PL 238.

48 Quinton, *op. cit.*, pp. 341–2.

49 It makes a great deal of difference to the sense of this passage whether and where one uses the articles 'a' and 'the' in translating into English. It seemed to me that the passage became much more intelligible once it occurred to me to translate it in the way that I have here. (Contrast HR I, 259.)

50 Cf. letter to More cited in note 47, above.

51 Leibniz sometimes indicates that ideas of sense fail to be clear and distinct precisely because they include a diversity of elements that we fail to recognize in them. Cf. for example *Nouveaux essais* II, xxix, §4: pp. 255–6 in Prussian Academy edition.

With respect to Descartes, however, I agree with Gueroult's observation that 'on ne doit pas confondre cette idée sensible, qui est obscure et confuse par nature, avec ces idées obscures et confuses par accident que sont des idées de l'entendement insuffisamment analysées, ou oblitérées par leur confusion avec des idées sensibies' (*Descartes selon l'ordre des raisons*, vol. II, p. 135).

52 Here we find further evidence that Descartes is prepared to embrace some kind of distinction between implicit and explicit knowing. (The issue is discussed at length in Chapter IV.) Descartes's discussion of his knowledge of the wax recalls the contrast in the *Rules* between 'the fluctuating faith of the senses' and 'the conception of a pure and attentive mind that is so easy and distinct that no doubt remains about that which we understand' (Rule iii, AT X, 368; HR I, 7).

53 See Roderick Firth, 'The Men Themselves . . . ,' in H.-N. Castañeda, ed., *Intentionality, Minds, and Perception*, pp. 357–82.

54 However, Descartes is really none too consistent in his pronouncements about the individuation and identity of bodies. Sometimes he can be subtle: cf. AT IV, 163–7; PL 155–7.

55 The contrast between intelligence and mechanism is developed from another point of view in Descartes's famous discussion, at the end of Part V of the *Discourse*, of the distinction between humans and animals. This passage is discussed in Chapter VI. See also J.-M. Beyssade, 'L'analyse du morceau de cire,' pp. 13f. I regret I read this sophisticated study too late to consider those of its claims which differ from my own.

56 This notion, though, would apparently involve a confusion of 'distinctness' with 'clarity': cf. AT VIII–1, 22; HR I, 237; but compare AT VII, 75; HR I, 188.

57 I take it Descartes's view that substances are only perceived through their attributes does not necessarily in itself imply a hidden 'inner structure.'

58 In the *Treatise of Man*, which is part of *The World*, Descartes repeatedly indicates that he is going to go on to describe the rational soul, and its union with the body, after he has finished with the business of describing the machine of the body and its actions. However, the *Treatise* was either unfinished in this respect, or its continuation has been lost. See T. S. Hall's footnote 157, on p. 113 of his translation. In the following footnote, Hall points out that Descartes's 'central contribution to the history of physiology' was to eliminate all the Aristotelian faculties of soul (nutritive, sensitive and motive) except the rational. Thus, by drawing the soul–matter distinction in terms of the thought–extension distinction, and assuming that 'thought' of any sort presupposed reason, Descartes claimed much new ground for mechanistic physiology. This observa-

tion of course does not illuminate Descartes's treatment of thought itself as outside science; however, it is useful to be reminded of the positive aspect of Descartes's dualism, with respect to scientific progress.

Chapter III Some Perspectives on the Third Meditation

1 'Thoughtless Brutes,' *Proceedings of the American Philosophical Association*, vol. XLVI, 1972–3, p. 7.

2 See, for example, AT VII, 40, ll. 10–20. Descartes uses 'exhibit' (*exhibere*) twice and 'represent' (*repraesentare*) several times in this passage. The alternation doesn't show up in HR, who, following the French translation, use 'represent' all the way through (HR I, 162; AT IX-1, 31–2).

3 Descartes distinguishes ideas from images for example in the Third Replies, AT VII, 178–83; HR II, 66–70. Hobbes, to whom Descartes is responding, was apparently led by Descartes's *'tanquam rerum imagines'* terminology, as well as his own biases, to take for granted that Descartes assimilated having an idea to having a sense-related image in the mind.

4 This passage foreshadows the claim of the Fourth Meditation, discussed in Chapter IV, that the locus of error is to be found in judgments, and that judgments depend on free will, as well as 'understanding.'

5 See, for example, *Rules for the Direction of the Mind*, Rule XIV (AT X, 438ff; HR I, 54ff). Descartes also discusses imagination in terms of geometrical representations in Meditations V and VI, which are discussed below. On the other hand, in Rule XII (for example) Descartes associates imagination with memory: AT X, 415–16; HR I, 39.

6 *Metaphysical Foundations of Modern Science*, pp. 117–18. While I think Burtt's meaning is clear, his use of 'inured' is unusual.

7 It is perhaps needless to point out that *'res'* is not in this context restricted to substances.

8 In the *Discourse* Descartes presents confused or obscure ideas as not merely epistemically inferior to clear and distinct ideas, but also as lower on an ontological scale of perfection. That is, they participate in 'negation.' See *Discourse*, Part IV: AT VI, 38–9; HR I, 105.

9 Gueroult takes Descartes's position to be that the ideas of sense have 'infinitely small' objective reality, rather than none: cf. *Descartes selon l'ordre des raisons*, vol. I, pp. 216ff and vol. II *passim* (e.g., p. 131). He takes this view partly because he tends to assimilate having objective reality to having representative character, and partly on the basis of a passage in the *Meditations* where Descartes says the ideas of heat or of stone must have causes with as much formal reality as the reality he conceives to exist in the heat or the stone. As I indicate in the text, however, I believe this passage is inconsistent with the main point Descartes wants to make about material falsity: cf. p. 112.

10 I set aside here further 'intentionality' problems that would arise, such as whether I need to have and apply the concept of degrees of reality, in order to conceive of, say a stone as having such and such amount of reality.

11 Cf. Kenny, p. 137.

12 An alternative explanation, that has been suggested to me, is that Descartes was trying to anticipate what he perceived as a possible response to his theological proof: i.e. that a critic might spontaneously object that the idea of God could, like sensations, represent nothing real. However, it seems that the distinction between the clear and distinct and the obscure should by itself be adequate basis

for an answer to this objection: we don't need the theory of material falsity.

13 From a philosophical and critical point of view, it would be interesting to pursue the following question: what sort of connection might there be between the concept of an idea's having representative character, and the concept of its having representative *content*, i.e. exhibiting *res* or something possible? For example, for an idea to be *tanquam rei imago*, must it in some sense *purport* (perhaps fallaciously) to exhibit a possibility to us? This question connects, I believe, with Descartes's claims that every idea contains the thought of the existence of its object, and that possibility is *really* contained in (not merely 'thought in') every distinct idea. But it would require a disproportionate amount of detail to pursue the question here.

14 Wilfrid Sellars observes that it is a 'categorical feature' of physical objects in the manifest image 'that they have color in the same literal sense in which they have shape.' See 'Science, Sense-Impressions, and Sensa: A Reply to Cornman,' *Review of Metaphysics*, March 1971, p. 394.

15 Kenny says Descartes has 'four main arguments' to prove that 'secondary qualities are mental entities and not real properties of external objects' (Kenny, p. 209). However, it is not at all clear that Descartes has *anything* as dignified as an 'argument'; Kenny's exposition certainly does not seem to establish that he does. Incidentally, Kenny is wrong, I think, in supposing that Descartes's rejection of real accidents bears directly on the primary–secondary quality issue (*ibid.*, pp. 210–11).

16 Cf. *Discourse*, Part IV: AT VI, 33; HR I, 102.

17 For example by Gouhier, in *La Pensée métaphysique de Descartes*, Ch. IX, §4, and Alan Gewirth, in 'The Cartesian Circle Reconsidered,' pp. 674–5.

18 Letters of 6 April, 6 May and 27 May 1630: AT I, 145–53; PL 11–15.

19 To Mesland, 2 May 1644: AT IV, 118–19; PL 150–1; to Arnauld, 29 July 1648: AT V, 223–4; PL 236–7; to More, 5 February 1649: AT V, 272–3; PL 240–1.

20 See Replies to the Fifth Objections, AT VII, 380; HR II, 226; Replies to the Sixth Objections, AT VII, 431–3; HR II, 248–9.

21 AT V, 159–60; B 22.

22 For instance, A. Boyce Gibson, in 'The Eternal Verities and the Will of God in the Philosophy of Descartes,' *Proceedings of the Aristotelian Society,* n.s. 30, 1929–30, pp. 40ff; and Harry Frankfurt, 'Descartes on the Creation of the Eternal Truths,' *Philosophical Review*, vol. LXXVI, January 1977, pp. 36–97. My own interest in the eternal truths issue derives from Frankfurt's work.

23 Leibniz condemns Descartes's position repeatedly: cf. for example *Discourse on Metaphysics*, §II, in *Die Philosophischen Schriften*, ed. Gerhardt, vol. IV, p. 428 (where he calls it 'altogether strange'), and passages from the *Theodicy* cited in n. 30, below.

24 E.g. by Gueroult, *Descartes selon l'ordre des raisons*, II, 26ff and by Boyce-Gibson, in the work cited in n. 22.

25 Cf. AT VII, 108–10 and 236ff; HR II, 14–16 and 108ff. (For this observation and the reference in the following note I'm indebted to Janet Broughton.) In both passages, however, Descartes does indicate that the power or essence of God is the 'positive cause' of his existence, in a manner *analogous to* efficient causality. Still, this would indicate *some* distinction between the sense in which God is cause of Himself and the sense in which He is the cause of creatures and the eternal truths—unless one supposes that Descartes is *also* speaking analogously when he says God is the efficient cause of the latter!

26 In a letter to Hyperaspistes of August 1641 (AT III, 429; PL 116). Descartes

explains that God would not be demonstrating His power if He made a creature that could continue to exist without Him; rather He would be showing that His power is finite.

27 A striking passage in this connection is Descartes's reply to Burman at AT V, 166, B 32–3, where Descartes says that although God is indifferent to all, nevertheless He made His decrees necessarily, 'for He necessarily willed the best.' Descartes here is reported as going on to say that God's decrees cannot be separated from Him, and 'God could not be without them.' On the face of it, these reported statements are difficult to reconcile with Descartes's own writings, including a number of passages cited in the text. Thus, Descartes writes to Mesland that we cannot know that God always does what He knows to be most perfect; that He cannot have been determined not to make contradictories true together; and that though He willed them to be necessary, it doesn't mean that He willed them necessarily (cf. AT IV, 113, 118; PL 148, 151). It may be, however, that contrary to appearances Descartes didn't really mean to be denying (to Burman) that God 'could have done otherwise,' in creating the eternal truths. Thus, *part* of the point may be that since God himself *determined* what is best, in determining what He would do, there is no sense in denying that He necessarily does the best. Of course here, as in other places, the question arises: how far can we trust Burman?

28 My way of stating this point was strongly influenced by a conversation with Jean-Marie Beyssade. (I do not mean to suggest that he would endorse this formulation.) Boyce-Gibson and J. Jalabert, among others, have also stressed the notion of *unity* (of will and understanding in God) in interpreting the creation doctrine. See the former's 'The Eternal Verities . . . ,' pp. 40ff and Jalabert's notes to his edition of Leibniz's *Essais de Théodicée*, p. 516, n. 29. Alquié offers the further gloss that while one can't *strictly* say that *in reality* will precedes understanding in God (since they are one), man cannot 'comprehend the situation of God with respect to the eternal truths,' except by according primacy to the will. See *Descartes: Oeuvres Philosophiques*, vol. I, p. 264, n. 2.

29 Is Descartes implying in the letter to More that God *can still* change the eternal truths? If so, his statement is inconsistent with others cited above. It seems possible, however, that he is here using 'cannot be brought about' [*fieri non posse*] *timelessly*, rather than with the sense of 'cannot be done *now*.'

30 Besides *Discourse* §2, cited above, see *Théodicée: Essais sur la Bonté de Dieu* §§175–92 (pp. 229–42 in Jalabert's edition; vol. VI, pp. 218–31 in Gerhardt). Part of Leibniz's distress is a *moral* distress: the Cartesian position puts God above the principles of justice and goodness, conceiving Him as an arbitrary dictator. Further, the conception of Divine 'liberty of indifference' '*choquerait le grand principe de la raison déterminante.*' But it is clear that Leibniz also regards the creation doctrine as an intellectual absurdity. Thus, in §185 he notes that Bayle, who generally opposes the doctrine, in one place expresses regret at not being able to understand it, together with the hope that '*le temps développera ce beau paradoxe.*' Bayle goes on to say that he wishes Malebranche had not rejected the doctrine. Leibniz comments:

> *Est-il possible que le plaisir de douter puisse tant sur un habile homme que lui faire souhaiter et de lui faire espérer de pouvoir croire que deux contradictoires ne se trouvent jamais ensemble, que parce que Dieu le leur a défendu, et qu'il aurait pu leur donner un ordre qui les aurait toujours fait aller de compagnie? Le beau paradoxe que voilà! Le R. P. Malebranche a fait fort sagement de prendre d'autres mesures.*

(In the next section, however, Leibniz argues that Descartes's expression of the doctrine was one of his '*ruses philosophiques*,' and that he actually intended something much less paradoxical, having to do with his theory of judgment.)

31 Hilary Putnam writes, with respect to the change from Euclidean to Riemannian cosmology, that '[s]omething literally *inconceivable* had turned out to be true . . .' (*Mind, Language and Reality*, p. xv). On the next page he continues:

> I was driven to the conclusion that there was such a thing as the overthrow of a proposition that was once *a priori* (or that once had the status of what we *call* an '*a priori*' truth). If it could be rational to give up claims as self-evident as the geometrical proposition just mentioned, then, it seemed to me that there was no basis for maintaining that there are *any absolutely a priori truths*, any truths that a rational man is *forbidden* to even doubt.

There are of course anti-Cartesian elements, as well as Cartesian ones, in the position adopted by Putnam (and related views expressed in W. V. Quine's seminal essay, 'Two Dogmas of Empiricism,' by which Putnam was influenced). The Cartesian ones, I think, lie in the generalized suspicion of 'inconceivability' as a basis for claims about what *cannot be*, and a consequent attenuation (at least) of the concept of 'necessary truth.' A principal difference between Descartes and Putnam is that Descartes does not link his position to any observation of 'conceptual revolutions,' and (as noted in the text) does not seem to let his creation doctrine ultimately interfere with his own reliance on conceivability as a present guide to certain truth.

32 As indicated in Meditation II: AT VII, 29; HR I, 153-4.

33 Cf. Meditation III, AT VII, 46; HR I, 166.

34 In the article cited in note 22, Frankfurt holds that 'no coherent meaning can be assigned to the notion of an infinitely powerful being as Descartes employs it— that is, to the notion of a being for whom the logically impossible is possible.' Since the notion is 'unintelligible' we cannot believe or know that God is such a being (*op. cit.*, p. 44). This is a potentially important objection, but it surely requires defense—including, perhaps, some account of the notion of 'coherent meaning.' Presented without argument, it seems merely question-begging against Descartes.

35 I believe that Frankfurt mistakenly conflates the epistemic and the metaphysical senses of 'God could have (or might have) made contradictory propositions true': *op. cit.*, p. 56.

36 Meditation I: AT VII, 21; HR I, 147.

37 See Willis Doney, 'Spinoza on Philosophical Skepticism,' in Mandelbaum and Freedman, eds, *Spinoza: Essays in Interpretation*, pp. 142-3. In the Second Replies and some other passages Descartes seems to stress (as relevant to the Circularity issue) that there are *certain propositions* that can't be thought of *without being* distinctly perceived, and that hence can *never* be doubted. But for the sake of minimal consistency with the First and Third Meditations he would have to mean that they can't be *attentively* thought of, without being distinctly perceived. When this concession is made, it is hard to see how the point in question adds much to the position as I have summarized it in the text.

It takes, I think, an *extremely* subtle reading of Meditation III to find in it much affinity with Descartes's account of the problem of knowledge in the Second Replies. However, the Fifth Meditation does come closer (AT VII, 69-70; HR I, 183-4; see also *Principles* I, xiii: AT VIII-1, 9-10; HR I, 224).

38 Cottingham stresses the *Conversation*'s importance for the Circularity issue (B

xxix–xxxii). (He also cites other relevant texts from the work.) My treatment has been influenced by his observations.

39 The issues here are admittedly very complex. For a more detailed critical pursual of some closely related questions, see Willis Doney, 'Descartes' Conception of Perfect Knowledge,' *Journal of the History of Philosophy*, vol. 8, October 1970.

40 You may object that my argument is fallacious, on the grounds that when I'm perceiving p as most manifest I'm knowing that God *is* not deceiving me about p; not that He couldn't have if He'd wanted to. Indeed, my argument takes the Burman position as implying that it's *essential* to something's seeming most manifest to Descartes that he knows he is not being deceived about it then. That is, if something seems most manifest to Descartes, then necessarily he knows he's not being deceived (and hence, necessarily, he's not being deceived). To which the reply might be: Descartes can subscribe to both the 'Burman position' on circularity and the doctrine of God's unlimited power, just because a feature of the latter is that God can make contradictories true together, and hence could bring it about that Descartes was deceived in his distinct perceptions even though when he's having them he necessarily knows he's not being deceived. I do not mind agreeing that the 'Burman position' is inconsistent with Descartes's position on God's unlimited power just up to the point where the latter itself impedes the free operation of the principle of logical consistency.

Views partially reminiscent of Descartes's 'Burman position' have been espoused by some modern anti-skeptics. For some classical approaches see Moore, 'Certainty' (*Philosophical Papers*, Ch. X), H. A. Prichard, 'Descartes's *Meditations*' (Doney, pp. 140–68), and N, Malcolm, 'Knowing and Believing' in *Knowledge and Belief*, ed. by A. Phillips Griffiths.

41 This interpretation is particularly identified with Harry Frankfurt, who originally presented it in an article, 'Descartes' Validation of Reason,' first published in the *American Philosophical Quarterly* in 1965, and later reprinted in Doney (see also DDM, Ch 15). As he notes, Frankfurt had been influenced by an earlier article by Alan Gewirth; see also Gewirth's subsequent discussion in 'The Cartesian Circle Revisited.'

42 As already noted above in considering the *cogito*, Frankfurt imputes to Descartes a distinction between concern with *certainty* and concern with *truth* that is not really borne out by the texts. Certainly Descartes's way of setting up his problem in Meditation III does not suggest he is doing what Frankfurt says he is doing: see especially AT VII, 36–7; HR I, 159. In the Second Replies Descartes does introduce and dismiss the point that someone might suppose that what we take for incontrovertibly evident might appear false to God or to an angel (AT VII, 145, 146; HR II, 41, 42). This could mean, as Frankfurt thinks, that Descartes is expressly rejecting a concern with 'absolute truth' in favor of a concern with 'certainty.' But Descartes may not mean this at all in the passages in question. He may already be reaching for the notion that in some circumstances our certainty *that we know the truth* is so 'firm' and perfect that we cannot but dismiss the notion that God has a different view as a *fiction*.

43 As long as falsity is distinguished from inconsistency itself.

44 Descartes seems nearly as preoccupied as Spinoza with the notion that God *is infinite*; the seventeenth-century preoccupation with infinity is further reflected in such diverse works as *Paradise Lost* and Pascal's *Pensées*. It does not seem surprising that the notion of God's infinity should be so powerful an intuition for Descartes as to make *any* limitation on His will seem unacceptable.

45 A view now associated with both Suarez and Aquinas—although I cannot claim detailed first-hand knowledge of their positions. On the scholastic background of Descartes's contention, see Norman J. Wells, 'Descartes and the Scholastics Briefly Revisited,' *New Scholasticism*, 1961, pp. 172–90; and Kenny, 'The Cartesian Circle and the Eternal Truths,' *Journal of Philosophy*, October 1970, pp. 695–8.

46 For example by E. Bréhier, 'The Creation of the Eternal Truths in Descartes's System' (Doney, pp. 192–208); by F. Alquié, *Descartes: Oeuvres Philosophiques*, vol. 1, p. 261, n. 2, pp. 265–6, ns. 2–3; and by Frankfurt in 'Descartes on the Creation of the Eternal Truths,' §11.

47 See *Principles* II, xxxvi–xxxvii: AT VIII-1, 61–3; *Le Monde*, Ch., VII: AT XI, 36–8; cf. letter to Mersenne, 26 April 1643: AT III, 649–50; PL 136.

48 A similar point is argued (in more detail) by G. Rodis-Lewis; see *Oeuvre de Descartes*, vol. I, Ch. III, §5, esp. pp. 131ff.

49 Though again from only one point of view. Descartes thinks of mathematics and the basic principles of physics as having the same epistemological and ontological status—and as being in some sense *not* ineluctable. However, he also thinks they are innate in our minds, and he certainly offers no suggestion that our view of them might be 'revised' or 'given-up'—once we have achieved the necessary (and available) Cartesian clarity with respect to them.

50 Throughout his discussion Descartes moves freely from 'infinite' to 'infinitely perfect' to 'infinitely real.' The part of the discussion I am commenting on occurs at AT VII, 40–6; HR I, 162–6.

Chapter IV Judgment, Ideas and Thought

1 Boyce-Gibson gives a detailed and fascinating account of the politico-theological struggles surrounding the issue in Descartes's time. See *The Philosophy of Descartes*, pp. 64ff.

2 By this remark Descartes seems to suggest that some creatures (angels?) have greater faculties of knowledge than his own.

3 Cf. *Conversation with Burman*, AT V, 158–9; B 20–1.

4 Descartes says that the cause of his errors doesn't come from the understanding, since 'whatever I understand . . . I rightly understand' (AT VII, 58; HR I, 174), but this is at best misleading, given other aspects of his doctrine (e.g. the conception of obscure ideas).

5 See especially Rule VIII: AT X, 392ff; HR I, 22ff; *Discourse* II: AT VI, 18; HR I 92.

6 A good example (despite the brief separation of 'clear' from 'distinct') is the following passage from Part IV of the Discourse:

> And having remarked that there is nothing at all in this: *I think, therefore I am*, that assures me that I say the truth, except that *I see very clearly that*, in order to think, it is necessary to be: I judged that I could take for a general rule, that the things that we conceive very clearly and distinctly are all true . . .
> (AT VI, 33; HR I, 102; emphasis added).

7 Cf. AT V, 224; PL 236; AT VII, 431–2; HR II, 248.

8 See for example Rule V: AT X, 379–80; HR I, 14–15.

9 'Descartes, Spinoza, and the Ethics of Belief,' in *Spinoza: Essays in Interpretation*, M. Mandelbaum and E. Freeman, eds, pp. 177–8; cf. 176.

10 Curley rightly points out that we must be careful to keep in mind a distinction

between (inwardly) judging and *saying*. We *can* just decide to say something, whether or not we believe (or perceive) it to be true (*ibid.*, p. 177).

11 In using this terminology I don't mean to suggest that there's nothing problematic about the notion of 'recognizing we perceive a thing inadequately.' For instance, on the interpretation or reconstruction of Descartes I develop below, an important—indeed crucial—issue is that without deliberate (i.e. voluntarily induced) reflection, we may take for granted that we perceive a thing adequately when we do not. (Indeed this is just the problem, on my account, that the *Meditations* is most concerned to combat.)

12 Spinoza, *Ethics* II, xlix; cited by Curley, *op. cit.*, p. 174.

13 *Ibid.*, p. 175.

14 Peirce writes, '[T]hus to make single individual absolute judges of truth is most pernicious' ('Some Consequences of Four Incapacities,' in *Values in a Universe of Chance*, ed. P. P. Wiener, p. 40). It could be argued that Descartes's view of warranted assent is *logically*, as well as historically and morally unsound, on the grounds that the notion of warrant or evidence logically involves some sort of interpersonal confirmability.

Incidentally, if Peirce is to be believed, the Cartesian distinctions between clear and obscure, and distinct and confused perceptions, were a prominent and proud feature of logic texts into the late nineteenth century. See 'How to Make Our Ideas Clear,' *ibid.*, p. 114.

15 Cf. for example Second Replies, AT VII, 143-4; HR II, 40-1. Sometimes the claim that God is not a deceiver seems to mean no more for Descartes than that we cannot be made so as to fall into errors we can never detect. There is a hint of that view in this passage. At other times he seems to intend the much stronger position that God could not have given me a faculty that will ever lead me into error 'if I use it rightly' (AT VII, 54; HR I, 172). It is, I think, a still stronger position to hold that I *can* always avoid using my faculties other than 'rightly.'

16 On the other hand, Descartes does rather frequently *forget* the point (which he concedes in the Preface to the *Meditations*) that the mind–body distinctness conclusion doesn't fall directly out of the *cogito*. (AT VII, 7-8; HR I, 137-8; cf. for example *Discourse* IV: AT VI, 32-3; HR I, 101. Compare AT VII, 225-6; HR II, 101-2).

17 Cf. Rodis-Lewis's pioneering work, *Le Problème de l'inconscient et le Cartésianisme*; also Zeno Vendler, *Res Cogitans*, Ch. VII, and R. McRae, 'Innate Ideas' and 'Descartes' Definition of Thought,' both in CS.

18 I *think* this is evident. How could an idea be in my mind and its aspects and internal features not be?

19 CS, pp. 67ff.

20 AT VII, 34; HR I, 157. It is of course a premiss of the Second Meditation that one is apt to start out with *completely* confused and erroneous conception of one's thinking self—assimilating it to material entities, etc.

21 Besides the wax passage (AT VII, 31; HR I, 155), see *Principles* I, xlvi: AT VIII-1, 22; HR I, 237. Actually the issue is a good deal more complicated than this formulation would suggest, since (as Alan Gewirth has pointed out) the notion of distinct cognition is tied up in Descartes's thinking with that of making the right 'interpretation' with respect to one's ideas—and it's not clear that this is the same as just being aware of what is in them. Cf. Gewirth, 'Clearness and Distinctness in Descartes,' in Doney, esp. pp. 257-62.

22 See Chapter III, §2. In *Passions of the Soul* I, xxviii Descartes remarks that 'those who are most agitated by their passions are not those who know them the best' (AT XI, 349-50; HR I, 344).

23 This problem has been dealt with in detail by Kenny ('Descartes on Ideas,' Doney, pp. 227–49): my treatment here will be simpler, with some different emphases.

24 Cf. First Replies: AT VII, 101–3; HR II, 9–10.

25 However, as noted above, he seems to think that a mental state like fearing a lion is analyzable into *two* forms—that of the thought of the lion, and that of the fear: cf. Meditation III (AT VII, 37; HR I, 159: 'Other thoughts have certain *other forms besides. . . .*' It is, incidentally, a curious question whether Descartes would regard *seeing* a lion as differing from thinking of a lion by virtue of possessing some additional 'form,' over and above the representation of the lion. (Perhaps the 'form' of passive or involuntary reception?)

26 As Kenny points out, there is some confusion in Descartes's writings as to whether the objects of one's thoughts, in the sense of what one *thinks of*, are things or the *ideas of* things. Cf. Doney, pp. 241–2.

27 Kenny gives many references that are apposite there; cf. Doney, p. 230.

28 On the other hand, Descartes sometimes seems to resist *any* assimilation of ideas to faculties: cf. McRae, 'Innate Ideas,' CS, p. 49.

29 Elsewhere Descartes *says* we can't know we are aware of everything in us: cf. AT VII, 129; HR II, 31; cf. AT VII, 219; HR II, 97. Compare letter to Gibieuf, 19 January 1642: 'I do not . . . deny that there can be in the soul or the body several properties of which I have no idea. . . .' (AT III, 478; PL 125).

30 See Thomas Nagel, 'Linguistics and Epistemology,' in G. Harman, ed., *On Noam Chomsky*, p. 223.

31 This is from the part of the *Search after Truth* that is preserved only in Latin translation.

32 *The Concept of Mind*, p. 159.

33 In a reply to Burman, however, Descartes seems to be saying that we become conscious of our thoughts only in so far as we 'please' to reflect on them—though this 'reflection' can take place while we still have the thought: AT V, 149; B, 7; cf. McRae, 'Descartes' Definition of Thought,' CS, p. 67.

34 There is, however, a certain lack of clarity in Descartes's writings as to *whether or not* attentive consciousness and explicit knowledge necessarily involve 'reflection' in the sense of the representation of an idea by means of another idea.

35 CS, pp. 67–8.

36 Also printed (with French translation) by G. Rodis-Lewis as Appendix I.B to her edition of Descartes's letters to Regius. McRae does not cite this letter: I am grateful to Mme. Rodis-Lewis for calling it to my attention.

Chapter V True and Immutable Natures

1 See for instance the letter to Hyperaspistes of August 1641: AT III, 423–4; PL 111.

2 See for instance the letter to Chanut of 6 June 1647: AT V, 51–2; PL 221; as well as *Principles* I, xxvi–xxvii: AT VIII-1, 14–15; HR I, 229–30. As the latter principle makes clear, Descartes withholds the term 'infinite' from *res extensa* primarily because one can't be metaphysically certain that *res extensa* has no bounds (whereas one can be metaphysically certain that God is absolutely unlimited). See also letter to More, 5 February 1649: AT V, 274–5; PL 242.

3 Descartes does, however, think of God as endowing matter with motion *at the time of* creating it. See *The World*, AT XI, 34, 36. It should further be noted that in at least one place (AT III, 665; PL 138) Descartes says the notions of figure

and motion 'follow from' [*suivent de*] the notion of extension. This might be explained by the fact that Descartes is in this passage concerned specifically with the issue of the mind–body union, and therefore is thinking of body as a determinate finite body (a human body), rather than thinking of *res extensa*. Alternatively, he could be seen as skipping over the fine point that what *strictly* 'follows from' extension is *divisibility*—and hence the *potentiality* of internal figures and motions.

4 On the scholastic notion of transcendental qualities in relation to Descartes see S. Schiffer, 'Descartes on His Essence,' *Philosophical Review*, vol. LXXXV, January 1976, pp. 22ff. Schiffer writes that 'Just as the property of being colored can be instantiated only in and by the instantiation of some particular color, so the essence of a substance can be instantiated only in and by the instantiation of one or another of its modes' (p. 23). As explained in the text, I believe this is correct only for *res cogitans*, not for *res extensa*.

5 My treatment of this issue has been influenced by some unpublished work of Eric Rosen. However, my account is both different from Rosen's, and less detailed and formal; I do not wish to suggest he would agree with it.

6 The language here—'*après y avoir fait assez de réflexion*'—recalls Descartes's stress on the issue of attentive consideration of our ideas, discussed in Chapter IV.

7 Cf. 'Innate Ideas,' CS, p. 43. McRae interprets Descartes's denial (to Gassendi) that he had claimed that 'the ideas of material things are deduced from the mind' as 'a denial that the idea of extension is innate.' However, the context (and indeed the quotation) makes clear that Descartes and Gassendi are talking about ideas of particular bodies, not the 'idea of extension.' Even of *these* all Descartes says is that they 'often' come from bodies. AT VII, 367; HR II, 217–18; cf. AT III, 666; PL 138–9. In the latter passage Descartes rather clearly implies that the idea of extension, together with the other 'simple natures' is innate. And of course a principal aim of the wax passage in Meditation II is to establish that our conception of the wax's extension is *intellectual*.

8 This point is discussed in some detail in Chapter VI, below.

9 Cf. Rule xiv, esp. AT X, 442–3; HR I, 57–8.

10 See Chapter VI, §2 below.

11 Cf. the continuation of Meditation V: '*possum enim alias innumeras figuras excogitare. . . .*'

12 The issue of Descartes's 'Platonism' has been debated by Gewirth and Kenny in the following series of papers: Gewirth, 'The Cartesian Circle Reconsidered,' and Kenny, 'The Cartesian Circle and the Eternal Truths,' both in the *Journal of Philosophy*, vol. LXVII, 8 October 1970; and Gewirth, 'Descartes: Two Disputed Questions,' *ibid.*, vol. LXVIII, 6 May 1971. Kenny maintains that Descartes's 'philosophy of mathematics is thoroughly Platonic' on the grounds that 'mathematical essences are distinct from the essence of God' (*op. cit.*, pp. 692, 695). Gewirth, who does not address this point directly, holds in his first article that 'Descartes seems to veer between Platonic and Aristotelian interpretations of . . . mathematical essences' (p. 678), and in the second article that Descartes's position combines Platonic and Aristotelian elements. The 'Aristotelianism' of Descartes's position lies (according to Gewirth's later statement) in his ontological view that mathematical essences are not substances, and the epistemological tenet that 'mathematical and other concepts' are derived 'by abstraction from sensory images' ('Disputed Questions,' pp. 289–90). Despite Gewirth's care in distinguishing ontological and epistemological issues, his interpretation involves serious difficulties, and raises a lot of questions. In

particular, it seems regrettable that Gewirth doesn't consider the question whether Descartes is *entitled* to deny that mathematical essences are substances, given the view (plausibly ascribed to him by Kenny) that they are neither attached to God's essence nor dependent for their reality on finite minds or *res extensa* itself. Neither Gewirth nor Kenny considers what seems to me the most fundamental and pervasive non-Platonic element in Descartes's philosophy of mathematics: the conception of the role of *imagination* in our physico-geometrical thinking. (The passages from the *Rules* that Gewirth cites (in both articles) as showing that Descartes thinks we derive mathematical concepts from the senses don't seem to me to show that at all. They are rather concerned with the role of imagination. Elsewhere, of course, Descartes *denies* we derive the ideas of geometrical figures from the senses. Besides AT VII, 64–5; HR I, 180, cf. AT VII, 381–2; HR II 227–8.)

13 Rule xiv: AT X, 442ff; HR I, 57ff. My suggestion about the development of Descartes's view on imagination between the *Rules* and the *Meditations* derives from conversations with Jim Alt.

14 Kenny, p. 151.

15 The criteria of 'life-form' are derived from a 1976 *New York Times* account of some Mars scientists' analysis of the concept.

16 The idea of a hippogryph is given as an example of a factitious idea in Meditation III, AT VII, 38; HR I, 160. Compare, however, AT V, 160; B 23.

17 Kenny, p. 162.

18 Kenny, pp. 170–1.

Chapter VI Mind, Body and Things Outside Us

1 For example, at a symposium on the Mind–Body Problem, held at Princeton University on 9 January 1975, the term 'Cartesian [or cartesian?] dualism' was repeatedly used as a label for the position that merely denies the *identity* (not necessarily the correlation) of physical and mental states. (Participants in the symposium were four major contributors to the literature on the subject.) However, the peculiarities of the historical Cartesian position have been accurately and concisely formulated by Wilfrid Sellars in 'Philosophy and the Scientific Image of Man.' For instance, Sellars writes:

> As for conceptual thinking, Descartes not only refused to identify it with neurophysiological processes, he did not see this as a live option, because it seemed obvious to him that no complex neurophysiological process could be sufficiently analogous to conceptual thinking to be a serious candidate for being what conceptual thinking 'really is.' It is not as though Descartes granted that there might well be neurophysiological processes which are strikingly analogous to conceptual thinking, but which it would be philosophically incorrect to *identify* with conceptual thinking. . . . He did not take seriously the idea that there *are* such neurophysiological processes. (*Science, Perception, and Reality*, p. 30)

Sellars goes on to remark that even if Descartes had taken the latter idea seriously, he still 'would have rejected' the identification 'on the grounds that we had a 'clear and distinct,' well-defined idea of what conceptual thinking is before we even suspected that the brain had anything to do with thinking.' And this, I believe, is questionable. I agree that Descartes *could* have maintained his dualism even in the face of increased appreciation of the complexities of neurophysiology: as indicated below, his main argument for mind–body distinctness seems (overtly at least) logically independent of this issue. But it is entirely possible that the *motivation* for his dualism was quite bound up with false preconceptions about the limitations of physical explanation.

2 See for instance J. Fodor, *Psychological Explanation*, pp. 55–6.

3 See for instance J. Locke, *Essay Concerning Human Understanding*, Book IV, Ch. iii, §6 (in Fraser edition, vol. II, pp. 192–3).

4 Chomsky, *Cartesian Linguistics*, Ch. I. For a more detailed discussion see K. Gunderson, *Mentality and Machines*, Ch. I. (Gunderson also examines the historical sequel of Descartes's arguments in the work of La Mettrie.)

5 *Cartesian Linguistics*, p. 4.

6 Cf. Gunderson, *op. cit.*, pp. 10–11: '[A]ll Descartes needs in order to show that S has not passed the . . . action test is that there is some (broad) range of actions where S (machine or beast, for example) fails to perform in ways comparable to the ways in which human beings perform.'

7 Of course it must be granted that Descartes vastly over-estimated the extent to which he *could* explain ordinary physical phenomena.

8 I mean in the English language literature. (An exception is Ch. 6 of Julius Weinberg's posthumously published *Ockham, Descartes, and Hume*. While published after the original version of the present section (see Acknowledgments), Weinberg's essay was written before it.) French accounts are generally quite knowledgeable. See for instance, Rodis-Lewis, *L'Oeuvre de Descartes*, vol. 1, pp. 335–40, for an excellent exposition of a central point.

9 AT VII, 225; HR II, 101. At times, however, Descartes allows that we can say that mind is *in a sense* extended: the extension of mind, unlike that of body, does not involve impenetrability. Cf. AT VII, 442–4; HR II, 255–6.

10 Another important text is the beginning of the Second Replies, AT VII, 128–33; HR II, 31–3, where Descartes stresses the role of the Second Meditation in developing clear and distinct ideas of mind and body, by bringing about the withdrawal of the mind from the senses. He is explaining the importance of this philosophical stage for the mind–body distinctness argument.

11 Cf. the beginning of the Fourth Replies, AT VII, 219; HR II, 96, where Descartes makes explicit the importance of the Divine guarantee to the mind–body distinctness argument.

12 Versions of the first and third objections considered here are found in Kenny, pp. 79–95, and Malcolm, 'Descartes's Proof That His Essence Is Thinking,' in Doney, pp. 312–37; the first is also stressed by Leibniz in 'Remarks on the General Part of Descartes's *Principles*' (Gerhardt, ed., *Die Philosophischen Schriften*, vol. IV, p. 359).

13 It must be conceded that in *The Search for Truth* Descartes's spokesman endorses the formulation, '[Were I a body,] if I doubted of body, I would also doubt of myself. . . .' (AT X, 518; HR I, 319). However, in view of the consistent line Descartes takes on this matter throughout the *Replies*, I'm inclined to think that the point he really means to be making in the *Search* passage is, again, that the character has a conception of himself (as doubting, etc.) that does not involve corporeal notions. If it is objected that this is not what the text *says*, I would also appeal to the following points as mitigating its authority: the discussion in the *Search* is exceedingly loose and informal; the work was not finished, and not published by Descartes; the passage in question exists only in Latin translation; and the prose is remarkably messy, in comparison with Descartes's usual conceptual and stylistic standards.

Leibniz reads the *Principles* passage on mind–body distinctness (AT VIII-1, 7; HR I, 221) as presenting a version of the Argument from Doubt, and Kenny cites the *Discourse* (AT VI, 33; HR I, 101; cf. Kenny, p. 79). However, these passages do not explicitly present an 'Argument from Doubt,' and I don't think it's necessary to read one into them. (One must suppose, however, that Descartes is suppressing a couple of premisses—especially in the *Discourse*.) See my 'Leibniz and Materialism,' *Canadian Journal of Philosophy*, vol. III, June 1974, p. 499.

14 Descartes's exposition of his dualism is so obviously and so closely reliant on (his adaptation of) the scholastic theory of distinctions, that it seems surprising the fact has not received more attention in the literature. Mark Sagoff and Alan Donagan have discussed his use of, and departures from, the scholastics, in so-far unpublished writings. Sandra Edwards has provided a useful survey and comparison of the differing views on distinctions among different scholastic philosophers in an unpublished Ph.D. dissertation, 'Medieval Theories of Distinction' (The University of Pennsylvania, 1974). See also the second and third articles by Norman J. Wells cited in the bibliography. The most direct scholastic influence on Descartes was probably the work of F. Suarez. See his *Disputationes Metaphysicae*, Disputatio 7, in *Disputaciones Metafisicas*, ed. Romeo, Sánchez and Zanón, vol. II, pp. 9–68. Section II of this Disputatio, 'By which Signs or Modes the various Distinctions of Things can be Discerned,' is of special interest in connection with Descartes.

An additional important passage in Descartes, besides those cited in the text, is from the Replies to the Sixth Objections, AT VII, 442–5; HR II, 255–7.

15 In the Sixth Meditation Descartes does speak of understanding himself distinctly as a 'whole' (*totum*) without the faculties of imagination and sense (AT VII, 78). The French version gives '*tout entier*' (AT IX-1, 62) and HR translate 'as a complete being' (HR I, 190).

16 We are here, of course, 'bracketing' the doctrine of the creation of the eternal truths. Descartes has done so himself with his initial statement that God can do *anything in which he perceives there is no contradiction*.

17 See Chapter IV, note 16—especially the last reference (AT VII, 226; HR II, 101).

18 A point I failed to recognize in a previous treatment of this subject ('Leibniz: Self-consciousness and Immortality in the Paris Notes and After,' *Archiv für Geschichte der Philosophie*, Sonderheft, January 1977; despite the title this paper also deals in some detail with Descartes, against whose views Leibniz reacts).

It is, incidentally, interesting to contemplate the vastly different ways in which Locke, Spinoza and Leibniz reacted to this serious problem in their predecessor's system: Locke by holding that we are probably enduring mental substances, but that the issue is irrelevant to personal identity; Spinoza by holding that our minds are, like our bodies, only dynamic, organized modes; and Leibniz by developing an elaborate theory of individual essences—while also partly agreeing with Locke! (The article just cited provides more details and references.)

19 It is not clear that this disclaimer is consistent with the position taken in Meditation III concerning his ability to recognize the powers of his own mind. See David Fate Norton, 'Descartes on Unknown Faculties: An Essential Inconsistency,' *Journal of the History of Philosophy*, vol. VI, July 1968, pp. 245–56.

20 He seems to come closer to saying this in *Principles* II, i: AT VIII-1, 40–41; HR I, 254–5.

21 Of course he does develop a scientific theory in the *Optics* (and elsewhere).

22 Gueroult has offered a more positive account of Descartes's treatment of the

mind–body union (*Descartes selon l'ordre des raisons*, vol. II, Chs XVII–XVIII). He stresses the passages in certain letters where Descartes says the body derives its 'identity' from its union with the soul. Gueroult takes this to mean that the body has no substantial unity, real identity, or 'finality' apart from its union with the soul. All parts of the body derive 'finality' from this union: that is (I think) they all contribute to maintaining the mind–body union, and in this respect only can be said to have a purpose. Gueroult thinks this perspective provides a way of understanding what I will call the Co-extension theory—one that avoids inconsistency with Descartes's claim that the mind's effects are primarily located in the pineal gland. However, I am unsatisfied with Gueroult's explanation for a number of reasons. First, I do not find very clear *Descartes's* claim that the human body derives its 'identity' from the union with the soul (except in the tautological sense that my body is identifiable as *my* body in so far as it is united with me—i.e., with my soul). Further, the claim is hard to reconcile, on Cartesian terms, with the fact that we do recognize *non-human* organic unities. (Gueroult gives some attention to this point.) Also, it isn't after all so clear how one can move from the position that the soul 'confers finality' on the body's parts to the claim that the soul is *extended through* those parts. But finally, and most important, I do not think it is really at all clear *what it means to say* (as Gueroult does over and over, in his exposition) that 'finality penetrates' the body's parts. This is no improvement over Descartes's own obscurities.

23 See Leibniz's 'Considerations on the Principles of Life, and on Plastic Natures . . .' in *Die Philosophischen Schriften*, ed. Gerhardt, vol. VI, pp. 539–55. Compare Curt Ducasse's discussion in 'In Defense of Dualism,' Wilson, Brock and Kuhns, eds, *Philosophy: An Introduction*, p. 232.

24 G. Vesey cites this passage as primary illustration of what he calls the Cartesian Impasse (*The Embodied Mind*, p. 11). He thinks the Impasse results from 'the inadequacy of Descartes' concept of substance,' though he doesn't explain this diagnosis very fully.

25 At the end of Part V of the *Discourse* Descartes says that a mind must be joined more closely to the body than a pilot to his ship, if it is to have sensations similar to our own (AT VI, 59; HR I, 118).

26 Descartes discusses this issue in a fascinating and revealing pair of letters to Regius in December 1641, and January 1642: AT III, 459–62, 491–510; PL 121–3, 126–30.

27 As Descartes remarks to Regius, 'always and wherever the occasion occurs, privately as well as publicly, you should take the opportunity of saying you believe that man is *a true ens per se, not per accidens*, and the mind is really and substantially united to the body, not by location or disposition, . . . but by the true mode of union, of the sort that all commonly admit, even though no one explains what sort it is, and therefore you don't have to explain it either. . . .' (AT III, 493; PL 127)

28 I've been persuaded of this by Janet Broughton.

29 See *The Concept of Mind*, Ch. I.

30 *Individuals*, Ch. 3.

31 *Ibid.*, p. 99; cf. pp. 104, 106. The claim in question is that 'there is no sense' (p. 106) in the idea of ascribing experiences or states of consciousness to oneself unless we 'already know how to ascribe' them (106), 'are prepared to ascribe them' (99), to others. Strawson takes this to imply that we must have 'logically adequate criteria' for ascribing states of consciousness to others (p. 105).

32 Cf. *Passions*, I, 1, AT XI, 368–70; HR I, 355–6, and *Principles* IV, cxcvii: AT VIII-1, 320–1; HR I 294–5.

Bibliography

*1. Other editions of Descartes's work, besides those listed under
'Editions and Abbreviations' (pp. xvi–xvii)*

Descartes, *Correspondence avec Arnauld et Morus*, texte latin et traduction, introduction et notes par Geneviève Rodis-Lewis, Paris: J. Vrin, 1953.
——, *Lettres à Regius et Remarques sur l'explication de l'esprit humain*, Texte latin, traduction, introduction et notes par Geneviève Rodis-Lewis, Paris: J. Vrin, 1959.
——, *Oeuvres et lettres*, introduction, chronologie, bibliographie, notes par André Bridoux, Gallimard (Pléiade), 1953.
——, *Oeuvres philosophiques*, textes établis, présentés et annotés par Ferdinand Alquié, Paris: Garnier Frères, 1963–73 (3 vols).
—— , *Treatise of Man*, French Text with Translation and Commentary by Thomas Steele Hall, Cambridge, Massachusetts: Harvard University Press, 1972.

*2. Works and editions of pre-twentieth-century philosophers
cited in the text and notes*

Galilei, Galileo, *Discoveries and Opinions of Galileo*, translated with introduction and notes by Stillman Drake, Garden City, New York: Doubleday (Anchor), 1957.
Leibniz, G. W., *Essais de Théodicée*, suivi de *La Monadologie*, préface et notes de J. Jalabert, Aubier (Editions Montaigne), 1962.
——, *Nouveaux Essais sur l'entendement humain*, in *Sämtliche Schriften und Briefe*, herausgegeben von der Deutschen Akademie der Wissenschaften zu Berlin, Reihe 6, Bd. 6, Berlin: Akademie-Verlag, 1962.
——, *Die Philosophischen Schriften*, herausgegeben von C. I. Gerhardt, Hildesheim: Olms, 1965 [first edition, Berlin, 1875–90] (7 vols).
Kant, Immanuel, *Critique of Pure Reason*, translated by Norman Kemp Smith, London: Macmillan, 1958.
Locke, John, *An Essay Concerning Human Understanding*, collated and annotated, with biographical, critical and historical prolegomena by Alexander Campbell Fraser, New York: Dover, 1959 [first edition, 1894] (2 vols).
Pascal, Blaise, *Pensées*, translated with an introduction by A. J. Krailsheimer, Penguin, 1966.

245

Peirce, Charles S., *Values in a Universe of Chance: Selected Writings of Charles S. Peirce (1839–1914)*, edited, with an introduction and notes by Philip P. Wiener, Garden City, New York: Doubleday (Anchor), 1958.

Spinoza, Benedictus de, *Chief Works*, translated from the Latin with introduction by R. H. M. Elwes, New York: Dover, 1951 [first edition, 1883] (2 vols).

Suarez, Francisco, *Disputaciones Metafísicas*, edición y traducción de Sergio Rábade Romeo, Salvador Caballero Sánchez, y Antonio Puigcerver Zanón, Madrid: Biblioteca Hispanica de Filosofia, 1960–3 (7 vols).

3. *Twentieth-century books (those cited in the text and some others of special relevance)*

Alquié, F., *Descartes,* Paris: Hatier, 1969 (nouvelle édition).

Beck, L. J., *The Metaphysics of Descartes: A Study of the Meditations*, Oxford: Clarendon Press, 1965.

——, *The Method of Descartes: A Study of the Regulae*, Oxford: Clarendon Press, 1952.

Belaval, Yvon, *Leibniz Critique de Descartes*, Paris: Gallimard, 1960.

Beyssade, Michelle, *Descartes*, Paris: Presses Universitaires de France, 1972.

Buchdahl, Gerd, *Metaphysics and the Philosophy of Science: The Classical Origins: Descartes to Kant*, Cambridge, Massachusetts: MIT Press, 1969.

Burtt, Edwin Arthur, *The Metaphysical Foundations of Modern Physical Science*, New York: Harcourt, Brace, 1925; London: Routledge & Kegan Paul.

Caton, Hiram, *The Origin of Subjectivity: An Essay on Descartes*, New Haven: Yale University Press, 1973.

Chomsky, Noam, *Cartesian Linguistics*, New York: Harper & Row, 1966.

Collins, James, *Descartes' Philosophy of Nature*, London: C. Tinling (American Philosophical Quarterly Monograph Series), 1971.

Curley, E. M., *Descartes Against the Skeptics*, Harvard University Press, 1978.

Edwards, Sandra, 'Medieval Theories of Distinctions,' University of Pennsylvania, 1974 [unpublished Ph.D. dissertation].

Fodor, Jerry A., *Psychological Explanation*, New York: Random House (Smithsonian Inst. Press), 1968.

Geach, Peter, *Mental Acts*, London: Routledge & Kegan Paul, 1957.

Gibson, A. Boyce, *The Philosophy of Descartes*, London: Methuen, 1932.

Gilson, Etienne, *Etudes sur le rôle de la pensée médiévale dans la formation du système Cartésien*, Paris: J. Vrin, 1951.

Gouhier, Henri, *Descartes: Essais sur le 'Discours de la méthode,' la Métaphysique et la Morale*, Paris: J. Vrin, 1973 [third edition].

——, *La Pensée métaphysique de Descartes*, Paris: J. Vrin, 1962.

——, *La Pensée religieuse de Descartes*, Paris: J. Vrin, 1924.

Gueroult, Martial, *Descartes selon l'ordre des raisons*, Paris: Aubier, 1953 (2 vols).

Gunderson, Keith, *Mentality and Machines*, Garden City, New York: Doubleday (Anchor), 1971.

Joachim, Harold H., *Descartes's Rules for the Direction of the Mind*, edited by Errol E. Harris, London: George Allen & Unwin, 1957.

Keeling, S. V., *Descartes*, London: Ernest Benn, 1934.

Koyfe, Alexandre, *From the Closed World to the Infinite Universe*, Baltimore: The Johns Hopkins Press, 1957.

Kuhn, Thomas S., *The Structure of Scientific Revolutions*, Chicago: University of Chicago Press, 1970.

BIBLIOGRAPHY

Malcolm, Norman, *Dreaming*, New York: Humanities Press, 1959; London: Routledge & Kegan Paul.

Mandelbaum, Maurice, *Science, Philosophy, and Sense Perception: Historical and Critical Studies*, Baltimore: The Johns Hopkins Press, 1964.

Popkin, Richard H., *The History of Scepticism from Erasmus to Descartes*, New York: Humanities Press, 1960.

Putnam, Hilary, *Philosophical Papers*: vol. 2: *Mind, Language and Reality*, Cambridge: Cambridge University Press, 1975.

Quine, W. V., *From a Logical Point of View*, Cambridge, Massachusetts: Harvard University Press, 1961 (second edition, revised).

Rodis-Lewis, Geneviève, *Le Problème de l'inconscient et le Cartésianisme*, Paris: Presses Universitaires de France, 1950.

——, *L'Oeuvre de Descartes*, Paris: J. Vrin, 1971 (2 vols).

Ryle, Gilbert, *The Concept of Mind*, New York: Barnes & Noble, 1949; also London: Hutchinson, 1949.

Sebba, Gregor, *Bibliographia Cartesiana*, The Hague: Martinus Nijhoff, 1964.

Sellars, Wilfrid, *Philosophical Perspectives*, Springfield, Illinois: Charles C. Thomas, 1967.

——, *Science, Perception, and Reality*, New York: The Humanities Press, 1963.

Sesonske, Alexander and Fleming, Noel (eds), *Meta-Meditations: Studies in Descartes*, Belmont, California: Wadsworth, 1965.

Smith, Norman Kemp, *New Studies in the Philosophy of Descartes; Descartes as Pioneer*, London: Macmillan, 1952.

Strawson, P. F., *Individuals*, London: Methuen, 1959.

——, *The Bounds of Sense*, London: Methuen, 1966.

Taliaferro, Robert C., *The Concept of Matter in Descartes and Leibniz*, Notre Dame, Indiana: University of Notre Dame Press, 1964.

Vendler, Zeno, *Res cogitans: An Essay in Rational Psychology*, Ithaca, New York: Cornell University Press, 1972.

Vesey, Godfrey N. A., *The Embodied Mind*, London: George Allen & Unwin, 1965.

Walsh, William Henry, *Metaphysics*, London: Hutchinson, 1963.

Wittgenstein, Ludwig, *On Certainty*, translated by Denis Paul and G. E. M. Anscombe, New York: Harper & Row, 1972.

——, *Philosophical Investigations*, translated by G. E. M. Anscombe, New York: Macmillan, 1953.

4. Articles: those cited in the text and others of special relevance

Allaire, Edwin B., 'The Circle of Ideas,' *Dialogue*, vol. V, no. 2, September 1966, pp. 131–53.

Austin, J. L., 'Other Minds,' in *Philosophical Papers*, Oxford: Clarendon Press, 1961, pp. 44–84.

Ayer, A. J., '"I think, therefore I am,"' in Doney [see p. xvii], pp. 80–7.

Beyssade, Jean-Marie, 'Mais quoi ce sont des fous,' *Revue de Métaphysique et de Morale*, 78ᵉ année, no. 3, Juillet-Septembre 1973, pp. 273–94.

——, 'L'analyse du morceau de cire,' in *Sinnlichkeit und Verstand in der Deutschen und Französischen Philosophie von Descartes bis Hegel*, herausg. v. Hans Wagner, Bonn: Bouvier Verlag Herbert Grundmann, 1976, pp. 9–25.

Bouwsma, O. K., 'Descartes' Evil Genius,' in *Meta-meditations*, edited by Alexander Sesonske and Noel Fleming, Belmont, California: Wadsworth, 1966, pp. 26–36.

——, '"On Many Occasions I Have in Sleep Been Deceived"—Descartes,' *Proceedings of the American Philosophical Association*, vol. XXX, 1956-7, pp. 25-44.

Bréhier, Emile, 'The Creation of the Eternal Truths in Descartes's System,' in Doney [see p. xvii], pp. 192-208.

Caton, Hiram, 'Will and Reason in Descartes's Theory of Error,' *Journal of Philosophy*, vol. LXXII, no. 4, 27 February 1975, pp. 87-104.

Donagan, Alan, 'Essence and the Distinction of Attributes in Spinoza's Metaphysics,' in *Spinoza: A Collection of Critical Essays*, edited by Marjorie Grene, Garden City, New York: Anchor Press/Doubleday, 1973, pp. 164-81.

Doney, Willis, 'Descartes's Conception of Perfect Knowledge,' *Journal of the History of Philosophy*, vol. VIII, no. 4, October 1970, pp. 387-403.

——, 'Spinoza on Philosophical Skepticism,' in *Spinoza: Essays in Interpretation*, edited by Eugene Freeman and Maurice Mandelbaum, LaSalle, Illinois: Open Court, 1975, pp. 139-57.

Ducasse, Curt, 'In Defense of Dualism,' in *Philosophy: an Introduction*, prepared under the editorial supervision of Margaret D. Wilson, Dan W. Brock and Richard F. Kuhns, Jr., New York: Appleton-Century-Crofts, 1972, pp. 229-33.

Evans, J. L., 'Error and the Will,' *Philosophy*, vol. XXXVII, no. 144, April 1963, pp. 136-48.

Feldman, Fred, 'On the Performatory Interpretation of the Cogito,' *Philosophical Review*, vol. LXXXII, no. 3, July 1973, pp. 345-63.

Firth, Roderick, 'The Men Themselves; or the Role of Causation in Our Concept of Seeing,' in *Intentionality, Minds, and Perception*, compiled with an introduction by Hector-Neri Castañeda, Detroit: Wayne State University Press, 1967, pp. 357-82.

Frankfurt, Harry G., 'Descartes's Discussion of His Existence in the Second Meditation,' *Philosophical Review*, vol. LXXV, no. 3, July 1966, pp. 329-56.

——, 'Descartes' Validation of Reason,' in Doney [see p. xvii], pp. 209-26.

——, 'Descartes on the Creation of the Eternal Truths,' *Philosophical Review*, vol. LXXXVI, no. 1, January 1977, pp. 36-57.

Funkenstein, Amos, 'Descartes, Eternal Truths, and the Divine Omnipotence,' *Studies in the History and Philosophy of Science*, vol. 6, no. 3, 1975, pp. 185-99.

Gewirth, Alan, 'Clearness and Distinctness in Descartes,' in Doney [see p. xvii], pp. 250-77.

——, 'The Cartesian Circle Reconsidered,' *Journal of Philosophy*, vol. LXVII, no. 19, 8 October 1970, pp. 668-85.

——, 'Descartes: Two Disputed Questions,' *Journal of Philosophy*, vol. LXVIII, no. 9, 6 May 1971, pp. 288-96.

Gibson, Alexander Boyce, 'The Eternal Verities and the Will of God in the Philosophy of Descartes,' *Proceedings of the Aristotelian Society*, new series 30, 1929-30, pp. 31-54.

Gombay, André, '"Cogito Ergo Sum": Inference or Argument?' in CS [see p. xxi], pp. 71-88.

Hart, Alan, 'Descartes on Reidentification,' *Journal of the History of Philosophy*, vol. XIII, no. 1, January 1975, pp. 17-26.

Hintikka, Jaakko, 'Cogito Ergo Sum: Inference or Performance?' in Doney [see p. xvii], pp. 108-39.

——, 'Cogito, Ergo Sum as an Inference and a Performance,' *Philosophical Review*, vol. LXXII, no. 4, October 1963, pp. 487-96.

BIBLIOGRAPHY

James, William, 'The Will to Believe,' in *The Will to Believe*, New York: Longmans Green, 1897, pp. 1–31.

Kenny, Anthony, 'The Cartesian Circle and the Eternal Truths,' *Journal of Philosophy*, vol. LXVII, no. 19, 8 October 1970, pp. 685–700.

——, 'Descartes on the Will,' in CS [see p. xvii], pp. 1–31.

Kripke, Saul, 'Naming and Necessity,' in *The Semantics of Natural Languages*, edited by D. Davidson and G. Harman, Dordrecht-Holland: Reidel, 1971, pp. 253–355.

Lucas, Peter G., 'Descartes and the Wax: A Rejoinder to Mr. Smart,' *Philosophical Quarterly*, vol. I, 4 July 1951, pp. 348–52.

MacDonald, Margaret, 'Sleeping and Waking,' *Mind*, vol. LXII, no. 246, April 1953, pp. 202–15.

McRae, Robert, 'Descartes' Definition of Thought,' in CS [see p. xvii], pp. 55–70.

——, 'Innate Ideas,' *ibid.*, pp. 32–54.

Malcolm, Norman, 'Descartes's Proof That His Essence Is Thinking,' in Doney [see p. xvii], pp. 312–37.

——, 'Dreaming and Skepticism,' *ibid.*, pp. 54–79.

——, 'Knowing and Believing,' in *Knowledge and Belief*, edited by A. Phillips Griffiths, London: Oxford University Press, 1967, pp. 69–81.

——, 'Thoughtless Brutes,' *Proceedings and Addresses of the American Philosophical Association*, vol. XLVI, 1972–3, pp. 5–20.

Margolis, Joseph, 'Locke and Scientific Realism,' *The Review of Metaphysics*, vol. XXII, 1968, pp. 359–70.

Marks, Charles E., Review of Hiram Caton, *The Origin of Subjectivity: An Essay on Descartes*, *Philosophical Review*, vol. LXXIV, no. 3, July 1975, pp. 457–60.

Miller, Leonard G., 'Descartes, Mathematics, and God,' in *Meta-meditations*, edited by Alexander Sesonske and Noel Fleming, Belmont, California: Wadsworth, 1965, pp. 37–49.

Nagel, Thomas, 'Physicalism,' *Philosophical Review*, vol. LXXIV, no. 3, July 1965, pp. 339–56.

——, 'Armstrong on the Mind,' *Philosophical Review*, vol. LXXIX, no. 3, July 1970, pp. 394–403.

——, 'Linguistics and Epistemology,' in *On Noam Chomsky: Critical Essays*, edited by Gilbert Harman, Garden City, New York: Doubleday (Anchor), 1974, pp. 219–28.

Norton, David Fate, 'Descartes on Unknown Faculties: An Essential Inconsistency,' *Journal of the History of Philosophy*, vol. VI, no. 3, July 1968, pp. 245–56.

Price, H. H., 'Belief and Will,' in *Philosophy of Mind*, edited by Stuart Hampshire, New York: Harper & Row, 1966, pp. 91–116.

Prichard, H. A., 'Descartes's Meditations,' in Doney [see p. xvii], pp. 140–68.

Quinton, Anthony, 'Matter and Space,' *Mind*, vol. LXXII, no. 291, July 1964, pp. 332–52.

Radner, Daisie, 'Descartes' Notion of the Union of Mind and Body,' *Journal of the History of Philosophy*, vol. IX, no. 2, April 1971, pp. 159–70.

Rescher, Nicholas, 'The Legitimacy of Doubt,' *Review of Metaphysics*, vol. XII, 2 December 1959, pp. 226–34.

Rorty, Richard, 'Incorrigibility as the Mark of the Mental,' *Journal of Philosophy*, vol. LXVII, no. 12, 25 June 1970, pp. 399–424.

Schiffer, Stephen, 'Descartes on His Essence,' *Philosophical Review*, vol. LXXXV, no. 1, January 1976, pp. 21–43.

Sellars, Wilfrid, 'Science, Sense-Impressions, and Sensa: A Reply to Cornman,' *Review of Metaphysics*, vol. XXIV, no. 3, March 1971, pp. 391–447.

Smart, J. J. C., 'Descartes and the Wax,' *Philosophical Quarterly*, vol. I, no. 1, October 1950, pp. 50–7.

Strawson, P. F., 'Self, Mind and Body,' in *Introduction to the Philosophy of Mind: Readings from Descartes to Strawson*, edited by Harold Morick, Glenview, Illinois: Scott, Foresman, 1970, pp. 89–108.

Watson, Richard A., 'In Defiance of Demons, Dreamers, and Madmen' [review of Frankfurt's book: see p. xvii]. *Journal of the History of Philosophy*, vol. XLV, no. 3, July 1976, pp. 342–53.

Weinberg, Julius R., 'Descartes on the Distinction of Mind and Body,' in Weinberg, *Ockham, Descartes, and Hume: Self-knowledge, Substance, and Causality*, Madison, Wisconsin: University of Wisconsin Press, 1977 (Ch. 6).

Wells, Norman J., 'Descartes and the Scholastics Briefly Revisited,' *New Scholasticism*, vol. 35, no. 2, April 1961, pp. 172–90.

——, 'Descartes and the Modal Distinction,' *Modern Schoolman*, vol. 43, 1965–6, pp. 1–22.

——, 'Descartes on Distinction,' in *The Quest for the Absolute*, edited by F. J. Adelmann, Chesnut Hill, Massachusetts: Boston College, 1966 (Boston College Studies in Philosophy), pp. 104–34.

——, 'Objective Being: Descartes and His Sources,' *Modern Schoolman*, vol. 45, 1967–8, pp. 49–61.

Williams, Bernard, 'The Certainty of the *Cogito*,' in Doney [see p. xvii], pp. 88–107.

Wilson, Margaret D., 'Leibniz and Locke on First Truths,' *Journal of the History of Ideas*, vol. XXVIII, no. 3, July–September 1967, pp. 347–66.

——, 'Leibniz and Materialism,' *Canadian Journal of Philosophy*, vol. 3, no. 4, June 1974, pp. 495–513.

——, 'Leibniz: Self-Consciousness and Immortality in the Paris Notes and After,' *Archiv für Geschichte der Philosophie*, January 1977: Sonderheft, pp. 335–52.

——, Review of *Descartes' Conversation with Burman*, trans. with intro. by John Cottingham, *Philosophical Review*, vol. LXXXVII, July (?) 1978.

Wright, J. N., 'Descartes and the Wax: Rejoinder to Mr. Smart,' *Philosophical Quarterly*, vol. I, no. 4, July 1951, pp. 352–5.

Index